BOOK OF TRUTH
And The Theory Everything

For Daniel,
With my best wishes,
Paul Zecos

Contributor: Dr. Robert Rose

Edited by Alexander Zecos

This book is dedicated to all the children but it is not intended to be read by children under 13.

All the author's proceeds from this book will go to charity.

Published by: Altrutech LLC

ADVANCE COPY

TABLE OF CONTENTS

INTRODUCTION

Global warming and the resulting **environmental** destructions are likely to be catastrophic to humanity within this century. USA's over $16 Trillion debt (in addition to the even larger unfunded liabilities,)and most nations' increasing **economic debts** are very likely to become so large within this decade that one or more nations will be unable to pay them, causing a bigger than ever economic collapse. The increasing **nuclear proliferation, militant enmity** and explicit war mongering by N. Korea, Islamic terrorists and Iran is likely to result in a nuclear attack at any time within the next 3 years.

The **political and social** (racial, gender, sexual orientation and wealth) **polarization,** dislike and internal debilitating antagonisms are likely to cause a huge economic crisis in 2016-2017. Underlying these there is a **hypocritical cultural and moral human state** in which everyone claims to be right and pretends to be moral while most know the truth that true spirituality, social morality and ethics are disintegrating fast.

How severe are these real and potential problems? Each of these problems on their own isn't too difficult to solve but they are interlinked like a Gordian knot, with most solutions to each of these being likely to aggravate the solution to the others; and a major disruption caused by any of these potential problems will trigger a vicious cycle by which several if not all the rest of the potential problems will become reality.

Because of these major challenges, humanity is unlikely to survive this century unless there is a dramatic change in the direction so as to adequately deal with all these challenges.

The probability is extremely high that by 2016-2017 there will be a greater than any of the previous hugely catastrophic event and a global economic collapse, unless the public and the government make significant changes. I am sorry to be bringing you a message that you may not want to hear but it is the truth.

The solution to these problems starts by admitting their existence.

Though the following subjects are often avoided in polite company, Physics, Psychology, Business, Economics, Politics, Philosophy and Religion are as diverse and incompatible disciplines as your body, emotions, work, finances, opinions, understanding and beliefs.

Don't you think that these disciplines shouldn't be incompatible, self-contradicted and contradicting each other as it has been but should be synthesized into a cohesive, coherent whole so that all the components of you are synthesized into a cohesive unbreakable Whole? It is that unifying synthesis into oneness, in simple common sense language that this book offers.

Whatever knowledge understanding or beliefs one claims to have they either come from God and/or from the physical and thus by the forces and laws of physics and/or they come by the functions of Man, as explained by psychology. If they come from Man they either come from the physical or from God or both. There is no other potential source of knowledge and of correct understanding.

This book explains both: The physics forces of the Universe, their laws, functions and their logic and the corresponding driving motives in psychology, business and economics thus the one potential source of all knowledge and of correct understanding; and it also explains the intent, reason and expressions of the One God, His Kingdom and the Seven Spirits of the Holy Spirit.

The Physics:

-There are 3 quantum (probabilistic in how they are perceived) forces—energy fields— (of light) the Strong, the Weak, and the Electromagnetic (E-M) that are unified at a very high energy level and are distinct at lower energy levels. Each Quantum force is symmetrical in 3, 2, 1 Dimensions respectively and causes changes on the surfaces, lines and points of objects.

-Those changes **are resisted by and reacted to** by the deterministic, gravitational 4D **inertial** mass of the object as described by General Relativity.

If one does not understand correctly the forces of physics, their laws and logic and/or does not Know or correctly understand God, then one does not know or understand correctly the sources, causes, direction and consequences of whatever they say, do or don't do and therefore one is extremely likely to be wrong.

Being extremely likely to be wrong, knowing it, having the choice to not be wrong and willingly continuing to be wrong and lying in claiming to be right or to be correct is evil, the 3 archetypes of which are shown through an entertaining fictitious story.

God is Good is Right and is True.

This book explains what Good, Love intends, means, is, and does, what Right, righteous and correct reasoning means is and does, and what being truthful and real means and is.

Those that truly believe in God are right or correct in their reasoning and express true love by their actions.

The book advocates the establishment of one small Independent Demilitarized, Disarmed, Democratic, Holy Land in your nation for the poor, the weak, those that are suffering in the current systems, the peace-loving and the righteous to live by love truly, and as an oasis of true love for the rest. That is the right solution.

A physics Theory of Everything is proposed and proven through a new equation. That theory is then shown to apply to Psychology, Business and Economics.

Using the Theory of Everything the book offers precise, coherent and correct solutions to the currently unsustainable imbalances and direction of the economy and among economies as well as for the environmental, relationship, political problems and for the religious conflicts.

"Don't read this if you don't want to get shocked by the secrets men keep from women and the secrets women keep from men," says my enemy, the secretly in charge global authority.

OVERVIEW

The Physics and Psychology Theory of Everything:

The Physics: There are 3 quantum (probabilistic) forces—energy fields— (of light) the strong, the weak, and the electromagnetic (E-M) that are unified at a very high energy level and are distinct at lower energy levels.

These 3 Quantum forces are symmetrical in 3, 2, 1 Dimensions respectively, are described by the Standard Model of Particle physics as SU (3) × SU (2) × U (1), and cause changes on the surfaces, lines and points of objects. Those changes **are resisted and reacted** to by the deterministic, gravitational 4D inertial mass of the object as described by General Relativity. Fractals are described by the Theory of Chaos.

Equation 2 (shown later) that is based on the first law of thermodynamics proves that the relationship between the 4 known forces is as described. The TOE is validated by and validates all 4 well proven (for their range of application) theories of physics i.e. General Relativity, Quantum Theory, Symmetry and the Theory of Chaos and integrates them into a single comprehensive Theory.

If the forces of change do not have the critical energy to exceed the inertial gravitational resistance, the changes are reflected back as information into the quantum fields and the motion of the object is unaffected. If the energy and speed from the forces of change exceeds the inertial (gravitational) resistance it changes the motions of objects.

The pace of change is accelerating throughout the Universe.

The change in the structure and form of space is caused by time. Time has a "lower limit" during which it automatically operates as a 4th space dimension, curving space. At speeds of change that are faster than the lower limit, time is dependent on the (timing and phase of the) of observation and the measuring device and thus on the measurer.

None of the above requires proof because each of the components of this theory has been proven already.

Nature also shows us this structure through three probabilistic in direction of motion states of matter, i.e. water (liquids); fire (plasma), wind (air, gases) causing changes and being resisted and reacted to over time by the (deterministic) solid (earth, rocks) state.

The Psychology: Causing changes in those 3 Quantum Forces of Physics, corresponding to them by dimensionality and synchronously responding to them, there are 3 quantum (probabilistic) spiritual (unseen) forces of Light.

They are: the thoughts that are like the words and the air we breathe, in and out, operating in 3 dimensions as the strong force; emotions, pulsing as the blood, radiating, operating in 2 Dimensions as the Weak force; and the unique soul and conscience, that is our Light, operating like a ray of light in a single dimension by and like electromagnetism, that are unified at very high energy level and are distinct at lower energy levels, each being symmetrical in 3, 2, 1 Dimensions respectively.

These three quantum fields of your Will are manifest as the needs for power, for affiliation and for achievement respectively that cause changes on the geometries of points, lines and surfaces (respectively) of the body that deterministically and by the instinctive by fear for loss of life fight-flight inertia, resists and visibly reacts to changes caused by your Will.

These 3 Universal Quantum probabilistic (that I use colors to distinguish) force fields that are strengthened by (in-phase) synchronicity, and the 4th ,gravity, that is the inertial resistance and reaction to them, that operates deterministically at the lower speed limit, are described by the Cross.

As shown, this structure is manifest in the four forces of the Universe, (is described in Revelation 4:6-9 as " the four beasts around the throne of God,") is in the states of matter in Nature, in the functions of humans, in business and actually in every aspect of the Universe and life, including for psychological disorders (Anxiety Disorders, Mood Disorders, Mental Disorders and Personality (character) Disorders; (such as the B.S.W. that I refer to,) (don't ask me how I am so familiar with all these disorders!) and for any economy, at any level of detail and any depth because it is the same pattern of the 4D Cross that one keeps finding.

The TOE confirms that the (action-reaction) cause-effect; and the (desired) effect-cause laws of reciprocity are the laws of the Universe proving the Wisdom of the Golden Rule.

If the spiritual speed of change is higher than the "lower limit," and only under those conditions, what will happen physically, can be foreseen (prophesied) and can be changed from its otherwise inevitable course, into what you choose. So, acting before it is too late is critical. For some, tomorrow will be too late.

Before rejecting this Physics and the correlated by dimensionality, synchronicity Psychology Theory of Everything (TOE) please consider what the alternative TOE's for Physics and for Psychology are; there aren't any. Absent this TOE, confusion reigns. In the context of nothing, something, even little, is infinity.

Business- Economics-Strategy: This same Theory of Everything that has metrics the vectors on The Cross applies fully and very usefully for all business and economic applications as has been shown. Current or past performance can be shown as single vector that has 4 major components. Any strategy can be shown as a single vector also on The Cross that has 4 major components that are operated independently (by a separate part of the structure) but are coordinated to happen synchronously. These are the coherent 4 track strategies that are most effective and efficient.

Every problem, disorder, dysfunction, disease and destruction has a spiritual (moral) and an intellectual and an emotional and a physical cause, component and implication, at varying degrees and as a result the solution to be correct requires understanding all of these 4 major components while forming a specific solution to each component.

For the resulting strategy to be most effective and efficient its implementation requires that all 4 major components are addressed synchronously but with different priority and intensity in 4 phases.

After accomplishing the objective and/or mission in the 3rd phase, (for brevity I skip explaining each phase because they are the same in any lifecycle,) the 4th phase of each strategy is the exit strategy that must be designed to sustain the benefits of what is accomplished after the exit.

Assumptions, beliefs and judgments: For judgments to be right or correct they must be fully honest and they must explicitly evaluate all

4 component judgments underlying any strategy on any decision or else they are likely to be hypocritical judgments with untested assumptions.

Therefore right judgment requires that one is able to evaluate the intent and motives of whoever and whatever is being evaluated. Is the motive pure, good and loving or is the intent in part for one's own self-interest, in which case it is the wrong motive? If the intent is self-interest to preserve one's physical survival in which case even though it is wrong, it is least wrong, necessary and correct; or is it or is it greedy self-interest that has little to do with legitimate self-defense, in which case it is very wrong and to the extent it causes harm to others it is evil?

Does the rational, logic and strategy make common sense or are there inconsistencies in the strategy and/or between the rational and the assumed intent? Is the logic righteous or is it wrong?

What are the emotional causes and implications to others and self and which part of those emotions are validly related to the current circumstance and which portion are "carry-over" emotions that one brings along with them-selves?

What are the physical causes and implications of whatever is evaluated or decided as evidenced by the facts and by rational well-tested theories?

Each of these 4 elements of judgment must be explicitly judged rightly for one's judgment to be right or correct and to the extent that it is not is the extent to which the potential hypocrisy of either the judge or the judged is not exposed.

Disease-Healthcare-Health: This holistic approach (that takes into account all 4 human components) applies also to disease-health and medicine. It was pioneered in recent times by Deepak Chopra, among others, and it is practiced and has proven to produce better outcomes with least harm and at less cost, through the multi-specialty team approach as is applied in Cleveland Clinic. (Cleveland Clinic's more ethical compensation system of doctors is also a critical component of their success.) The holistic approach to medicine and to health is the one of "first, do no harm," as was intended by Hippocrates and has gained significant acceptance but still it is not common practice, as it should be.

The Philosophy: R. W. Emerson wrote that philosophy is "footnotes to Plato." This TOE supports that Plato's assertion, that our bodies and the visible world are the 'shadows' of the (important, positive) light and life that are our invisible soul, eternally living Ideas, thoughts, and emotions, **is right**.

The Politics: The TOE supports that Aristotle is **correct** about **democratic** politics being the best (least wrong) in dealing with the (necessary, negative,) physical, shadows, images of the worldly, and the balances of their numbers.

As to **the appropriate ethics** it confirms that Aristotle is correct (least wrong) in noting in the Ethics, "...virtue is concerned with passions and actions, in which **excess** is a form of failure, and so is defect, while the **intermediate** is praised and is a form of success."

That is why, in the context of those staying in the current societies, I stand firmly in support of the mostly compromising, restored moderate modest, straight, honest s., w. and b's.!

My modest mostly endorsement of these beautifully moderate ladies and men, is because they are how by the necessities of life they mostly had to be; they are the best there is, and as modest salt makes food tastier, they are the salt of the earth.

Currently the media and the political structures encourage, promote, represent and are represented by excess.

That is why there is a need for a **Moderate Independent Party** that supports moderate Independent Candidates, offers sustainably beneficial to the public bi-partisan solutions (as above), and endorses the moderate candidates of the other political Parties.

International politics-economics: The only explanation for the people of Spain, Portugal and Greece continuing to suffer an economic depression by choosing to submit to the ECB and to Germany rather than managing their own currencies, is intense masochism.

Growth in manufacturing must shift from China to the rest of the world, as I show how, (that includes declaring China a currency manipulator, as it is,) or else the US, the free world and you are all in fully predictable immense trouble, economically, politically, environmentally and militarily no matter what democracies do to reduce their own fiscal deficits.

The solutions: The global warming; the military (N. Korea, terrorism, Iran); the economic growth and the fiscal and trade deficits/debts; and the sociopolitical problems also form the Cross of humanity. This book has offered the correct solutions that work together in dealing with each and all of them, with the solution of each enhancing the solutions to the others.

The faith and Knowledge: The book and I validate and confirm Christ Jesus's claim that He was the embodiment of, the eternal who, what and why Right intends, is, means and does.

A central advantage of understanding what right means and therefore that you or any of the politicians are not right but are in part wrong (other than it is true) is that it allows for, in fact it makes it an intellectual imperative that you and politicians co-operate and compromise in reducing wrongs.

The alternatives to this clear simple complete coherent understanding of Life and of the Universe, are incoherent theories by multiple disciplines, each theory being different and incompatible with the other disciplines, in confusion.

Accepting the truthfulness of the TOE and/or its philosophy without accepting the truthfulness of its source, Christ Jesus through me, is wrong.

During my travels, I realized that I didn't need to speak the language of the locals so long as what I communicated about was physical, because no matter how dog is called in any language, I could point to it and that is all I needed to communicate.

However when it comes to emotions, thoughts, ideas, any word, even a seemingly straight forward word such as "go" can mean a very wide range of things with fuzzy boundaries and so any word is like a cloud, depending on many factors, including the context and interpreter, but here I want to emphasize the difference that the same word can mean depending on the Spirit in which it is said. There can be a loving and a hating "go." Even the word 'bitch' can be meant lovingly, as the short comedian with the self-proclaimed "luxurious hair" convincingly exclaims: "I love the bitches; I do everything for the bitches..."

And almost irrelevant how the written 'go' was meant, it can be interpreted as a hating, a loving 'go' and in many in between ways as any actor can show you. For example, the exact same Holy Scriptures have been interpreted differently enough as to trigger real wars between... believers of Love! This is part of the evidence that communication, as all the spiritual functions including consciousness, obey the principles of Quantum Mechanics and not of General Relativity.

So, the Spirit in which something is interpreted, said, and/or done is critical as to what it means to you.

I claim to know and to have felt your pain; I know and have felt your anxieties; your fears, your shame, your guilt, your suffering, your greed, your lust, your ambitions, your disappointments, your loneliness, your confusion, your dissatisfaction, your frustration, your exhaustion, your sadness, your boredom, your anger, your hate and your wrath. I am truly sorry because I know how painful each of these is. But I also know that I can and do escape any and all these at my will. I do so by letting the Holy Spirit by His Loving Spirits raise me into God's Kingdom. And I know that you can do it too if you choose, every human can; because all humans are created equal.

Even though we each use our capacity and rights unequally we are each created with the same (eternal infinite divine) capacity and rights and are judged equally by God's Commandments and by God's Laws of Nature.

I clarify this because I do not want you to feel superior for not be a Greek watching what to you may appear as a comedy but to me is a real Greek tragedy of the demise, economic depression and willful enslavement of the cradle of Western Civilization to the spiritually barbaric Germs. That demise is a harbinger of what is about to happen to the rest of the West unless they change to as I show, now.

You have the God given right and should say f. off to any tyrant or self-serving leader, as I do to all of them now.

I also emphasize that we are created equal so that if you were born in the US or in China or in Europe you don't feel inferior just because you weren't born in Ethiopia as I was!

Finally and to start with, this book explains the One God's Spiritual Kingdom of Love and who Love is, means and does that validates all the Loving Spirits of the seven great religions of the world, (not necessarily the actions of their institutions).

Those that are part of the religions of the world better understand what the Resurrected Christ says in Revelation to His Churches.

The loving intent is needed most toward those whom you do not like. I will repeat, viewed "from bottom up," the Loving Spirits of the Glorious Holy Spirit, which are the Eternal Values and Principles of Life, are the Eternal Truths that have been, are and will be and are the Gifts that He has given us by which we are lifted into the eternal Heavens.

"The ladders" to and from the heavens start with Knowledge of Self, self-reliance, self- governance, self-accountability, mutual respect and then rise by helping those trapped by inter-dependences and co-dependencies through (ego) self-sacrifice to:

THE ETERNAL TRUTHS OF TRUTH

Faith in God, (and faithfulness in Loving), Honesty, fear of God, Discernment, Endurance, Integrity, **Just Justice**;
Compassion, Understanding, Courage, **Wisdom**;
Kindness Goodness, Hope, Charity, **Forgiveness**;
Humility, Mercy, Peace, Separation **Holiness**;
Thanksgiving, Perseverance, Harmony, **Grace;**
Competence Excellence, Joy, **Enlightenment**;
Freedom Liberty, Creativity Innovation, Renewal of Life, **Righteousness**.

These Self-evident Truths, Gifts of the Holy Spirit, and inalienable rights "are endowed to us by our Creator." These Harmonious Expressions of the Holy Spirit of Love and Life are the pillars of the Holy of holies of the Spiritual Temple of God.

Usually if one's spirit is at a certain stage the Intellectual and emotional states are the ones that correspond as above to that stage.

So whatever you interpret, say or do, if you do it in the any of the loving Spirits as above, you are in the eternal Spirit of God, you are a Child of God, are pure at heart, are blessed, a blessing and will live forever, as you wish when you wish, even if you die. God wants you to live in absolute joy forever; do you?

If you live within God's Kingdom, within that Holy of holies, you are Seen as sinless. It is in that Holy of holies that the 12 Commandments are kept.

There are two opposing processes going on simultaneously in any interaction among living things. One is from one's own spirit through their body to the outside world and the other is from the outside world through your bodily senses to your spirit.

So while the priority, preference and pre-requisite sequence from the Spirit through the material is from Righteousness, to Deliverance, to Grace....to Justice the sequence is reversed, like in the formulation vs. execution of strategy, and there has to be Justice perceived from the outside world through their senses for people to then start elevating themselves to being understanding and wise and then know when and how and to whom to be forgiving... and then find their separate, unique, Holy Wholeness and then to humble Grace, Enlightened Liberty and Righteousness.

1. "Life and death" or Eternal Life?

"What is the most important decision and choice that I or you have to make in life and why?" asks an old friend.

The central choice in life is: Do you choose your life and your children's **life to be eternal**; or do you want your and their lives to end with death? All the other choices follow from this choice.

The difference between living forever versus surviving in fear and loneliness to exhaustion and death is immense.

It is the difference between living eternally in joy by the Spirit of God-Love vs. "living and dying" while struggling to survive a little longer in fear, loneliness and suffering to death, as animals.

Living primarily in God's Spirit vs. in the animalistic ego, is the difference between the spiritually Alive vs. the spiritually Dead that like animals feel free but whose fate to death is predestined.

The Divine Spirit and the animalistic instinctive body are both within each child, making a **dual**ity, like the left and/vs. the right side of your body.

That synchronously self-conflicted **dual**ity is in all Nature, is caused by the opposing forces of the Universe and is in the nature of each indivi-**dual**.

Life (eternal) vs. "living and dying" is the central and most important choice for each to make while alive because it determines not just all your other choices but also the Life or death of your and our children.

The only ones that live and will live forever are those living in God's Kingdom of Love.

"What-Where is the Kingdom of God?" asks the old long lost friend.

2. The Kingdom of God, who is Love

Love is **Righteous** and others saves, love is eternal and resurrects, love is creative, innovates and impregnates, love is Free and others Liberates (Christ Jesus); love is kind and **Enlightens**, love is competent and leads, love is joyful and delights (Buddha); love is **Graceful** and harmonizes with its undeserving opposites, love is thankful for the opportunity to love, love is humble and others elevates, love is patient, persists and despite failures perseveres (The Vedas); love is **Holy**, is separate and the holy from the unholy separates, love is discerning and distinguishes right from wrong and truth from lies, love is in peace and makes peace (Lao Tzu); love is merciful and **Forgives**, love is hopeful and inspires, love is compassionate and the needy helps, (Mohammed); love is **Wise** and rightly teaches, love is courageous and conquers, love is Sovereign and self-governs (Confucius); love is faithful and endures, love is honest, truthful and integrity restores, love is **Just,** lawful, and the unjustly injured redeems(Moses and the prophets.)

These are the Righteous Ways by which God loves you. These are the righteous expressions of Love by which God wants you to love others. It is by these Spirits of Love that the founders of the seven great religions were inspired and lived.

"I love whatever I need and express it by my willingness to have sex for it. Their love is shown by how much they give me. My preferred price is

commitment to exclusive sex from me till death but I'm open to negotiation. Most people consider love to be whatever they like. Your explanation of love is like trying to teach poetry to Camels," says my enemy, the secretly ruling authority of the world, laughing while sitting on her golden throne in her amazingly opulent palace that's in a highly classified location.

Love's expressions are by the seven Spirits of God (Rev. 4.5), each of which inspire each of the seven great righteous religions of the world, as above, is in the sequence of: Christianity; Buddhism; Hinduism; Taoism; Islam; Confucianism; and Judaism.

Even though each religion refers to every expression of love, each Spirit of love and each faith is focused on the particular expressions of love as shown in the above sequence, as they manifest into the soul, reason and emotion of a person, at each level.

Each religion is self-divided to some extent by various sects placing a different emphasis on their "central" expression of love.

Other 'religions' that also preach some of the expressions of love as above, include Sheik (a combination of Hinduism and Islam,) Shinto (in Japan,) Jainism (in India; rejects all violence) and Baha'i (from and persecuted in Iran).

(Older, mostly obsolete belief systems about the existence and importance of more than just matter spiritual forces, are multiple and include the 12 Greek and then Roman gods, the Zoroastrians, and Shamanism.)

Just the (basic) single "headline" evidence is provided here confirming that each founder of the seven great religions of the world did indeed express and live by the Spirit of Love as described.

- "Take this **book of the law** and put it beside the arc of the covenant of the Lord your God; let it remain there as a witness against you." (Deut. 31. 24-26) This is part of the evidence that Judaism is in the Spirit of **Justice.**

- "**Wisdom**, compassion and courage, are the three universally recognized moral qualities of man," said Confucius, from THE WISDOM OF CONFUCIUS, p.118, showing self-evidently that Confucius is in the Spirit of Wisdom.

- Every Chapter in the Koran starts with: "In the name of Allah the Compassionate, the Merciful." This should be a clear clue to Muslims that God is asking them to be in the Spirit of **forgiveness**, asking forgiveness when wrong and being compassionate, merciful and forgiving.

- "Righteousness is kindly, and kindness divine and divinity is the Way that is final." (From THE WAY OF LIFE, Lao Tzu, Chapter 16, p.68) confirming that Lao Tzu is in the Spirit of (divinity) **holiness** and that is the Spirit that Taoist are asked to operate through.

- The Lord Krishna (that is derived from the Greek 'Christos', as is Christ), said: "At the end of each millennium all material manifestations enter my nature and in the new millennium I create them again; I deliver the holy, destroy the sin of the sinner and establish the righteous." That is the Spirit of **Grace** and that is the Spirit that Hindus are asked to operate by.

- Buddha means **Enlightened,** (by The Light), and is about the joy in being liberated from the life-death cycle and delivered into the "pre-existing" Absolute (God). "There is an unborn, neither become nor created nor formed; were it not there would be no deliverance from the formed and created," said the Buddha, (UD.80-81.)

- "The Advocate will prove the world wrong about **Righteousness**… because I (Righteousness) am going to the Father and you will not see me (Righteousness) any longer…" (John 16.8). If you don't believe that Jesus is a liar, he is **Righteousness**, and you had not Seen him until now.

Now, the Lord Christ Jesus is "shepherding all his flocks;" all those mentioned above that are in His righteous paths, as He said He will.

Further explanation of the above along with examples and the further supporting quotes from the primary holy text of each religion can be found in the First Section of the 2006 book: "The World Anew" by Paul Zecos.

The biggest problem of all of the seven great religions of the world is (too much emphasis on religious rituals and traditions and) too little emphasis on the Spirit of Loving others by which believers are being asked to live.

There are many expressions of Love because different times, circumstances and people need different expressions of love.

It is a Kingdom because Love is, as above, hierarchical with a sequence of preference and priority; the **first expression, righteousness, being a rational pre-requisite of and inclusive of the next and so forth.**

Some fail to understand that the eternal Truths of their religion such as forgiveness, kindness, courage, compassion, humility, joy etc. come from love. Others fail to recognize that the synthesis of truths (even of material truths) into "greater truths" is and must be hierarchical; for e.g. potatoes and carrots are part of vegetables, which are part of...

There are no arguments among the true expressions of love. There is no one that truly lovingly says that expressing love by, for example, compassion is garbage but by humility is not garbage. The expressions of love, as above, are mutually supportive and thus are in harmony; they are the Harmony of the Cosmos.

God is the same One God of every religion, though expressed through a different Spirit, i.e. Expression of Love.

God loves and likes any true believer irrelevant of the religion though which they believe in Him. God loves and likes even those that do not believe in Him yet do operate by a Loving Spirit rather than by self-absorbed and self-interested spirits.

Instead of arguing, fighting and killing in the name of religion, God and love, (as part of the controlling each other human power games) believers should understand and be inspired by the Spirit of love of their own faith, as explained above, so that in being faithful to the Spirit of their faith **love and like the Spirit of every other faith of the One God and of anyone that expresses and acts by any of the Spirits of Love.**

"Woe to you hypocrites, how are you going to escape damnation; because you fuss over details and ignore the weightier matters of Justice, Mercy and Love," said Christ Jesus.

It is only the hypocrites, who are sinners, are wrong and deny it and have been condemned to hell, as Jesus warned, by the Holy Spirit of God, that make up arguments among expressions of love to get attention, power and authority over others.

"I'm offended. Aren't you? Stop asking questions and go make some money," says my enemy, the world's greatest villain, pointing her finger somewhere.

"How do I choose which expression of love is right for and/or by me?" asks my old friend who does not remember me yet.

The Righteousness of God

The means by which love chooses its **right** expression for the particular individual circumstance-time and acts on it, is self-evidently **Right**eousness, Christ Jesus, who is the ruler, The Most High, the king of kings and Lord of Lords in God's Kingdom.

The righteousness of God is the intending, thinking, feeling and acting in the best interest of others while clearly excluding one's own self-interest.

If one's self-interests are not clearly excluded, the answer about what "is right for you" cannot be and is not objectively right for you.

Righteousness, Christ Jesus, is the highest expression of love because it is the only rational means and the necessary pre-requisite by which to choose whom to love, when and how. He is the most High also because He embodied the **love of the enemy** and that is **the only way to make two opposing entities, which is inevitable given the conflicted forces of Nature, into One.**

Righteousness, Christ Jesus, is also the most preferred expression of love because righteousness saves others from death. And Justice is least desirable because despite all other efforts of the more preferred expressions of love to prevent harm, not-forgiven harm has already occurred for Justice to start operating.

Within Christianity there is Ap. Paul's beautiful description: Love is patient, love is kind. It does not envy, it does not boast, it is not proud. It does not dishonor others, it is not self-seeking, it is not easily angered, it keeps no record of wrongs. Love does not delight in evil but rejoices with the truth. It always protects, always trusts, always hopes, always perseveres. Love never fails. (First Corinthians 13:4-8).

And there are expressions of the sequence and hierarchy, as I describe it, of love's "seven heavens" by Ap. Paul in Galatians 5:22 as 'Fruits' or Gifts of the Holy Spirit (that start from love, joy, peace… to faithfulness….) And from the perspective of a 'bottom up' order (starting from faith, to goodness… to love) by Ap. Peter in his Second Letter (1:5) as "stages of Sainthood."

"For we know only in part and we prophesy only in part but when the complete comes the partial will come to an end." (First Corinthians 13: 9-11)

The seven Spirits of God are also symbolized in some religions such as in Judaism by the seven candles of the Menorah.

Finally, the sequence is as above also because of the **degree of self - sacrifice** required to get from <u>Justice, to Wisdom, to Forgiveness, to Holiness, to Grace, to Enlightenment, and to Righteousness.</u>

THESE ARE THE SEVEN SPIRITS OF GOD.

Intellectually the rational sequence and preference is from righteousness to Justice because one must understand what right is before they can make any right or Just (i.e. correct, least wrong, least inconsistent or most consistent with right) judgment.

In practice however the sequence is reversed with Justice being at the foundation and a necessary prerequisite for others to get to the next stage of wisdom that is in turn a pre-requisite to successfully sustain being forgiving….

Each of the seven religions that correspond to each of these stages as I showed above have the common understanding of the reciprocity embedded in the laws of the Universe. And so they each preach the "golden rule" **of treating others as you want to be treated**, that many atheists also believe in.

The law of reciprocity within the Universe and the golden rule do have a minor flaw in my view. Masochists or sadists shouldn't treat others with the pain that they like to be treated. For masochists and sadists there is a special treatment that I discuss later.

The expressions of Love can also be thought of as branches of God's Righteousness, as in the Kabbalah's "Tree of Life."

Righteousness is not instinctive to humans and that is why it is called "the righteousness of God," but righteousness is intuitive and it is objectively right.

Humans have many opinions and disagreements about everything yet no one has, and not even the best attorneys can credibly argue that evil is better than good or that hate is better than love or that wrong is better than right or that lies are better than truth. The arguments fail on their face.

There is no opposition from anyone in the heavens, in Spirit, **to the rule of the Good (absolutely, completely and only good towards each and all) Loving** (the Conscience, Father**)** Right (Reason, Son, Christ Jesus) and True (Expressions, Holy Spirit) One God and His Kingdom of Love. (Unless one argues that evil is better than good, or that a little good is better than Absolute Good, or that there is no Oneness in Good Right True.)

God, the Father, is all powerful but is in His Nature Free and does not impose or oppress; if He did He would not be Absolutely Good and the only Good.

Because the evil, wrong, liars cannot argue that it is preferable to be wrong rather than right, the evil **hypocritically hide behind** religion and laws, claiming falsely to be right while doing wrong and evil and causing suffering and destruction.

So, there is much suffering, unnecessary destructions and deaths caused by humans, contrary to God's Will.

The disasters that are experienced are the inevitable results, by the God Designed laws of Nature that contain reciprocity, of the wrong actions of people's ancestors and of one's own wrong actions. There are no accidents.

The seven Spirits of God are the Spirits of the Holy Spirit. God's Spirit is the Source and Judge of each and all life. The Holy Spirit is not Good, the Father only is Good; The Holy Spirit is True; He is all the Truth and nothing but the Truth.

If the truth is that you are wrong, you are wrong. If the damage you caused is X, X will be what you get. If you lived a lie, you die and no longer exist. If you become righteous you are rewarded. The Holy Spirit determines the destiny of each soul after death. Souls go to

Paradise or Recycling (Reincarnation, Purgatory) or hell or no longer exist ("scatter.")

The decision is made by you while you are alive. (After you die you can no longer change.) The Holy Spirit is the truth about what your decision truly was, as expressed by the totality of your actions, irrelevant of what you think, feel or say.

Because of the great unnecessary suffering caused by humans, the Holy Spirit always has the last word and He recovers, relieves, redeems, repairs, revives, reconciles, restores and resurrects the unjustly harmed; redirects the sinners and condemns the not repenting criminals, and particularly the hypocrites that falsely claim that their judgment is right while being wrong and sinners.

God intervenes and inspires the human spirit through The Holy Spirit to prevent harm, to warn of impending destructions, that unless people change will happen and to teach and guide, as He is doing now.

"**First** seek the Kingdom of God and righteousness." (Mat. 6:33) Have you done so? Did you understand of what is the Kingdom of God and what-who is righteousness? Or are you deceived and distracted to destruction and death?

"I told you that this book is heavy. Despite being an engineer and an inventor, the author ignores our brilliant technological advances that allow super-fast global communications of human silliness, tragedy and confusion. The world is perfect as it is; it needs no major change.

Even the uglier than monkey s. Bill Maher knows enough to not believe in God. Did you take care of your nails, shoes, buy lingerie, brush your hair, and make dinner? Do those. Junk this book," says our loveless enemy lying down on her golden bed.

*"How may I live in God's Kingdom **on earth**?" asks my old friend.*

God's Kingdom on earth

The Kingdom of God, that is the main subject of the three synoptic Gospels (of Mathew, Mark, Luke,) on earth is not intended as a utopian fantasy but as a real kingdom of Independent and sovereign Lands from the current governments of nations of the world, for the weak, poor, suffering, alienated and the resurrected righteous that choose to know the Good God, and only good.

Any small land within a nation, even if a village or piece of desert (to be purchased,) is enough for God's Kingdom, so long as it is recognized as a **demilitarized, disarmed and Independent Land**.

These Lands of God must be Independent from the current national governments or else they are bound to be operated and oppressed by power (over others),money (more than others) and fame (as better than others) and self-entertainment driven by **fears, selfishness, greed**, ignorance, loneliness, boredom, sex, hurt, anger confusion and laziness, as it has been.

Many attempts by small communities or denominations to live by love have failed because these communities have had to be dependent on the current power-money-fame structures and so they ultimately had to play those control of each other games to survive resulting in them becoming hypocrites and failing.

The one and only one Independent Demilitarized, Disarmed Land of God within each nation is not intended to be the dominant system of a nation or to compete with the current system of government, but rather to help those within the nation with chronic problems that current governments cannot solve.

These disarmed Lands of God are not intended for the rich, strong and happy who obviously like the current systems, but rather for the weak that feel oppressed, the poor that cannot or are not willing to do what they have to within the current systems to be affluent, the sad or depressed that find no joy in operating in the current societies, the refugees, the homeless, potentially the prisoners (who want to be rehabilitated), the alienated and disenfranchised, the religious extremists, those that are suffering from some harm and need a temporary respite of love, and the truly righteous believers that want to live by co-operating by love rather than by the current competitive survivalist systems of power-money-fame.

God's Kingdom of Love on earth will not be imposed by God but will be voluntarily established by people, as prophesied by the three Abrahamic religions, on the Day of Resurrection and of Judgment.

"Our people can't handle the truth. Tell him not to waste our time with trying to tell all of the truth because no one wants to hear it and he will get hurt," says my enemy in anger.

"When is the Resurrection and Judgment Day?" asks my old friend.

3.   The Resurrection of the Dead

The dead are resurrected as you become Aware and conscious of them.

The dead in body from the very beginning of life are alive **without discontinuity**, in the DNA of every cell of your mind, heart and body and are distinctly identifiable. You are their children; their future. Those that valued most their body have the remnant of what they most valued about themselves "alive and kicking" in your body.

The Dead in God's Spirit, those "living and dying" in the world, are also being resurrected now by becoming Aware and understanding eternal living.

The righteous with Christ Jesus, from your own ancestries, that were wrongly injured and killed in body but live eternally are also Present here-now seeking to live on earth again.

Will you allow them to live in peace and safely on earth?

The righteous are not of this world, do not operate for self-interest, did not and cannot survive in the world without the establishment of a sovereign, independent, kingdom of love on earth, through independent, demilitarized, disarmed, anti-violent, sovereign Lands for those that voluntarily choose to live by loving and by mercy; rather than living by money, power, force, judgments by appearances and Justice as the world necessarily does.

Acting righteously among those that believe in their own self-interest is like feeding sheep to wolves; it punishes the righteous deeds, strengthens the evil, and at best causes co-dependency. Let the dead Resurrect.

Are there any dead that you know that are not resurrected?

"My time costs money; my love costs a lot of money. Authors are disturbed people. The density of hairs on the author's back is evidence of the missing link. You are beautiful. Don't pay attention to him," says my enemy while putting her make-up on.

4.   The World is Wrong

Many worship God hypocritically in words only but contrary to God's Will (and people's "beliefs") not even one small Land within this world is ruled by love and by Right, but all are ruled by might (power, and by money, which is also a form of power) though governments of nations each acting explicitly in their own self-interest.

What is even worst and is blasphemous against God is that many abuse religion to hurt and/or to kill others. If one says that they are a believer in God and one is a murderer, then one is not just a murderer but one also blasphemes God because who would want to believe in God, if murder is what God's believers do?

Blasphemy against the Holy Spirit in any form is the unforgivable sin that gets one to eternal hell without forgiveness ever, as Christ Jesus, the most forgiving, said (Mark 3. 28) and as you should know.

Even a small pain (like the Chinese torture by drops of water,) if it is forever it is immense torment in which case death becomes a merciful relief.

Both the truly righteous and the condemned to hell hypocrites say that they are right and are righteous.

For right to be right it must be provable and verifiable. Even the scientific standard requires that for anything to be right, it must provably exclude self-interest, and be **verifiable** by any objective observer.

As a past skeptic I can understand if some disagree with Jesus's teachings but no one can deny that he provably excluded his self-interest and was at least a righteous, moral man.

Once one understands the righteousness of God as above then it is clear that governments of nations that operate by necessity in self-interest act wrongly every time.

No matter what politicians say, they are acting in self-interest (even the few most altruistic that go beyond narrow self-interest and beyond political Party interest and act in the self-interest of their nation) so when they say that they are right, they are lying; in truth they mean the Babylonian, confusion inducing, "right for themselves" or (of their idea of) "the nation" in the abstract but they are always wrong towards you.

Understanding how wrong each action is, relative to the alternatives, is quite complex and requires understanding and **knowledge of the relative good and evil of various evils,** because unlike the Absolute Good God, **all evil and all worldly issues including animal life are relative and temporary. So that even the 'most evil' person is still a relative and includes some goodness.**

Yet, that knowledge of evils and their relative harm, burdens scars and finally kills the knower.

This has been told to you by the Spirit of God from the beginning in the form of: "do not eat from the fruit of knowledge of good and evil because you will die."

-The world is wrong because people misunderstand what righteousness is; **what right must be, to be right.**

People wrongly and falsely call their judgments and actions right without evidence of having excluded their self-interest.

As a Greek, with an exceptional tradition of great teachers and leaders it is not in my self-interest or national interest to claim that a Jew, Jesus, is more than a righteous man; that He is Righteousness.

-The world is provably wrong and sinful; look at the news. Most people say that they believe in God, in love, and/or in Righteousness, The Son, but their actions and lives prove that they are sinning, harming others, and are self-destroying hypocrites. It is bad to be wrong or sinners; it is **twice as evil** to deny it and keep doing wrong and calling it right as the hypocrites do.

Hypocrites make wrong judgments that are for their own self-interest, sin, and then use scriptures, laws and **deceit** to make it look that their judgment is right (for others). People sin because they don't truly believe in Jesus, Right enough and to do what is right for others.

Yet if there was no Right, there would be no point in any communication, and life would be meaningless.

-And the world is proven wrong because the Presidents and political leaders of the national governments are ruling the world wrongly, oppressively, and then falsely claim to have good and/or right judgment while the evidence —by what they get for themselves, while others continue suffering — is that they make wrong, self-interested, by the spirit of Babylon, judgments every time. Being sinners, wrong and not admitting it **doubles** the wrong **which is why these leaders have been condemned to hell.**

Have I done my job described in John 16:8-12?

The righteous, as their first priority, will work for the establishment of God's Independent Kingdom on earth showing that they are not hypocrites. The condemned to hell hypocrites have done, do and will do nothing about it.

The record of implementation so far of the righteous Teachings of the Holy Spirit by the seven great religions is mixed. Revelation 2, 3 is to the Seven Religions (Congregations; "Churches;" Assemblies) of Asia, as each founder established his religion in Asia. Their record and what they should do, is described in Revelation 2, 3, in the "bottom up" sequence of: Judaism, Confucianism, Islam, Taoism, Hinduism, Buddhism and Christianity. Heed God's words.

God did not give his first begotten Son for the sinners to keep sinning while lying in claiming to have been saved.

Unlike the liar, deceiver who claimed that you will not die, God is truthful and is The Truth. Humans did die and will die **except those that truly believe in righteousness and thus live righteously in God's Kingdom on earth.**

When I was younger I was not religious nor had much faith. A major reason for it is that when I would ask anyone knowledgeable about what their religion says about when and how humanity will start doing well, the answer I got from Christians, Jews and Muslims is that life is expected to get more difficult until the coming (or second coming) of the Messiah on the "clouds of heaven." That there is nothing I or anyone else could do effectively, until then, was highly unsatisfactory for me. Now I understand that Jesus Christ has been and is on the 'clouds of heaven' now and the only waiting that is happening is for humans to meet Him.

I am sorry I had to, but didn't I just prove the world and you wrong? The positive side of this is that learning is about correcting your wrongs and there is joy in becoming better.

Jesus forgave the sinners but not the hypocrites; how and why can they be forgiven while they don't admit that they are wrong?

Jesus warned the hypocrites: "How are you going to escape being sentenced to hell?" (Mat. 22. 33) "Woe to you hypocrites because you are like whitewashed tombs, which on the outside look beautiful but inside (in your spirit) you are full of filth."

"Sin is wrong and results in suffering of others and of one-self; and if one does not truly repent to get forgiveness it results in death. Grave sin, such as murder or war, while claiming to be right, as national leaders do, is hypocrisy that is condemned to hell. Terrorists who commit grave sin in the name of God are hypocrites and also blaspheme God, so they will end up in fiery hell forever without forgiveness," says Allah.

Potential Islamic terrorists must be informed of their sentence to eternal hell without forgiveness by Allah prior to committing any such act. Please help them and yourself by informing them, now. Allah the compassionate and merciful shows them here the correct way of meeting their objectives without destruction and death but constructively that will get them to the 'afterlife' here on earth.

"I feel that you are preaching and that is not going to work for me," *says my long lost friend looking somewhat dismayed.*

The main villain, my enemy, intervenes and says: *"We can't let this bozo get away with calling us all wrong. Theories; our prophet, the attorney, says to ask about his specific solution and Constitution."*

"What are the characteristics and Constitution of God's Lands, and how are they to be established?" asks my old friend.

5. Constitutions for the Lands of God

-God's Holy Lands should be demilitarized, verifiably by its affiliated secular government. No one should be allowed to bear arms in those Lands. The government of God's Lands should not be allowed to use physical force either.

All physical violence by any human against any human is wrong.

-The Lands of God (no more than one within each nation) must be Democratic and chose the political structures that the people within them wish, yet their government should attempt to be minimal.

The only recourse for injustice that is not forgiven is an, after a trial, extradition of the offender by a formal request of the government of the Land of God, to be implemented (if force is needed) by an affiliated national (i.e. current—mostly secular) government.

- Even though charity workers and believers of any faith of God should be most welcome, organized religious institutions should not be allowed in the Lands of God because there should be no need for any preaching. If one doesn't Know God, His Laws and Principles they should not be there.

The purpose of the Lands of God is not to preach about love as is needed in the world and as religious Institutions do, but to live by love with others that love, as is most needed.

- The only laws necessary, written in and guiding peoples' hearts and minds, are the Ten Commandments and Jesus's 11th Command of loving others as He loves. He is the Spirit one needs to be in, to keep the Ten.

The preferred three co-equal branches of Government are: **Righteous**; working with Charities for economic support of the needy; **Joy**; for spiritual, social, educational, emotional and physical help; **Justice**; helping with the issues of work, arbitrations, the Judiciary and extraditions.

- Anyone from any nation including non-believers, particularly any refugee (of the currently approx. 35 million and I count myself amongst them) should be allowed to visit and after a year become a citizen of the Lands of God, except lawyers. (Except for my friend Craig Andrews who was the brilliant attorney advising me when I was in business because I am grateful to him for his excellent advice that the best legal strategy is avoidance of litigation.)

Lawyers should not be allowed in, except any who significantly help in establishing the Lands of God, **because there should be no need for any lawyering that the accused or a friend can't do.**

- The economic system in God's Lands is preferably **"the other side"** from the (usually) capitalistic system that is most useful for secular States.

It needs to be "the other side" i.e. relatively socialistic, community, family like, hopefully by culture through charities, rather than by taxes but if charities fail, then by taxes that are re-distributed directly in cash not through programs that benefit mostly the government, **so that it provides an alternative system and government within each nation** thus allowing the most alienated, most dissatisfied, weakest, poorest and most disapproving of current systems, an option out. (For socialistic—communist nations as China, the relatively Independent capitalistic Hong Kong is what they needed.)

This will allow the leftist extremists who will not change their mind and currently imbalance the economy to go in the Independent unarmed Holy Lands and will allow the current societies to become more competitive. This also provides a safe sovereign place for "right wing" religious extremists to go, if they do not like the current 'mostly secular' systems, thus stabilizing the relatively secular societies.

Preferably no corporations will be allowed. To do business, people may form proprietorships or partnerships that have the same liability as persons do.

-Unlike the secular systems that become more globally interdependent, the Independent unarmed Demilitarized Lands of God should be as autonomous economically as achievable and therefore should each have its own currency.

For most people it is clear that capitalism is the most useful economic system generating the most wealth. Unfortunately most of that wealth is concentrated in few hands. For example, the top 5% in the US own about 65% of the wealth (pay about 60% of the taxes) and control over 90% of the wealth. Despite its problems, that can be better managed as I discuss later, the advantages of capitalism are much greater than the disadvantages for most (not for all) so I am not in any way suggesting rejection or replacement of the current systems but I am suggesting a supplemental Independent system for those, that are many, that don't feel helped by capitalism but hurt by it, such as the poor, weak, depressed, the disenfranchised, the oppressed, the peace-loving and the righteous.

So, given the targeted people for God's Disarmed Lands, using the currency only for interactions with the "outside world" and not using any money in the interactions amongst them-selves, the same way that money is not used to allocate resources within a family is the preferred economic system within those Holy Lands.

Those in the Independent Disarmed Demilitarized Democratic should be remembering Jesus Christ and righteousness not by the "Eucharist" as a ritual but by thankfully (which is what Eucharist means) sharing freely with others food (spiritual and physical) and joy.

By leaving the current human systems, all that you will lose financially is the huge debt that your current government owes and your children will have to pay.

- Marriage is appropriate and even central for those of the world because family is the only place where love has a decent chance of being experienced in the world as it has been. However, the Disarmed Independent Lands of God aren't primarily for those that are married or for those that want to get married, as Jesus explained in Mark 12:25, because there is no need for any ceremony or financial commitments for people to truly love.

Preferably, women in those Lands are "married" to the Christ. Marry in Spirit the Christ Jesus; the only Right One. Become Mrs. Right. I invite all to His Wedding.

As to a woman doing what is righteous towards men, it is not complex nor unpleasant nor difficult.

In Maslow's hierarchy of needs, sex is listed at the lowest level as a physiological need for both men and women. My hypothesis is that sex is much more of a physiological need for men than it is for women. It seems that sex is more of an emotional (social, love-belonging, intimacy) rather than physical need for women than for men. It may be a physical need for women also at least for some days a month yet the 'satisfaction time' ("the length of the waves") and rhythms are quite different. Whether the above is correct or not, all the data indicate that there is a significant statistical imbalance in the sexuality of men vs. women causing a series of psychological, behavioral imbalances and often wrongful sexual acts mostly by men. Ask Darwin, Freud, Maslow or any honest man.

So that some of the single women voluntarily, freely, being physically affectionate and offering without being asked, to make love (have safe, with contraceptives, clean physical sex) with any (not-married, not "celibate") adult man in God's Lands, excluding me, and excluding the elected leader(s) at the time in the Holy Lands, that seems to need it without asking or expecting anything in return, is what meets the needs of man, and what helping the needy is.

Sex and the words associated with sex have a pretty bad reputation not because the act itself is bad but because it is used uncleanly spiritually and physically. Sex is used as a means to get money by a certain group or for power by another group or for selfish pleasure just as money power and entertainment are used to attract sexual partners. It is this unclean spiritual intent and/or physical use of sex that caused and causes humans to cover their genitals in shame.

I don't encourage fornication because the intent of fornication is primarily the pleasure for one's own self, and it is wrong, as the Bible says. However given the current availability of hygiene, quite effective contraceptives, pills, tests and medicines that significantly reduce many of the potential major damages from uncommitted sex and because the intent of the sex that I suggest is primarily for the benefit of the other, it is probably the best way to reduce the imbalance and the abundance of fornication, masturbation and sexual crimes currently going on. I know that many will disagree with this part of my recommendation and those don't have to do it and I don't even recommend this behavior within these societies but only in the Independent unarmed Demilitarized Holy Lands. Only a few (nice looking ones) need to agree to make a significant difference.

If the intent for sex, the process and act is clean and by pure love, sex is a very positive act. Sex must not continue being used as an instrument of power/control because it results in competitions of power. Rather, sex must be an expression of compassion for those who you know are righteous, kind and/or in need.

There is no need to increase human population with more children but if a woman asks any man to raise (or help raise or mentor or babysit) her child, that man should gladly accept the honor and financial responsibility, whether that child is his or not, whether she chooses to also marry him or not, without asking or expecting anything in return.

The better "their children" do, the better "the environment" for 'our children.' Halleluiah, from the Hebrew, means 'Praise the Lord;' if it was also derived from Greek it would also mean: 'For our children.'

Even though men should work, their primary role in the Father's Lands is to be fathers who actually do as the ones in current societies talk about and actually spend more time with the children than their work.

I support the view on "celibacy or marriage" as the only defense in the self-interested W. houses produced by the systems of the world but neither is sustainably achievable by most. In my view, only children that grow up in the Lands of Love as I describe them will be able to maintain their integrity and joy while in celibacy, if they get plenty of non-sexual physical affection.

It is assumed that rape should be illegal and is a sin. And sex by an adult with any under-aged (18 years old) person should be illegal, including in Muslim nations despite the bad example of (in my view despicable) pedophilia by Mohammed. There is no justification in the Koran for pedophilia or for child rape that I can find.

The immense life-long damage done to hundreds of millions of young women in Muslim nations is based on wrongly idealizing Mohammed and thus considering correct whatever he did including his consummation of marriage (by all Muslim accounts) with a 9-10 year old (Aisha,) which is by definition pedophilia and which is and should be illegal and criminal in any civilized society. Children can be easily manipulated and no child at those ages can make an informed independent decision about sex.

In defense of Mohammed given that he lived during the Dark Ages, if the alternative in those times was to rape and leave children (as is still happening in some places) raping a child in the context of at least being married was an advance (an improvement) for those societies at those times but pedophilia is completely unacceptable in these times and in any civilized society of any time.

Muslims must choose between believing in Mohammed vs. believing in Allah because Allah says that "the prophet Mohammed is far from an ideal man and is illiterate, ignorant, wrong, and a sinner."

Mohammed himself said that he should not be idealized and that he was just another man subject to the ignorance, (and lies) incompetence (and wrongfulness) and immorality (and malice) of humans and is counting on God's forgiveness which is what believers in him and his **lousy and terrible Sharia law** better ask for, because they are wrong and are sinners.

There is indeed a holy war, (Jihad) that has been going on, and I am in that war, against the self-loving filthy evil spirits (within and amongst us) but that holy war is, by definition, strictly and only spiritual. When this holy war for the rule of and by good and right is made into a physical war it becomes another dirty war.

If they like the lousy Sharia law, Muslim nations may encourage it as a private code of ethics but it must not be imposed by either the government or anyone else, because the by violence imposition, even if it is the perfect Law as are God's 12 Commandments can cause almost as much harm as it produces benefits.

A few months prior to the Arab Spring I wrote an intentionally provocative article on the net, entitled: "Are the Muslim b'.s righteous?" that I hope contributed in causing the Arab revolt. The answer is that unless one is righteous by their free will, and not by being forced by the government or anyone else, one maybe a well behaved b. but is not righteous.

There are many valid reasons for Arabs and most others to revolt against their government or other governments but committing sin or violence in the name of God is condemned hypocrisy that invalidates all of them.

Muslims who by their complicity allow or encourage terrorism in the name of God are hypocrites that are condemned to hell.

Instead of the delusionary hope for "Virgins" by committing murder in the name of Allah which gets them to burning in hell forever, Muslims should look for the Virgins in an inclusive of any that so chooses Holy Demilitarized Disarmed Democratic Land that they establish here on earth.

The purpose of the governments in God's Lands is to help remove the obstacles —**fears, selfishness, greed**— that inhibit people from loving others truly, so while keeping the Eleven Commandments in mind, they can make up rules for their particular Land, including if they so believe "marriage or celibacy" recognizing that they will need to, in time, change those "rules."

Given the current horribly immoral spiritual condition of humanity, what is achievable at this time? In the areas where God's Lands are most urgently needed because they are contested or are in 'religious war' such as in Kandahar, Judea-Palestine, the Golan and Kashmir, the best that can be done now probably includes little of the above **but it must include being demilitarized and disarmed.**

As it has been until now the "converts" into "religion" are likely to be **"twice the children of hell," as Jesus said**, because they pretend to have been saved, while if they do not establish not even one Independent Sovereign, disarmed demilitarized Land of God on earth they will be hypocrites that are more sinful wrong evil and disgusting than diseased ugly prostitutes and they deny it.

"I'll be darn; I found an honest man asking for evidence by actions that one's beliefs are true!" says the founder of the Cynicism, Diogenes, who lives on the streets, while blowing off the lit candle that he carries during the day claiming that he is looking for an honest man and continues: "I am fed up; life is not worth living for me; death is better."

The whole world and you in it are currently rushing towards immense suffering, anguish, death and hell. No saint would want to live in the current murderous, violent, deceitful, destructive, hurtful, whorish and hypocritical societies.

As it is has been until now, there is no way that any of those leading the nations will get anywhere near God or heaven but will end up in hell.

Without an Independent, Demilitarized, disarmed, anti-violent, democratic Land of Love, (I use Love because in some places the word God has been wrongly defamed) within your nation, humanity's sufferings will increase.

Those of the American Congressional Churches are likely to be among the first to rush to God's Independent Disarmed Land.

There are two main examples of similar Independent Demilitarized lands that have been operating successfully, (with over a billion followers each), for a very long time, (that have a somewhat different function) and they are the Vatican, in Italy and Mecca in Saudi Arabia, and they have proven that they can be safe even if Demilitarized because people are afraid (and should be) to mess with Holy Lands. Actually Independent holy lands are the safest places in the world and even all the rest bomb each other to oblivion the Independent Disarmed Holy Lands will be the last places standing. (It's a shame that there are no women and children in the current two holy lands which would help preserve humanity.)

So, who wants to argue that a holy Land of your nation as I describe it, which is much more inclusive (in fact inclusive of all that choose) and in which love is practiced rather than just preached (often hypocritically) is not the Will of God?

And who wants to argue that God believes that the Saudis and the Italians should be entrusted with a holy Disarmed Demilitarized land of God within their nation (and I don't believe that either of these Lands is truly operating by any of God's Spirits because they really haven't seen righteousness and haven't known what it means, and so they don't really know how to be righteous) but that Americans or other Europeans or the Chinese or Africans should not be entrusted with a holy land within their nation because either there aren't enough holy people in your nation or because everyone in your nation is holy (in which case I will smack you and will expect you to turn the other cheek) or because you are more brutal that the Saudis and the Italians and will overrun the Independence or sanctity of your holy land?

Only with this solution, that God has called you to do, humanity you and your children will be delivered from suffering and evil.

"The bozo wants an Independent Land of free love and free sex; fat chance. Has hell frozen over and I missed it? Go make money baby, sell your-self the best you can and ignore him. Did you see on Y-tube a kitty dreaming she's in heaven? It's hilarious. People will not change even with these Lands," says our enemy while sipping Champaign. "Ask: What difference will this form of governance make?"

"What are the benefits to me and to my children?" asks my old friend hesitantly.

6.   Love is Free and Liberates

The poor, the depressed, the alienated, the refugees, the disenfranchised, the weak and the oppressed by definition don't have the know-how, the resources or the political power to make such a major socio-political change that they need; and are suffering the oppression in silence. The truly righteous is their only hope for this change and is the only way for them to be empowered, to be free and to relieve their suffering.

Only when the central tools for the animalistic competition of power (security, force, money, fame) for sex, through marriage or otherwise, are neither available nor needed in separate, Independent Sovereign unarmed demilitarized societies designed to eliminate these motives will humanity escape the fears, oppression, suffering and deaths that it is currently experiencing.

The Natural selection process, explained by Darwin in "THE DESCENT OF MAN, AND SELECTION IN RELATION TO SEX" (1871), (30) and procreation, is driven by whom and why you have sex.

Until men are loved freely and honestly including sexually by women they will try to **dominate** to deal with their loneliness, frustration and misery.

When and only when men are loved (freely-truly) by women for real, including physically, **the "scarcity" that is only in the human spirit, minds and hearts,** and the competition, oppression along with the associated abuse, crimes, damage and deceit will disappear. (Being so utterly small in the context of the Universe and claiming that there is scarcity can be true only for economists because there is much scarcity of light in their mind.)

With increasing civility, the role of physical force decreases and the role of economic power and of woman increases.

Ladies, because the life or death of humanity is now your choice, the Resurrected Jesus, who is now leading more people's lives than any of your "living now but dying," in His second Presence, is focused on teaching you. If there are no women willing to be separated into an Independent sovereign disarmed land of God where being righteous by action is the norm and self-reinforcing, rather than abused as it has been inevitably, pain and death to all is inevitable.

In God's Kingdom men should be spiritual and thus reduce their drive for power, money and fame to get enough descent sex. At the same time, the women that offer to make love to men not to get married or because they are married and not for getting power, security, fame, entertainment for themselves or for money but because of divine love **should** (if they wish) **be called Virgins** (and treated with outmost respect), because they **are Virgins, pure, in Spirit and should have the primary,** but not exclusive, **role in the governments of God's Lands.**

Some Beautiful (and pure in heart) Virgins in Spirit have existed from the beginning. These glorious Virgins in Spirit were central to advancing humanity even before the Parthenon—the word means "a place for the Virgin(s)." Where are my Virgins?

You heard of the "bad words" men use in private for women, that God can hear, because these men feel that women really want them for the money, the W. word relating to the first profession; or for their success, fame and for entertainment, **an S. word that rhymes with glut**; or for power, security and control, the B. word used for female doggies.

These 'bad words' are about the well-known human needs for achievement, for affiliation, and for power respectively that when pursued to excess or are out of balance and are out of control, **causing crippling psychological disorders to people who act what these bad words say**.

These psychological character disorders are narcissistic personality disorder (characterized by self-love, homosexuality, rejection of criticism) and mood disorders for the "financially overachieving" W. first professionals; histrionic and anxiety disorders for the over-controlling "dog like" B.; and borderline personality disorder, bi-polar mood disorder and addictions for the affiliation fanatic S.'s, that make it difficult for any man who gets close to such women to not say these bad words or leave. These are also the same personality disorders that cause women to leave men.

I can address these groups with personality disorders by their psychiatric name but I prefer to address them by how a common person experiences them which are as a W. and/or a B. and/or a S. There are male equivalent terms (describing the same disorders) which I disclose later but I use the feminine terms for both males and females with these disorders because from my prospective they are more descriptive.

As a statistical generalization I believe and the evidence shows that women are more balanced and cause less harm than men in each of these areas. So, I do not intend to be offensive particularly to women but rather to men, even though I use feminine common language terms to describe the character of their egos' psychiatric disorders.

Men that are truly loved and freely made love to (safely-cleanly) by women even if they did not believe in God before…will believe and will cry out like Muslims that God is great! And they will honor Man, me, that sent you to them, as a… great bozo!

If you want relationships that last forever, love rightly truly and freely.

Don't do so in the world as it is; you will get badly screwed for no benefit to any. Do so safely only in God's Lands, that women should primarily govern, either by living there or by temporarily going there to help, and you will be loved truly forever.

It was mentioned that the central problem of people in Churches, Mosques, and other attempts (and there have been many,) to live by their true beliefs, is that they are subordinate to a nation that is ruled by power-money and as a result they either succumb to that power-money struggle or become a part of it.

That problem of being controlled under the power-money-fame authorities has been exaggerated over time, even though governments have become less tyrannical, because of technological improvements that allowed the reach and power of governments to dramatically increase to the point that they are (almost) monitoring everything and everyone, everywhere on earth all the time.

Only an Independent, Disarmed, Demilitarized Land within a nation, and supported by that nation, can solve that central problem of being slaves to the powerful, power driven big governments and to the wealthy money driven big corporations.

IN A PRIVATE "Classified" meeting, **the United Nations Security Council** of top professionals is discussing the request.

"There's a revolutionary that wants a place in the world where sex is not paid; not even through dates or drinks or gifts or jobs or marriages and divorces; he must be nuts. He would like a sovereign place thus challenging the rule of the world by the self-interested spirits of the first profession. What should we do?"

"Who is he?" asks our enemy clearly upset.

"I don't know him; he is not paying for me; I think that he is Greek."

"Oh! No! Not that Easterner, (the meaning of the Latin word 'Greek'); He is back again. I was afraid of that. Placate him, talk, ask, argue with him, distract, do anything but don't let him go to war. **He is the most dangerous warrior ever**," says your mortal enemy.

"**Your Excellency, Queen Babylon,** I cannot handle him; he keeps making sense. I am afraid you have to deal with him yourself," says my old friend that has still not woken up.

"*There is no sense in any part of the world not being ruled by us; by our money and by force. I'll take care of it.*"

"*What if I choose to not help in establishing the Lands of God?*" asks Babylon the Great, that is described in Revelation as "The mother of whores and of earths abominations....with whom the kings of the world have fornicated," (Rev. 17) while stretching her legs.

When suffering becomes intolerable

Ladies,

Men know that you need security, prosperity, entertainment, to be well known and well liked, in exchange for your affection and that is what they try to offer and usually that's all they offer.

So, the chances that you will find true eternal love in these competitive power-money societies are as low as finding a porn star that is a virgin.

You may get a false temporary sense of strength, security, affluence, fun and fame from those in power, rich and famous. In these power driven beastly systems you may be pursued, your body may be admired and needed —a need that feels like a partial loss of self-control that is often unexpressed and so gets manifested in the form of addictions— but the chances that you will love truly and be loved truly, are minimal.

Imagine providing food and shelter to your children on the basis of money they have to earn and everything within your family was done through money. You may indeed produce more survivalist and survivable children but the depth of your relationship with them would get destroyed.

Loveless life is joyless life and after a while the fire of craving true love with no way to quench the fire of that passion is hell, so death becomes a relief.

After almost 40 years of praying almost daily that I die now, (in the mornings mostly,) if I was not able to ascend into the heavens from time to time, where we are now, and did not believe that the worldly experience is temporary and that my life will soon be in Paradise I would not be able to bear one more minute in this world. (That is why I thank God in my evening prayer for not answering my morning prayer literally but only letting my ego die.)

Billions of people and children are suffering greatly and are dying unnecessarily and unjustly, for the pleasure of very few prostitutes in spirit that like acids seek their base "soul-mates" in body. Suicides in the US kill more (than double the) people than murders do. Too many in this world, including me, find current human life so deceitful, loveless and destructive that we would rather die than participate in the violent competition of, by, and for deceitful hypocritical and disordered ugly prostitutes (W's), B's, and S.'s as humanity does.

"You think you know it all but baby you don't know a thing about me. Am I free to do as I chose or is there no choice in life to what God says?" asks Babylon while putting lipstick on.

"It has been written that the Truth will set us free. That presumes that we are not free yet. Are we free or not?" asks, my old friend.

BEING TRULY FREE

Creation, humanity and each is only as free as the truth about self that one can handle, admit to in honest remorse and change.

Most hide a part of themselves by keeping some secret from each of their relationships. The result is that they live in darkness and are bound to remain unknown, lonely and scared in Darkness, unless they change.

There is more freedom because there is more honesty, in democracies vs. in dictatorships, akin to the difference in the freedom of motion of a drop of water in a river vs. of a spec of sand in a rock. As a drop of water in a river there is a chance of not ending up where the river goes but you are far from Free. You are not free yet from oppression from force and from money; not free yet from fears, anxiety, depression, suffering and death.

Without the establishment of the Independent, demilitarized sovereign Lands of God, all, even the righteous, will inevitably die. All will die because the cumulative suffering from "living" becomes so great that at some point people would rather die. This is not theory; it is history. Did anyone escape death?

Unless **you truly change** how, where and why you think, feel and live, now, you and all others will die.

Do you know of any place where people live by love? Given your belief in love and God shouldn't there be at least one small land in the world where you or your children can go as strangers and experience true love?

I, like many, have been around the world several times but haven't found any place where people live by true love nor a place where I experienced love as a stranger.

Is there at least a place of Peace? Suppose that I being a pacifist, in the Spirit of the American Congregational Churches, live in a town of Texas where everyone carries a gun and it is Constitutional, with the chances that the Constitution will be changed being minimal, and it is even wrong to demilitarize and disarm a whole nation that feels threatened. So, what are my choices?

Submit to every scum with a gun; move somewhere else and submit or pretend (lie) to respect different scums with guns; or put aside my pacifism and carry a bazooka? All choices are unacceptable; **being free to choose among evils as you have to do now is not being truly free.** Where is your freedom to live safely without having to be amidst violence from people or governments?

Most people accept and defend the status quo because that is the natural inertial state. And many, particularly those with most of the power and money are actually quite happy with the current state of humanity and defend it.

Yet there are few that do understand that they can be in much greater freedom and much greater sustained joy in life and they want to experience it.

This is the time for an Exodus, again.

Humans can't claim to be doing right while having all the lands of the world be ruled by might (while lying and saying they're right) and not allow even one small Land to be truly ruled by Right; that is deadly, condemned to hell hypocrisy.

Until there are Demilitarized, Disarmed Lands of God, destructive, deceitful and self-destructing huge hypocrites dominate, resulting in increasing torment by anxiety and suffering to all humanity.

Whether you will choose to live there or not, set up one small Demilitarized Disarmed Independent Sovereign Holy Land, available to anyone to live there or leave or visit as they choose, in your nation, now, to avoid death and to be truly free. Even if you don't believe in God or in such holy lands having that option is much better than not having any option.

These lands should be called Holy because holy people will found it. They should each (at most one within each nation,) be recognized by their national government and by the U.N., as an Independent non-member observer State, (as is the Vatican and now Palestine.)

Actually, humanity's and your freedom is still very limited. Set yourself truly free and live in sustained joy as you believe is right by giving you and your children the choice of Good and only good, in an Independent unarmed Demilitarized Holy Land.

Your Deliverance from evil and suffering, was is and will be God's Will.

7.   "What is best for the world?"

Living righteously and so not for self-interest is diametrically opposed to surviving by self-interest. For example, living righteously is living without defenses, as Jesus did; while surviving the longest possible, delaying one's death the most, is operated by evolutionary principles, by being (or if female by having sex with) the strongest (to deter aggression), the most adaptable, and the fittest (most competent).

Just as there is a hierarchy of Love, with the most desirable being Righteousness, embodied in Christ Jesus, there are levels and degrees of wrongfulness.

These are the two inverted hierarchies (like triangles) of Truth, of Right and of wrong, that are symbolized by the Star of David.

The wrongfulness of calling someone a 'bad name' is no-where near the wrongfulness of those that do what the bad-name says.

The wrongfulness in Democracies (even the plutocracy that the US nears) is much less to the wrongfulness in dictatorships.

The wrongfulness, hypocrisy and commitment to self-interest of the powerful rich and famous, is much greater than the wrongfulness and pursuit of self-interest of the weak, poor and of the mourning.

That's why the "first," at the top of the current social hierarchies, are "last" in the eyes of God.

That is why the Christ Jesus lives within and among the weak, poor and depressed; that is why He blessed them; that is why He is with me, one of the least amongst you (a jobless alien with no office); and **that is why you are being judged now by how you will, from now on, treat the least.**

You are not judged by what you have done so far, because you didn't know what you were doing, per the Savior, and because you haven't been truly free.

But those mitigating excuses for your sins are no longer available; you must know by now the impact on others of what you don't do or do, and can and are urged to choose Life, Liberty and Joy.

God is judging you now by what your next actions are, with the corresponding repercussions.

"Who needs God's Kingdom on earth?"

Even if the major media, supposedly expressing public opinion, (but actually expressing their own self-interest) show no interest for such Independent, Disarmed Holy Lands, there are hundreds of millions and maybe billions of people who are weak, (like children and some who were abused as children, others because they are old or because of gender discrimination) have no voice, have little money, are not known, are alienated so usually they don't even bother to vote, and need these Demilitarized, Disarmed Democratic Independent Holy Lands in which to be free.

Also, there are millions in the US that want their State to secede from the US and have signed petitions for it and even though their numbers within each state is small, combined are in the millions.

And the pacifists, the righteous and the true believers in God pray for by the Lord's Prayer and need as their first priority an Independent sovereign unarmed Demilitarized Holy Land for the Father's Kingdom on earth.

Finally, if one considers what Muslim extremists and Islamic terrorist say their beliefs and objectives are: they say that they do what they do for the glory of Allah. They say that they believe in Peace, (part of what Islam means); they say that they believe in the surrender of their will to Allah's Will (the other meaning of Islam). They say they believe in the afterlife after (the spiritual death of the ego) in the Judgment Day. They say that their God is the same God as yours because He is the Only One God. Their objective they say is to live by what they believe. Yet, their methods are in complete opposition to their beliefs and objectives which is why they self-destroy and destroy Justice, Peace, compassion and Mercy. "Islamic terrorists are damned hypocrites and blasphemers of Allah. Violent Muslim terrorists are in hell and because they blaspheme Allah they are never to be forgiven," says the Angel Michael.

Killing Bin Laden was accomplished and destroying Al Qaeda has been mostly accomplished but their ideology through Islamic (Jihad) violent extremism i.e. terrorism, has in no way ended, until Muslims get informed that the ideology of Islamic violent extremism has been murdered permanently by this book.

The Demilitarized Disarmed Democratic Lands of God do give glory to Allah, (Al-Elih) are fully consistent with the stated beliefs and objectives of even Islamic extremists and will end the last remains of Islamic terrorism, leaving it with no spiritual, intellectual or practical foundation.

I am aware that writing about an Independent Demilitarized, Disarmed Land for the Kingdom of God on earth sounds unrealistic and irrelevant to most people who are concerned about their jobs and what they will eat and wear today to improve their mating chances but it is the only solution that will move humanity forward.

The problem of believers is that they live in the **wrong structure and systems**.

Like playing basketball in a soccer field during a soccer game or vice versa being a Christian or a believer in God of any faith within the power—money—self—pleasure structures and systems does not work. It is like everyone is trying to catch a killer and someone "righteous" is trying to protect the killer. Being a believer in God while living in a house of disrepute actually multiplies the problems, the same way that multiplying negatives with a positive does.

"Babe, as you know the word hypo**crisy** comes from your Hellenic, that is Alien to most, and means under-**judgment**; a judgment for self-interest that in deceit claims to be right; and when the truth comes out there is a **crisis; requiring an urgent judgment, in truth,**" says Babylon.

Correct: **Hypocrisy always results in a crisis. All crises were, are and will be caused by hypocritical judgments; (as opposed to honest and correct judgments or right judgment.)**

"They may say whatever but in truth most, particularly those in power, love and like living in my W. houses that they call Nations. I'm nice and meet their needs. It is their emotion and instinct versus right reasoning, and I win. That is why nothing changes despite what God Jesus and they pray or say.

You're wasting your time. Your suggestion is no more than what the Branch Dividians and those in Jonestown, Guyana tried to do," says my enemy on Skype from Washington D.C., shaving her legs.

You are wrong. These sects were never Independent and were not recognized by the government. I advocate not a plethora of fringe and splinter groups doing their own thing but only one authorized (verifiably Disarmed) or accepted Independent Holy Land in a nation.

These groups you mentioned were led and dominated by "charismatic leaders," who were interested in their own power. I have no interest whatsoever in leading anyone in the Holy Lands or anywhere else. That's why I teach about God's Kingdom on earth and don't "do" it. Also, the structure of Independent Demilitarized Disarmed Democratic Holy Lands does not allow for any individual to dominate over others because dominance comes by force and no one having arms makes it extremely difficult for anyone to dominate.

Currently what and how you think is controlled by whoever pays you in your job; what you desire and admire is controlled through the media and what you can't say or do is regulated by a big-big government.

The people that will choose to go in the Independent Unarmed Demilitarized Democratic Holy Lands are doing so to leave these power games and being told what to do, as is happening in these societies, so that they are not looking for or accept any hero or leader to "save them," because they already Know God, who leads them from "within" each. The multiple failed efforts to live righteously are not evidence that such way of life is not achievable but are evidence of the need that many people feel to live in a truly loving Independent community.

The central human fear is the fear of death. The reason for the need for power, for achievement and for affiliation and the corresponding power, money and fame systems are efforts to cope with death, yet ironically they lead to death. The only way to overcome the fear of death and overcome all fear is to be reborn spiritually into an eternal loving spirit by living by God's Eternal Truths.

The question you and all humans have to face is whether you will live separately from the worldly, as God has been consistently calling for, (e.g. the "cities of refuge" through Moses and as Lao Tzu did by leaving that society all together) through every true apostle and every true prophet, by love, in God's kingdom on earth, eternally, as you say you believe, in disarmed, Independent sovereign Lands or will you condemn yourself and your children to death by hypocritically claiming to be a believer in right while living in systems, with no alternative available, that require you to operate by self-interest and/or suffer and die prematurely?

Do not be a condemned to death, by God, hypocrite.

Either believe in God and live righteously by love as you say you believe; or don't believe and have as much sustainable fun within ethical limits as you can before you die because that is all you will get.

If you have been gifted by God with a healthy body, then even that short moment in the Light is not too bad of a deal, either. Enjoy it; don't waste it in conflict, fear, confusion and deceit.

Nor is what you do during this short time irrelevant. There have been millions of "human years" of divine work that have been invested in you.

Even if you remain a non-believer and no matter what your sins (except for the unforgivable sin) your soul will learn and you will contribute uniquely to others even if you don't know it yet or don't intend it.

Babylon asks then in a derogatory way: "And what are you doing to establish God's Kingdom on earth?"

I am at war

The summary of all of last century's News and of all Drama and of Entertainment is **stunning stupidity**!

For example consider through this link how the outrageously stupid is what makes for "good drama": Dose of Drama

Until we are let free—from the thousands of laws and tens of thousands of regulations that are practically impossible for anyone to even fully read, of the mad and violent systems by men for barely decent sex— and we are into God's Sovereign unarmed Lands, I am officially at war against every celebrity because they get all the attention for offering things with little and temporary value while I Enlighten the path to true eternal life in happiness.

Saving humans is more than delaying death as is the case with what doctors and others do; saving is about saving from death permanently. Righteousness, the Son, Christ Jesus is the only one who saves.

And Liberty is more than putting in your two cents as to who will rule you. Liberty is about being delivered permanently from evil that oppresses, enslaves and kills.

Isn't there something very profoundly wrong with a society when Katy Perry, Britney, Shakira, Rihanna, C. Perri, Paris Hilton, M. Streep, Leslie Stahl, Erin Burnett, the models of Victoria's Secret (we all know the secret of the covered part), Julianne Moore, Oprah, Barbara Walters (and even kitties) get thousands of times more attention, mostly for showing and/or shaking their derrieres, than the Resurrected Christ gets by writing to you through me?

I am now officially at war for attention against these 'celebrity' idols, my named adversaries, and I will win even though I won't shake or show my behind.

(Unless you keep insisting that I don't exist, in which case I might be forced to privately show you my ugly behind and you'll cry out... oh...my God!). You have been warned!

I don't blame pretty women for thinking that they deserve more attention than abstract thoughts because if I looked like them I probably would make that mistake also the voice of God is being drowned within you and from outside you by massive amounts of meaningless, stunningly stupid fruitless trivia of the gossipy media.

But the same way that your body is more important than its clothing, your spirit is more important than its clothing i.e. your body, and its food. Modified, (Mat. 6.25.)

Not all the righteous will go to the Demilitarized, Disarmed Lands of God, (that should be available to each and all,) and not all that are in those Lands are going to be righteous but **there will be a critical mass** of righteous to get a self—reinforcing culture.

A few beloved heroes will accept dying to reduce evil among those that remain in the world, so they will stay behind with the ignorant or incompetent or immoral rest to keep protecting the world from itself. The religious institutions will stay also to preach love. Those that will move in God's Independent Disarmed Lands are the "First Fruits."

"If you quit this war for Jesus nonsense I'll give you the world to rule...what do you mean no? Who are you? What are your qualifications?

*I'm happy with my life as it is, even if in time I die. Who died and made you king of anything? **I disagree,"*** says Babylon frowning, pointing her finger at him while shaking her head sideways.

8.   I care if you disagree

Even if you disagree with all the above, the question is whether you will allow those that truly do believe in God to live without threatening you independently and with sovereignty from your worldly, ruled by force, national governments? Why wouldn't you let us free?

Democracies can survive only when the ruling majority respects the rights of the minorities.

Even if you are "right" and I am wrong, do we not have the right to live by our beliefs, separately from you, particularly since we are disarmed and are no threat to you, your current government and nation?

Even if all that has been explained is over some people's head, consider the Independent, Sovereign **Demilitarized, Disarmed Lands of God as humanity's insurance from extinction** because the current governments are inevitably becoming more interdependent, with some benefits, but with the big disadvantage that, as was shown in the financial crisis of 2008 and recently by Greece, if any nation goes down then all will go down and if that involves weapons of mass destruction it will cause the extinction of humanity, if the Disarmed Lands of God aren't established now.

Since you have plenty of lands to preserve potentially endangered animal species shouldn't you have at least one land to preserve the almost extinct among humans love and at least preserve humanity? No nation will bomb people that are in a demilitarized, Independent Land. Not N. Korea, not Iran, not China, not Russia, even if there is WWIII. Ask them. It can be a Treaty, but they will not anyway. Not allowing for the preservation of humanity, other than as rats underground, is way too mad. Are you that mad?

"That is a good point. But I don't see how it can be done within the US Constitution. Also by the U.N rules, unless you can by force defend a territory, it's not yours," says Babylon.

Isn't it our right to live by true Liberty and thus independently from worldly governments our religious right protected by the First Amendment? Aren't all the laws that Congress has established prohibiting the Independent and Free exercise of our religion unconstitutional?

Do we have to go to real war to gain Independence?

Do not insist that people with dangerous knowledge, like me, should stay in these competitive brutal societies because if forced to use force we will screw the daylights out of all the rest.

Even though operating in God's Spirits can be applied and should be applied in any circumstance and system, the use of religion and God to justify the choices among wrongs that is what all power-money-fame choices and what all your dilemmas and choices are, is using God for the vanity of people and is a sin.

Using the name of God for issues that are about the vanity of man is also obviously wrong and causes extreme fanaticism that makes finding and implementing the least wrong practical solutions, which is the best that can be done in worldly societies, much more difficult.

"Fine, but I care mostly about my money issues," says Babylon.

Look at http://www.lifeanew.org for answers to the current money, power-egos problems of the world. Don't look at my website if you do not like "bad words." I was unable until now to honestly write about the world without cussing my brains out!

At their core these problems of power— money **are concentrated on how badly public corporations are governed.**

External regulation of corporations does not alter how they operate; it only adds attorneys that make sure that the corporation keeps doing what it does i.e. operates in the short term self-interests of the CEO.

Public Corporations must get regulated "from within."

I wrote (an obviously unsuccessful) book about 24 years ago, "THE CORPORATE REPUBLIC" advocating that "public" corporations should not be run for the short-term interests of the CEO, (with crony Boards and crony Consultants) dictatorially as they are now, but should add some, limited democratization, for the long term interest of the public (i.e. Re-public), particularly since they are funded by the public.

I implemented successfully the first phase of democratizing in the last company I run, but after we sold the company the buyers ignored my advice so I left in 1989 and they reversed that direction, with tragic consequences two years later.

After three major recessions in three decades caused each time by CEOs gone wild screwing everyone with impunity, a few are concentrating on the central economic problem, which is the ethics of the corporate governance of public corporations.

Steve Jobs shows that the best CEOs are confident enough to have a salary of $1/ year and have all their benefits be derived from a share of the performance improvements that they produce.

The higher the salary, the short-term bonuses and the lower and shorter-timed the claw-back clauses, the more likely that shareholders, customers, employees and communities pay many billions of dollars for CEOs of their public corporations, whose primary expertise is kissing behinds while covering their own behind.

Carl Icahn has repeatedly spoken about has made billions out of the dysfunctions of the dictator-CEO's and the very corrupt corporate governance of public corporations and seems willing to help solve the problem even if that solution reduces the opportunities of profiting from identifying and intervening in cases of such abusive CEO-Board practices.

The SEC recently announced some positive rules for "say on pay" through Dodd-Frank, but they are not enough.

The SEC should make a ruling requiring public (and only public) corporations to provide an acceptable simple, substantive plan of how they will change their Corporate Governance, to allow for the voice, preferably through one elected —by one person one vote real elections that includes shareholders and employees— Board Seat of a (non-executive) in the Board (preferably of the Chair of the Ethics and Compensation Committee) and how they will ethically account for all stakeholders (including workers, community interests, National and the interests of democracies vs. dictatorships) through Executive Compensation incentives and disincentives.

Until the regulation of corporations is done "from within" by requiring the change of Corporate Board governance, as has been explained, the worsening wealth distribution problems, the excessive and very costly, to both the private sector and the government, external regulations will bankrupt this nation, and even if the nation escapes it, the regulations will keep proving inadequate and will keep resulting in immense economic crises.

Only when public corporations are regulated "from within" as above, the need for and the pressures from labor Unions will be reduced and governmental regulation can also be safely reduced and better focused thus allowing sustainable and well balanced high economic growth.

I run out cusses against the leading politicians of all nations because they are the most hypocritical, most pretending to be right and to Know while being Blind like Oedipus, do most harm which they deny having done and get most for themselves. I welcome any suggestions on new and improved cusses, to get them to re-think and avoid the hell that their souls are rushing to.

"And you are?" asks Babylon looking at him suspiciously.

I was born in Eritrea, (means Red land,) like a red heifer. My Greek in ancestry animalistic ego is aggressive with deadly instincts honed by swimming with sharks and pirates in the Red Sea. I grew up, in Ethiopia and enjoyed hunting in the plains and jungles of the Horn of Africa. Ethiopia is beautiful, it is probably the oldest human culture (as shown by the oldest Homo Sapiens fossils found such as "Lucy" of about 3.2 million years and the more recent find of the Ardipithicus radimus of about 4.2 million years.) Ethiopia's history is well recorded, for example like the Queen of Sheba that went to meet Solomon, and is unique in Africa because it has been a mostly Christian nation from the earliest times of Christianity and was never colonized.

After finishing high school in Addis Ababa, I studied Engineering in Athens at the National Polytechnic. During that time I participated in revolting against the dictators In Greece in 1973. I gained personal experience with what happened in Egypt many decades later, i.e. starting a revolution with other non-partisan students and then having the old political establishment wrongly get most of the credit for it and the power. My family got kicked out of Ethiopia in 1975, by a then communist government, for not being black and our factories and home were nationalized without compensation, still. So, while completing my studies I built a couple of buildings to make a living.

My ego then got bigger by receiving Masters Degrees from both Columbia and from Harvard Universities. My ego then got shrewder by running, buying growing and selling very successful small, medium and large electronics businesses.

I quit and retired at 34 because having gotten a clear view of 'the system' having been a part of it, I decided that I want to be outside of these systems and want nothing to do with these governments.

I have been single parenting my two children since. I find that raising children correctly to be more difficult and important work than any of my previous work. I need to be efficient because I am quite lazy even for a Greek. I retired for longer than most retire, for 23 years so far, and statistically I should have been dead by now, even though I am 57 years old. Is that enough about me?

"A real John Galt or Atlas?" she wonders. You quit because you became conscious of the most dangerous enemy: your huge ego-self. You got horrified by your ego and you've been fighting you since," she says while perfuming herself.

Let me Free or else I will be forced to fight you. To fight you, per Sun Tzu ('Know your enemy') I will need to know you, which if taken Biblically means that I will be forced to have sex with you, and then you will be asking for more! (I'm kidding!)

To avoid "getting known" please write a five star review for this book.

"What if I still I'm not convinced?" asks Babylon while feeling her hair...

Please don't force me to have sex with your mind!

If you are still not convinced consider:

Self-interested non-believers allowing the right of believers within their nation to live as they believe Independently in a Sovereign Land is a righteous act (and it is safe for them particularly since they are demilitarized, disarmed and against any physical violence) so that God will treat those non-believers that stay behind in the current systems, as if they are righteous.

God's Kingdom is not for all; many aren't ready yet. These systems would not have lasted if they didn't have the consent of the majority.

True believers only by allowing non-believers and the mostly secular States to pursue what they believe are in their self-interest, freely, independently and with sovereignty in their nations and by governments they choose makes the believers righteous and not hypocrites.

As it has been until now, both the believers and the non-believers confuse, polarize each other and become deceiving hypocrites, resulting in all suffering and slowly dying.

Become "whole" rather than being broken identities that end up scattered. Have integrity and be holy in Spirit. Holy means also separate; so be separated from the world and from the worldly 'survival of fittest' struggles.

There is no compromise between believers in God's Absolutes and those believing that all is relative and temporal. There is no in-between between eternal living and dying.

Even basic communication between the two groups is very difficult because the same words mean opposing things when thinking in absolute vs. in relative terms.

For example, "good" in relative terms is at the bottom of the levels of goodness with better and best being better while that same word "good" in absolute terms means the highest and Absolute Good, God. No wonder you are confused when the same **critical words** mean opposing things to different people.

You've done what I do when you separate children that keep fighting and say 'go to your rooms.'

Don't hurt each other but separate enough so as to each be free independently, in peace and clarity.

The two separate governments within each nation, (that could be called the "Church"—except that it does not allow any religious institution because as M. Gandhi said: "God has no religion"— vs. the mostly secular "State" —except that the religious institutions will still be preaching within the secular societies as they do now and with much better understanding of what they are talking about and with at least one sovereign Land where Love is practiced, to show or to direct their converts— will no longer need to be and should no longer be antagonistic, because they will no longer **need** to interact, but will choose to become complementary and co-operating.

"To the **United Nations Security Council:** *We have a problem. We may need to allow a place in the world that is not ruled by us the classy, elegant, sexy, admired, beautiful, rich and glorious first of all professionals; the wild Greek has declared war. He does not even pretend to be pretty or nice yet the bozo still demands a sovereign*

Land of free love and free sex. It may be unreasonable but I've seen him fight before; he doesn't just defeat and conquer, he obliterates his enemies. Only the unemployed and poor will go there. No self-loving professional will go there. Since the most of the pretty will stay, if we increase their prices and with the savings from fewer bums we reduce the taxes to our girls and corporations, it will grow our economy so we probably should compromise."

"If I help establishing these Demilitarized Lands, even if I don't really believe in God, (I go rarely to Church or Mosque or Temple, just in case there is God and to cover all the bases because I go with people of any religion so long as they pay) and I disagree with you, what are the benefits to me, my nation and the world," asks Babylon sipping some Champaign.

9.   The benefits to you and your nations

The Independent, sovereign Lands are also a necessary oasis of love for those in secular societies that may want to visit for a respite to recover from their pretentious competitive struggles.

The righteous that live in the Independent Lands of God (that need to have a support structure with "critical mass" to be self-sustaining) should continue helping, primarily through the current religious institutions, the people that stay within the current systems and governments.

The current religious institutions when they preach love will have place that they can point to as examples of what they preach, rather than just keep pointing to…hope.

The measure of success of current religious institutions is how many of their flock will go to God's Lands on earth. Otherwise their "converts" are extremely likely to be "twice the children of hell." (Mat. 23.15)

This structure of two co-operative systems; one of love, mercy; and the other of enlightened civilized survival (of the current societies) by judgment and justice is the only way a nation that is otherwise very divided in reality despite the rhetoric and laws; can convert that duality and become truly One nation under God.

There are territories where the religious conflicts are intense and in which this separation is urgently needed. Kandahar (Afghanistan), **the Golan Heights** (Syria)**, Judea-West Bank-Palestine, a part in Uganda-Congo, Kashmir,** (Pakistan-India), **part of Iran, somewhere in the US** (or else I will leave, to avoid having any part with this country's demise, **and hopefully Patmos for an island of sanity in Greece), Cuba, Tibet, Chechnya, the occupied part of Cyprus,** a part of Istanbul, potentially Taiwan, N. Korea and maybe even Medina, are prioritized examples of Lands in **misguided religiously** fueled conflict causing **much suffering and increasingly likely to cause huge numbers of deaths, if each isn't recognized and accepted as a Sovereign, Independent (or autonomous,) Demilitarized, (Disarmed?)Land fast.**

In the case of Judea-West Bank an agreement on being Demilitarized and Independent, with Israel as the only guarantor of Judea-West Bank's Independence, makes other problems such as refugees, borders and Jerusalem easy to solve, with the easiest and least destabilizing solutions to them being the status quo including leaving the headquarters of Fatah in Ramallah.

Gaza must be dealt separately, as it is separated both physically and politically, and it may, a couple of years after the West bank agreement, become a "Palestinian State." Without this, the current cease fire will not last more than 7 years and will probably last only 3 and half years. The next war is very likely to be much more catastrophic.

B. Netanyahu and M. Abbas should stop leading to resolution through war and get on, now, with this path to lasting Peace.

In your negotiations remember that both spouses and prostitutes have sex; their difference is their spirit; whether the intent, the motive, is love or money.

Only once at least some of these conflict (with strong religious component) areas are resolved as above, the nuclear proliferation issues can be easily solved. Otherwise, the WMD proliferation problem is not solvable and the probability of truly apocalyptic destructions, suffering and deaths is unacceptably huge.

The increasing political polarization that has been crippling this nation and its Democracy as it has been doing across many democracies **is driven from both the "left" and "right" extremes by religious (and some anti-religious) fanatics that are right for an Independent Disarmed Holy Land of God but are very wrong for practical co-operative, compromise based, correct solutions necessary for surviving in the current systems.**

Once and only once this separation is established the rest of the problems that currently plague the nations can easily be solved because **most religious extremists that currently polarize both "the right" (currently focused on theology of the genitals) and "the left" (focused on government unsuccessfully "enforcing help" to the poor)** will be living separately in God's Lands thus allowing the **strengthening of the moderates from both the "right" and the "left"** which is a necessary condition to solve your society's problems.

This is the only way to safely and rightly remove extremists from both political sides and restore a sustainable balance and middle ground to the secular societies that is so central to their prosperity and peace.

Only once one Independent Demilitarized Disarmed Land of God is established for any pacifist, refugee, poor, weak or suffering and is available to live in somewhere on earth, and recognized by the host nation and the UN I will give you the correct solution to WMD proliferation and to Global Security.

You don't like us extremists anyway, so let us go and be disarmed and free and so free yourselves also. What do you have to lose? Nothing! Try it in small scale at least. Why not?

"Dear UN Security Council, It looks like I'm going to "be known" again.

The Wildest Warrior demands at least one sovereign Demilitarized Land in the world for the poor and weak who choose to live in it that is not run with the same motives as your national houses of assignation. His arguments devastate. I'll sleep with the king that gets me the Man's head on a tablet. Until then I'll distract him."

"Other than by God's Kingdom, how can those relatively happy with the current societies who choose to stay in them make their lives better and make the best of their problems?" she asks while brushing her hair.

10. HOW TO BE THE BEST

One cannot know what they do without understanding the long term consequences of one's inaction and actions towards others.

The majority that will probably stay in the current societies and defend their lives, but now also giving the right of the righteous in their nation to live with sovereignty without defenses, will be blessed and can dramatically reduce how wrong they are by taking a longer term prospective for the impact of their current actions.

This is so because the longer one's time horizon is, the less wrong one is.

So, judging priorities and actions by their impact to your and our children is the best criterion to use.

All the **correct i.e. least wrong**, answers about the worldly relative issues have been taught by Homer and by all great teachers, **are through the central—Straight path that isn't bent towards either of the two evils i.e. power, symbolized as the Beast i.e. B. and money, symbolized as the Whore i.e. W., that cause each and all crises.**

THE WORLD ANEW published in 2006 predicted the 2008 economic collapse. In the Introduction (p. xiv) THE WORLD ANEW says: "A confluence of factors brings the worst economic depression."

In hoping to be proven wrong THE WORLD ANEW offered the solutions on the first page of the Economics-Politics Section, i.e. on p.386 (See for free on Google Books) that would have averted that economic collapse. If in 2006, the Federal Reserve did **"increase the capital reserve requirements of Banks to reduce the probability of an economic collapse"** as was suggested on p.386 the economic collapse would have been averted.

As the President of the New York Federal Reserve since 2002, the major bozo T. Geithner, (groomed by the Whore to the Chinese Henry Kissinger) was doing the opposite thus causing the economic collapse. The increase in Bank reserve requirements had to happen and happened (through "Bazel III") **but because it was done too late, in 2010, (after the economic collapse)** hundreds of millions of people suffered significantly unnecessarily.

THE WORLD ANEW was not noticed and remains a voice in the wilderness because the major media gain influence (power), money and audiences by gossiping on (while smooching with) the "powerful" politicians, the rich and famous, thus perpetuating a self-serving cycle for those that are the worst and their cronies, while causing a down ward spiral of death for humanity.

The "two system one nation" structure is successfully implemented for a long time in Italy by the Vatican and more recently (with wrong intent) in China, (through Hong Kong) but it works very well.

To understand the nature of the dilemmas, contradictions, conflicts, imbalances and necessary separations in all of Nature one needs to understand some basics about physics.

Each of the known four forces of the Universe, (i.e. the Strong, Weak, Electromagnetic, and Gravity) operates in different number of dimensions at a time, as are the corresponding human functions as shown below:

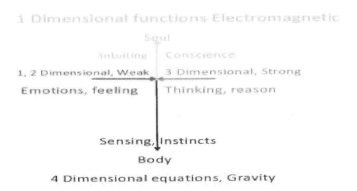

Note: The Strong force that holds nuclei together and the Weak force that radiates nucleus decay, are short range "within" nuclear forces.

The four known forces of the Universe as above, the corresponding four functions of humans, per Carl Jung, of intuiting, thinking, feeling and sensing; and four constituents of humans i.e. soul—conscience, mind—thoughts, passion—feelings, and body—instincts; are in directional opposition with each other as in the Cross above.

The correspondence as above extends to the *four states of matter; and to the primary colors and black* reflecting their frequencies.

Please note that the Cross isn't the classic Cartesian diagram with 2 variables but rather is a description of 4 independent, orthogonal to each other variables, each of which is represented by a vector (in either direction on its axis to represent positive vs. negative numbers.)

"Up" is where your **conscience is;** this is the right moral compass.

The Straight-Central path is the path of fastest growth with the best balance and causes an upward spiral that lifts your Cross and elevates.

It is these up and down spirals (helixes) over time on THE CROSS that the four bases of the DNA encode in time, recording history.

The Straight, least wrong, correct, fair, Just, beautiful, **best advance-balance path** requires a strong "middle ground" for compromise through respectful honest collaborative friendly long term relationships among the conflicted that find and increase mutually beneficial, 'win-win,' actions and reduce actions that imperil others.

That moderate path is the least wrong, straight, correct and best path for those that stay behind in the worldly and for those that deal with worldly issues, such as money, business, politics, pleasure and the physical.

"I hate moderation and 'the normal.' They are so boring and terribly dispassionate. I like being the best.

We the W.'s, the TV pundits, lawyers and politician hypocrites (who are wrong and lie in claiming that their judgments are right) *are experts in playing either **or "both sides"** of people, facts, laws and issues for our benefit while insisting that we're on your side, which is why we rule the world. But even I can't see how the heck you went from an extreme extremist to the moderate, straight path and claiming that moderation is best?*

I did not go anywhere nor did I do anything. I teach that God is Absolute (extreme) and those extremists that truly believe in Him should follow Him separately, safely, independently in God's disarmed Lands, to avert the unavoidable conflict with and abuse from those that see everything as relative, because other than God (Good-Love, Right, Truth), it indeed is all relative including evil, wrong, money, we, power, lands, the galaxy and everything else and it is compromise-able and should be compromised; including the $\pm$ 5% differences of the 'left' vs. 'right' that politicians pretend are issues of 'principle.'

Because the intent is to help both the righteous (primarily) but also the sinners (secondarily but necessarily as they need it most,) **I teach both sides.**

But there is no way to live as a necessarily 'extremist' believer in God and in righteousness; and to also act in moderation, straight through the social middle without hypocrisy and **befalling borderline personality disorder or schizophrenia** and/or **bi-polar disorder.** (I had much difficulty with this, just teaching both sides, let alone trying to act on both sides.)

The irreconcilable opposition of these two paths and the disorders it causes in trying to do both is another reason why there is a need for two separate and independent systems.

Finally, as Jesus explained, one either loves God and hates money or loves money and hates God. All attempts to live by God and for money, in a single government, result in confusion, deceit, whoring, hypocrisy, disorders and death to all. **So, separate.**

"You sound pompous to me my friend," says Diogenes *and runs a marathon introducing some action to this action less script.*

"Do you believe in evolution or creation?" asks Babylon.

"What, where, who is the 'divinity' within me?" asks my old friend.

11.   The Christ is my and your conscience.

If I showed you a car, a house, a computer or an airplane and said that they evolved by accident over billions of years without having been designed, you would say that I am nuts, because it is quite obvious that they must have been designed because you can decipher the design, the logic and their purpose. So, how would you call those that look at themselves, who are a much superior design to any human designs, other life, plants, flowers, trees, the earth, air, wind, oceans, rivers, sun, moon and stars and say that they were not designed?

The Universe was created, intelligently designed and made by God through "the Big Bang" that first let light be.

The bodies of humans were created and designed to be built from matter, 'dust', then animal life through **evolution and revolutions.**

It is during the revolutionary periods, that in contrast to Darwin's original theory of small incremental steps, the trend reverses direction and the change is drastic —punctuated mutation— that the Spirit of God has intervened.

There are clear revolutionary times (during which there is more than a step-by step quantitative change but also a qualitative change) in biology (including the destruction of dinosaurs, and birth and death) and in all physical and human history. For a nation that has come into existence by a revolution it is very inconsistent, in fact it is insane, to be teaching that the historical record is only of evolution.

Whether one believes in God or not, whether one can recognize the existence of a design, meaning and purpose or not, evolution is a very inadequate (misleading, wrong and false) theory on its own because all the historical record is clearly one of both evolutionary change and of revolutionary change; and it must be taught so in both biology and in history.

Also, **only humans have the Divine Spirit that is the consciousness of the consciousness of others, which is our conscience.**

For example, you now have consciousness of my consciousness by reading this, which no animal can.

Know yourself: There is the rational You; there is your lower body-self of your ancestral soul; expressed by instincts and by passions, likes and dislikes of the ego; **and there is your highest Self, your Christ conscience,** (that is moved by the Spirit of Christ Jesus.)

The Resurrected Christ is my and your conscience.

That is why and how he was and is always with us.

Either your animalistic ego **or the Christ within you** will die. Kill your ego and Live forever.

If you can't kill your ego (spiritually of course, as 'kill' is meant in all spiritual texts, to avoid having to physically die for it) yet, and so become an eternal Spirit that lives in any and all without an individualized soul (at the Buddha level), then at least submit, surrender or subjugate your ego to either God's Will or at least to reason; and reason for your long term interests while considering your impact to others.

Don't silence the Christ within you; don't silence your conscience.

Do not kill the Christ within you.

"Cute theories; It's too bad they don't have a chance in heck to become real. If there was any chance, it'd be by you getting out of retirement and doing it yourself. But you refuse to take charge of the world by politics and money, so only the miracle of miracles would make what you write become real. Your skills aren't in writing, particularly not in your 5th language, English; your last three books make you the most failed author ever! Books about crap have higher Amazon rankings than yours.

(By the ranking method of what sells most, toilet paper rather than books is by far the best paper to buy and pornos are the best digital data to buy.)

No one in America wants you here. Writing is not doing. Junk this book. Stop being a lazy looser and get a real job.

Having retired from business for over 20 years, you are running out of money and may not even be able to get your daughter through College. Forget about God's Kingdom on earth; do you see anyone else asking for it? Quit writing and go get a real job.

You're self-destructive, smoking, and ugly. Look at your fat belly; the permanent frown on your face for having learned more than you can handle. You're a failed husband, failing parent, old, ugly, worthless, lazy, self-destructive, moody, lonely, sexually deprived, vulgar, dysfunctional, sad, mad, jobless, bozo; go get therapy.

Sell your mind. You were the best CEO because you know how to make strengths out of your (and your people's) many weaknesses and make weaknesses out of your enemy's strengths and because you know how to make the best out of the worst. Quit writing and go make money."

"How do I access the divinity within me?" asks my long lost friend.

Prayer is a conversation with God.

I am so glad you asked. If you aren't clear yet about which action is right for you to take, then pray, have a conversation with God.

God is Spirit, so that just like the waves from a pebble thrown in water are in many places at the same time, in co-centric circles, God is in many places at the same time and like the invisible air He is fully accessible by each.

My Spirit is the Spirit of Truth that Jesus Christ spoke of.

Mine is "the sword" that is here to separate, as Jesus said must be done and is doing now in this, His Second Presence.

The separation is 'like that of sheep and goats' neither of which is too bad. It is their wrongful and deceitful interactions by not being separated that makes both sides destructive and suffer. (Goats are worse, but feta cheese isn't too stinky, even if my, beloved forever, American children disagree!)

I would much prefer accomplishing what I must do, —the job defined by Jesus in John 14, 15, 16, 17 — in this life without having to intervene forcefully and without having the fate of the prophets. God's prophets became well known after they died and are worshiped hypocritically by the hypocrites that the prophets despise. This adds continuing insult to injury on them and on the Christ Jesus.

So, it'd be nice if you help establish God's kingdom on earth now rather than kill me first and then agree with me; as people have done with all of God's prophets and with Jesus Christ.

"Repent for the kingdom of heaven is at hand." (The Baptist; Jesus Christ)

Repent, repent, repent; repent. Stop intending, thinking, feeling and acting for your interest. Start intending, thinking, feeling and acting for what is best for others excluding your self-interest. That is what right intent, right reason, right thinking, right feeling and right action means that are part of the eightfold path that Buddha and **the Enlightened, by The Light**, teach.

You and I, know that you can't do it and survive in the current systems designed by and for self-interest which is why you should also repent about waiting for God to do —establish His Kingdom on earth through Independent, Sovereign, Demilitarized, Disarmed Lands— what is and must be done by women and men.

As JFK explained, "Here on earth, God's work must truly be our own." Do it.

Asking "Kyrie Eleison" (that is Greek meaning: Lord have Mercy) is not going to be enough for the leaders of the governments that will not establish now any, not even one, small refuge of a Sovereign Demilitarized, Disarmed Land— for those that want to stay in their nation (or at least in their Continent) but do not want to submit to the rule by force and money or to their current or another secular government— because they are condemned and will be thrown in the eternal hell of fire.

"How can you claim to be able to measure and Judge the level of wrongfulness of each precisely?" asks Babylon while shaving her legs.

"How do I achieve best whatever I believe in?" asks my old friend that still doesn't recognize me.

12.   The right solution and the correct solutions

There is some value to both sides of the conflicted.

<u>There is eternal value to being righteous; and there is also value in reducing wrong</u> that civil societies attempt (to reduce poverty, crimes, abuses even if by forceful and thus wrong means and by dividing powers and by competition among the negatives, i.e. wrongs to produce positive results) **but that value is there, only if these two groups are fully separated.**

Without this separation—by Christ Jesus' Second Presence now— (a much greater separation than the current Constitutional "sort of separation" of Church and State) the two sides cancel each other out with both sides unnecessarily, unwisely and unjustly suffering and dying.

There is great value in being righteous and there is value in reducing wrong through another wrong but their methods are diametrically opposed for the same reason that in a straight line increasing a positive number (right) and reducing a negative (wrong) number are still opposites.

(wrong) -_____0_____+ (right)

Righteousness and wrongfulness can be measured in a straight line. There is always a right answer when it comes to the positive side of any issue; and on the negative side of any issue there is a very small range of correct, co-erect, i.e. consistent with what is right (but not right) least wrong answers about converting the negative to positive, by competition of negative vs. negative.

Getting from negative to positive requires passing through zero, nothing; through being a 'nobody' as was Odysseus. Socrates knew (the richness of flaws in) nothing and Knew One. It is through that same nothingness and selflessness that Buddhists meditate to empty them-selves of the negativity and get to "the other side of the shore."

The Buddha was asked, (I suspect by a Bactrian Greek that later helped preserve Buddhism,) "What have you gained by meditating?"

The Buddha answered: "Nothing. I have gained nothing, but I have lost a lot! I have lost anger, sadness, disease, fear of old age, and fear of death."

Losing those by meditation or otherwise is a very worthwhile loss. The Nothingness that you may meditate into is a great place to lose all of one's negativity.

But if passion still "burns you" to accomplish what you truly want by converting (negative) problems into (positive) solutions, the process is simple and always the same whether it is for an individual, a relationship, a business, a non-profit or for a government.

Start from what you truly believe in; that becomes your **mission** (purpose). That mission requires that certain longer term **objectives** (goals) are met; the objectives require you to lead others into supporting those objectives; those people become your "team" or **organizational hierarchical structure**, i.e. "the Means" to get you to the objectives; the organization, (in the context of a culture about the nature of relationships as I discussed above i.e. friendly, with respect, considerate, honest, compromising, demonstrated in action by you), requires a calmly thought out **strategy and plans i.e.** "the Ways."

The strategy is focused against whatever, whoever is on your way to achieving the objectives. The strategy includes a system of correct incentives, disincentives and measurement criteria **to align the team's (structure's) interests towards the objectives;** those become your **systems**; the organization then defines the **short term individual goals and action plans** with the time tables necessary to achieve the longer term objectives.

Looking for your errors and quickly correcting them is critical to being a successful executive so once you completed the planning as above, and you **start implementing, (executing), i.e. doing it, you go through the reverse process, i.e. from bottom up now**, by first acting with urgency and helping to make the action plans work, by, by-passing your whole organizational structure and focusing the whole management, by example, on personally finding ways to help (**not boss**) those at the bottom, in the front lines, doing the hardest work, and in doing so, change as needed the systems, measurements and organizational structure (means) to achieve the strategy and then you allow change of the strategy (Ways) and objectives coming from bottom up to more effectively and efficiently achieve the mission.

Starting with what (in whom) you truly believe in, is most critical because working hard to achieve something that you don't truly believe in, is stupid.

Also, unless you truly believe in your mission, you are unlikely to be committed enough to succeed; and failing is not nice.

May I suggest that you avoid believing in things that are temporal, (as money-power-fame-things- body-looks) because as the word says they are temporary, will in time be gone and you will find yourselves having believed lies and having turned into a W.B.S. to achieve them. Believe in the eternal Truths, (Values, Principles described here) that have been, are and will remain True for ever and thus you will live forever.

Some consider the eternal Truths that I described as "ideals" but they are wrong. These eternal truths were actually lived by humans like you, at least by the founders of the righteous faiths, and that is why their spirit still moves us, many tens of centuries after their "death" more so than most of the "living."

Physically and in terms of space and time because our galaxy is a miniscule part of the Universe and earth a miniscule part of our galaxy and each of us a miniscule part of the earth, we are each extremely irrelevant. Though our small bodies are necessary, all our great value comes from our spirit that **can** understand the Universe, experience and be in the Spirit of the Omnipotent, Omnipresent and Omniscient Creator.

If you still believe in material things rather than the spirit first, go to a morgue to check the value of any human body without its spirit.

The methods "Ways" as to right vs. the least wrong ways to reduce wrong are in full opposition, even though they are both well intentioned and valuable. I repeat that this is so for the same reason that increasing a positive number and reducing a negative number, arithmetically, are in opposition.

Even if one is on the Straight, least wrong path because there is still some wrong involved, one better still be asking for forgiveness.

What **should not continue happening** is for most to be hypocritically talking, preaching, worshiping and/or saying they believe in God and/or the Christ; in Love and/or Righteousness and in doing what is right while actually thinking, feeling and practicing wrongdoing, living in fears, worries, hurts, loneliness, unsatisfied needs, cravings and confusion that result in hellish suffering, death and in some cases in eternal torment of the soul.

If any President king or leader was objectively right wouldn't it have been obvious to all and would the result of their actions be this current mess?

The Resurrected Christ Jesus, Abraham, Moses, David, the Archangel Michael, the Apostles, the prophets, the Buddha, Krishna, (Hare is also derived from Greek and depending on how it is pronounced it means Grace or Joy) Lao Tzu, Mohammed (even though I disliked Mohammed after he moved from Medina through Ethiopia to Mecca to rule by force and… became a hypocrite), Confucius and all the righteous from the beginning of time are all with me, Elijah, as I am with them, asking for God's Sovereign Kingdom on earth through one Independent Demilitarized, Disarmed Land.

"Seek His Kingdom and His righteousness **First** and all else will be added."(Mat. 6.33) Truly, truly.

God's Kingdom coming on earth is what you pray for weekly. Don't pray, talk, preach or argue about it; Do it.

The Gospels have been preached already in all the nations. Now is the time to truly live by them, somewhere.

"Let us love not in words and speech but in truth and action."(1 John 3.18)

The Resurrection and Judgment Day is now.

Now that all the dead are resurrected and you know and understand what you do and the grave impact of inaction, your and then my judgment is about who lives **within you** and who dies.

By the Mercy of Lord Jesus you are now forgiven for all your past sins because you did not know what you do in choosing Darkness instead of Light and death over Life. If you accept my words you and each human are forgiven and free from all your sins until now and from your past.

But now you Know so if you knowingly choose Darkness and death that is what you will get. **You are judged by your next actions.**

Not helping establish God's Kingdom on earth as it is describe here, will make you knowingly guilty with no excuses.

Your children will know by this book that you had the chance to give them Life but you chose Death for them.

If you are not resurrected, restored and risen yet with a changed mind about what you must do **first**, now, why and how, wait and you will be soon **born again, re-born in spirit,** because I had wild spiritual sex (metaphorically speaking) with your beliefs, soul, thoughts and emotions and impregnated you. You did not respond when I told you to act, so sorry but I had to, as I said I would. Why did you force me to have sex with your mind!?

"How are you so sure that the Judgment Day is now?" asks Babylon, moving her hands around.

I am not sure what you think you are doing but I know and admit that I am judging, today, this Day. Actually most adults are also judging, because there is no way to make any decision without judging, however being hypocrites most do not admit that they judge.

The Mysteries that you heard in parables only, without understanding their meaning, have now been explained.

Look at the news; humanity is suffering and on a fast track to great destructions, great suffering and deaths...there is no time to waste. Help. You are called by God to help others.

Truly truly (vs. the common, pretend, false "truly")

Polydoros (pronounced Poly'thoros) but now that we are closer than many you are 'close with' and given the stress that Americans suffer when confronting words that have more than three syllables, you may call me whatever you like!

"Ok, fine; what specifically do you want me to do?" my old friend asks.

Please send the following message to as many as you can, starting from your President or Prime Minister, to your Congress and media members.

"The Book of Truth provides evidence that proves you wrong and not just least wrong but very wrong in every policy that you pursued.

The author claims that you lie (hypocritically) in calling your wrong choices among wrongs, right, thus nullifying the meaning of right. For example claiming to have made the right decision of an issue of war such as Afghanistan is a lie. All options involve some people getting hurt. Try telling the families of those that got killed, even if only one, that you are right and they getting killed was right.

'Start being honest and as Confucius says, **call things by their right name**. Admit that your political plans and judgments are by definition in part wrong because they are about what seems to you, (by unspecified criteria,) as less wrong at this time.

The "leaders" have chosen, in fact fought for the responsibility and so have the responsibility for fixing the suffering humans endure. Yet there are at least 70 million people in the US and at least two billion people around the world that are suffering greatly and dying with no prospects for a solution, except through an Independent Demilitarized, Disarmed Holy Land somewhere in the US, where people are given the option to live righteously without getting punished by the ignorant human structures and systems.

Politicians rather than keep lying about their 'definitively to be successful or right plans' that they sell yet they never pan out, better be honest about being necessarily in part wrong and so start gaining credibility.

An easy way to identify a 'twice child of hell' hypocrite is by the difference in what they say or promise vs. what actually happens. (There is plenty of evidence for their hypocrisy.) Another is by their emphasis on details while neglecting Justice, mercy and love.

The author challenges you to war at Armsgetdown.

He also accuses you for attempting to silence him and calls you personally bad names, including the B. and the W. words. If you don't admit to being wrong, he accuses you of being a God condemned hypocrite that is wrong, sinful, and doesn't admit it.

Please respond publicly by either supporting one Independent Demilitarized Disarmed Holy Land or responding to these very serious allegations against your character and behavior. If you do not respond, I may have to assume that you cannot and that the really bad names that the author has called you must be true. Thank you."

"Ok; it's done."

Thank you.

"What should our children be taught?" asks my good old friend.

13.　The Right Education

Until those of God are gathered and one larger more appropriate, mutually agreed location is established for God's kingdom on earth**, I Declare the Independence of my land on Crestview Court, from California, the USA and from all governments and declare it an Independent, Sovereign, demilitarized, disarmed Land of God;** on the basis of scruples of conscience.

"Man, where are you? I can't see; I have questions," says Babylon.

Esteemed Professors (Scribes) and Professionals,

The whole truth and nothing but the truth:

The first draft of this book was about 20 years ago and was 935 pages (and I dislike writing because I prefer being or doing!) That version went into too much unnecessary complexity in each subject. When I finished writing it and printed it, (instead of calling it "law" given that many of your laws are that massive) I threw it in the trash! If something including laws are not short and simple, one doesn't Know (fully know) or fully understand what one does or is intending confusion.

-**The intent**: If you are not righteous, you are not an Educator; you make money in the name of educating and make sure people remain uneducated so that you can steal more in the name of education. If you make money by pretending to educate what intent are you teaching? Evil?

-The Logic: What is right or good education? What are the clearly stated Criteria of what you are trying to teach? If you are not teaching what good and love means is and does, what right means is and does and what truth means and is, in various contexts, you teach falsity and are wrong.

What other criteria are of any value if they are false and/or are wrong and/or are into hate and/or are evil?

If you do not understand that these same critical Criteria mean practically opposing things if they are taken in absolute context, in which one fully, absolutely and deterministically means them vs. in the context of relatives in which case their relative "sort of" statistical, probabilistic meanings and relationships get reversed in sequence and importance, what the heck do you understand?

Because if true, right, love and good mean opposing things to different people and in different contexts how can you not end up confused in Babel and rushing into the first and the following professions for temporary survival?

-The Expression and relationships: **If one is an expert in one subject and one subject only, as most have had to, they are likely to be very wrong** because there is no aspect of life that is not interdependent and interconnected to and from all other aspects, and "experts" ignore the impact from all these interconnections. So, in optimizing a sub-set they sub-optimize the whole.

What are the relationships between religion, science, arts—humanities and the professions? The "scribes" neither know nor have explained those relationships. If you understand the Cross as above, these relationships have been explained simply and clearly. How do you expect your students to integrate their beliefs with their logic in their relationships and their actions while you offer no way for that integration and no place where true integrity is valued?

The current educational systems take children that are Whole beings with integrity and break them into disintegrated confused, deceived pieces, whose souls are bound to get broken and scattered, as are the souls of most of their blind teachers.

Most people have to go to work, sell and are sold as in the first profession but often selling things more important than their body such as their mind, affections and sometimes even their conscience. Then they act as parents at "family time." After 10 p.m. their screens or mind is into pornos; on weekend in the day they pretend to be virgins in Churches, Temples, Mosques etc.; on weekend nights they try to escape (get drunk or somehow be as "out of it" as acceptable), be silly, see or do something silly; on their spare time or for a living they complain about the bad non-believers that don't believe in God or the bad believers of a different and wrong faith that are hypocrites; and then go back to pornos, to selling themselves and trying to escape. How disintegrated and nuts is that?

Is that an integrated person in oneness, integrity or is it a legion of confused unclean spirits?

- The actions and results. Knowing what you do is about knowing the impact of your actions and all the resulting reactions from those affected.

There was a tablet saying: 'Know your-self,' for the (Mystic's) Virgin Oracles of Delphi, before entering the Temple. Knowing self, is to know who you were (without choice), who you are, who you are becoming and knowing who **by your choice you will be** and by the impact of your actions, how you choose to be known. Do you?

How can anyone of any profession claim that they know what they do, while being ignorant of the significant and precise effects to and from each and all the other professions, sciences, humanities and religions?

"You have explained what Good means, what Love is, what Right and Righteousness is, but you have not explained what truth is. So,

What is Truth?" asks my old friend that is still in a state of "not-Awake" and still does not remember me.

Truth is what is consistent with and fully expresses The Truth. The Truth is God. The Seven Spirits of God express all The Truth. The Seven Spirits of the Holy Spirit of Truth express all the Eternal Truths of Truth. The Truth, God was, is and will be.

"What is, is?" she asks.

The Truth is self-evident. The Truth is evidenced by Himself. Is, is what is. Is, is existence. Is, is what is real in physical reality, truth, that can be evidenced and verified by anyone who exists; and Is, Truth, is the spiritual reality, the spiritual truth who perceives, expresses accurately, correctly and validates both what exists physically and what exists spiritually.

"Do lies exist?" she asks.

Lies exist temporarily and only in the imaginations of humans and die along with the death of the human. Lies have no physical reality, i.e. no physical existence of their own. Their temporarily spiritual existence is contradicted by and is inconsistent with both physical reality and God.

"Can truth exist without it being perceived by anyone?"

No. Schlesinger's cat imaginary experiment answers this. Physical truth exists only to the extent that someone has, is or will perceive it. Perception is by consciousness and consciousness comes from the Holy Spirit of God.

"How do I find the Truth?" she asks.

God is The Truth. You find Truth, God, within you by being moved by the True Spirits of God that are described here. Once you are in the Spirit of Truth then it is easy to perceive which spiritual statements are lies. Once you are in the Spirit of Truth you will find contradiction and will be in contradiction with the lies, whether those lies are about the true intent of someone, or about their true reasoning and judgments, or about what happened, happens or will happen in physical reality.

"How do I find out if someone is lying?" she asks.

Ask for evidence. I repeat that the truth has and is its own evidence. If there is no clear evidence, either physical evidence or spiritual evidence, by validation by independent others, the chances that someone is lying are very high.

"So a liar cannot perceive The Truth, and distorts what was, is, or will be physically true also," correct?

Correct. That is why human spirits who were born physically into the physical reality and perceive everything from a material point of view, which is in itself a distortion because material things have no truth of their own, but whatever truth someone with consciousness, with spirit, assigns to them, need to be reborn into a true spiritual existence to survive and Be.

"What is consciousness?" asks my friend.

Consciousness is the recognition of and response to truth. Life is the experience and expression of truth.

Depending on the level of one's consciousness, consciousness is the experience, recognition and expression of all the spiritual Truths and of all the physical truth i.e. physical reality.

If one's consciousness is not raised into recognizing and correctly understanding all of the truth, both all of the spiritual truth, both the temporary (lies) and the eternal and all of the physical truth that is temporary and the eternal laws that drive it, they are operating with limited information, do not know or See the "big picture" and so they are bound to keep making wrong judgments and wrong decisions, leading to destruction, no matter what they say.

Have you violated any of God's Ten Commandments? Even though you claim to be believer in God? I believe that the true answer is yes and so you are guilty. Pretending to believe in Christ Jesus is not enough for Salvation. Truly believing in Christ Jesus, righteousness, so as to live truly righteously in Holy Demilitarized, Disarmed, Democratic Lands, is Salvation. I assert (by Jesus's suggestion) that you have been ignorant, and did not know what you do. You did wrong and caused serious damage primarily by your inaction.

Accept and rejoice in being proven ignorant and a slave to your sinfulness because they are the best defenses you can get for being wrong and guilty.

"So can you explain all of the physical reality, truth, and the eternal laws that drive it?" asks my old lost friend with a "got you" smile.

"Oh. No; not physics. I get hives just thinking about what I went through in the last class of physics I took. I'd rather that you slap me. Go ahead... slap me...slap me please but no fn. physics," says Diogenes.

THE PHYSICS

The two great theories of physics are: Quantum Theory that accurately describes the 3 Quantum forces and General Relativity that accurately describes gravity.

All previous attempts to unify gravity and Quantum Theory such as by "quantum gravity" have failed. Other attempts for unifying gravity and the quantum forces end up in 10 or 11 Dimensions in the Universe, which if not interpreted as suggested here, is less provable and less reasonable than UFO's of aliens having sex in the sky.

These two well proven Theories just have not been synthesized correctly because gravity has not been viewed correctly as the resistance and reaction to the three quantum forces over a prolonged period, but as an independent fourth force that somehow operates by the incompatible (opposing in many ways) to Quantum Theory (QT), rules of General Relativity (GR).

We live in a four dimensional Universe one of the dimensions of which, time, can be stretched or shortened depending on the relative speed of the observer to the subject.

It is because of the quantum forces that not everything in the Universe is balls.

As a result we, the living, also operate on 2 dimensions at a time (like our 5 senses do; each for a different distance range) and spiritually on 1 dimension at a time, in either direction and therefore we can change the effects of the otherwise deterministic four-dimensionality.

So, the structure of the Universe allows for worlds within the world.

The Cross (as above) applies, as expected given that it applies in physics and in human nature, (and as my proprietary software program can show,) on any subject and for any level of detail.

As the Cross shows, gravity governing the mass of matter is in opposition to Electromagnetism, (that is "charged by light" matter) as we know from Newton's constant having the opposite sign to Coulomb's.

The deterministic (for large objects, operating at very slow speeds, matter) 4 Dimensional world obeys strict "action-reaction" **reciprocity**, is operated by gravity that is best described by General Relativity.

While the (3) Dimensional (2 dimensions at any time), (2+1) Dimensional and (1) Dimensional —in two directions) worlds of the other 3 forces are Quantum, probabilistic, are by small **dual** "particle-waves" (waveforms) operating at speeds that are orders of magnitude faster, are described by Quantum Mechanics and per the Standard Model obey certain **symmetries**, (as above), —**that is reciprocity** in Quantum terms—stretch space (as opposed to curving space into itself that gravity does) become active only when observed so that the function of time is not constant but by choice, whenever created and/or observed, and so they alter the net effects to matter caused by deterministic gravity.

Modern "physicists" have become meta-physicists because instead of explaining the real and physical they are building super-colliders and other super-devices to find out if the metaphysical figments of their imagination are real. For example, they are in search of "super-strings" that if they existed, which cannot be proven, they could explain a lot.

At the macro-level, the cosmologist are in search of "dark matter" (attractive) and "dark energy" (repulsive) **that if they existed** (there is no evidence of them) they would explain their miscalculations and their data misinterpretations. There is no need to assume that there is an additional repulsive force (dark energy) if one adds back the cosmological constant in Einstein's gravity equation, as he originally had. That "constant" is due to the Second Law of Thermo-Dynamics that over time converts all energy (including mass) to heat and thus reduces gravitational attractions. For example, the acceleration of Universal expansion is caused by mass to energy conversions from the weak and the strong forces.

(It maybe that "the cosmological constant" isn't really a constant but is proportional to the distance from the primary gravitational source. This would explain the increased speed of outer stars in some helix like galaxies).

As to the need to assume that there is a new, not proven, attractive force caused by "dark matter:" they miscalculate the gravitational pull of black holes which is in 1 and 2 and 3 dimensions and not in four dimensions; and the gravitational pull of interstellar material; and the "attraction" caused from Electro-Magnetism.

Also, the margins of error from the spectroscopic measurements (of differences in intensity and color) have much higher error margins than assumed due to absorptions of interstellar matter, temperatures, lack of 3-D prospective, wrong assumption of a "locally flat" Universe, (which we know is curved,) directions of star motions, and the assumption that they are measuring "balanced state" conditions which is not true; the information about the actual current condition of the star motions they measure will take thousands of years to get here. (Even looking at the stars is looking into the past).

If physicists stick to explaining the real as is their job and leave the 'metaphysical' inventing of the unproven and mysterious to artists, then they will realize that the Universe can and has been fully explained with no need of imaginary strings (other than those used in writing) or of imaginary dimensions or of dark energy or of dark matter, (other than in imagination) but with the unfortunate consequence that some physicists will have to look for other jobs to do their inventing.

So, it is much simpler and more rational to explain the observed differences in speeds of stars within Galaxies and the acceleration among Galaxies by assuming that the intra-galactic mass is 20 times or so (whatever the observed differences are) greater than intergalactic matter. However, even if dark energy and dark matter exist causing these differences in speeds of motions of stars they do not invalidate this theory, they just require incorporating them into it.

The mathematics of 'super-symmetry' requiring 10 or 11 Dimensions to get to a 'unified' force are correct; it's their physical interpretation of undetectable 'very small or very large' 'extra' 6-7 dimensions that is wrong. It is wrong for many reasons the main of which is that it makes the so called string or M Theory not provable and thus puts these theories in the realm of philosophy not of physics.

This Theory is not dependent in proving the understanding of these extra 7 dimensions as real visible dimensions. They can be interpreted as undetectably high frequency spiritual dimensions, in which case I would say that they are the 7 Spiritual dimensions.

However, I submit that the more reasonable explanation is that these extra 7 dimensions are the sub-4D real dimensions, such as 2D waves, that become "real" only and at the time that they are observed, such as the waves emitted by this page.

The self-repeating order in what appears chaotic during Dimensional transitions and for fractal dimensions is described by the Theory of Chaos. (The positive side of operating in chaos is that if you know what you do, you can fly a little like a butterfly and cause a huge storm in a Continent on the other side of the ocean.)

If the "Dimensionality" of each of the 4 known force fields was understood as shown here, then the "extra 6-7 dimensions" are the known less than 4D dimensions i.e. the 3 D, (2+1)D and 1D dimensions; operated independently by each quantum force, at the same time; to which the 4D gravity resists and reacts.

While the strong force operates on the volume (3D) of an object, the weak operates on its (2D) surfaces and lines (1D) and electromagnetism on points (0-1D) of the same object at the same time and they are resisted and responded to by the object's inertia in 4D. Those 3+(2+1)+1+ 4 are the 11 Dimensions.

There is a single (Quantum) Force of change in the Universe; and rationally and inevitably there was and is the resistance and reaction to that change manifest as inertial gravity.

The three Quantum Forces, that are unified by the Standard Model, and are in perpetual motion (even though light appears as if static) cause change in motion.

The reason gravitational mass is always equal to inertial mass is because gravity is the **deceleration of time** relative to the time of light (in General Relativity by curving space) (that appears as acceleration of objects) due to inertia. Inertia is the resistance to change in motion.

The inertia of Universe; its resistance to being created and to life is manifest primarily through inertial mass but that dark resistance to change in motion and to life is also manifest in empty space (of what the Ancient Greeks called 'ether' and is now called "dark matter") and in every aspect of life but it is being scattered and reduced over time by the Quantum Forces.

Inertial mass increases, i.e. particles gain mass, in the transition (Higgs field) from the electromagnetic to the Weak force fields. I would expect that the relevant Higgs like particles gain dimensionality i.e. become more than 0 dimensional points, (but that is a hypothesis that may be tested.)

This hypothesis is because, as Special Relativity is a 4D extension of the Pythagorean, so is General Relativity an extension into 4D space-time of Archimedes' displacement of water by mass theory and calculus. So, a particle-wave with mass must occupy some space.

So, the Theory of Everything (TOE) that explains the Universe by a single force is that Creation by the Big Bang unleashed a single, Unified as per the Standard Model, Quantum (probabilistic) force of change in motion, creating light, space and matter (the 12 leptons-hadrons) that we experience as the 'disinfectant' elements: light; fire-water; and air; and causing a (deterministic) reaction to that change in motion from Gravity, that is the result of the pre-existing inertial resistance to change, manifest as inertial mass, and results in time delays and the relative 4D space-time, as per General Relativity, (GR.)

This Theory of Everything is proven by the first law of thermodynamics of conservation of energy. The conservation of energy is because as per The Cross each of the forces acts as the resistance and reaction to the other three.

The first law of thermodynamics can be expressed as:

Eg=- Eq,   (1)

Where Eg is the energy released and stored by gravity and Eq the energy released and stored by the quantum forces.

The Mathematical Theory of Everything (TOE)

A force field is a function of the number of space dimensions occupied by the objects or particle waves that it acts upon.

We define z as the number of the space dimensions occupied by the object or particle wave whose properties are being measured and call it the 'dimensionality' of the object.

-Objects that are 3 dimensional (3D) (space dimensions they occupy) have $z \equiv 3$
and particle-waves that are 0 dimensional (0D) have $z \equiv 0$.
Therefore, one could assume all the aspects of Riemannian 4D space-time and GR as correct for 3D objects,
and can also assume that the Hilbert space and the Quantum Theory (QT) as correct for 0D particle-waves.
The rules allowing this mathematical TOE to identify specific mathematical objects for possible measurements are:
-When $z= 3$, GR, its equations (EFE equations) and Riemannian 4D space-time apply; and QT and Hilbert space geometry does not apply;
- When $z= 0$, Hilbert space geometry and QT and its equations apply; and GR and Riemannian geometry does not apply.

This way, GR and QT combined become a Unified Theory. Yet, that is not enough.
General Relativity and Quantum Theory are two limiting cases for 0 dimensional particle waves and 3 dimensional objects of a deeper mathematical theory that also allows for different theories to accurately describe objects or particle waves that have a dimensionality between 0 and 3D. For example, string theories assume that the fundamental sub-particles are "one-dimensional curves called strings."

As a result, the mathematical rules are expanded to include string and super-symmetry theories, the Theory of Chaos and potential new theories, as follows:

-If and when $z=1$ then the string theory applies.

-If and when $z=2$ then the "M Theory", (membranes) and super-symmetry in 11 Dimensions applies.

-If $0< z < 3$ and is a fractional dimension then the Theory of Chaos (TC) applies.

As a result all these fully accepted theories of physics, (and there is no other) that have been extensively proven for their respective range of applications are integrated and consistent with the others by being referenced to the dimensionality of each of the force s and of the particles they act upon.

The Physics Theory of Everything

Equation (1) from the first law of thermodynamics can yield an equation, which, if I did correctly, results in or is consistent with all the other equations of physics.

G is the force of gravity as measured or as calculated by General Relativity or by Newton's equations.

$\Delta U(z)$ is the change in the energy from each of the other three forces as measured or as calculated by QT through the 1, 2, 3D Schrödinger's equations and/or through the Standard Model.

α_z as the a1, a2 and a3 are the effective coupling constants (See Bibliography book 42, page 442) corresponding to each of the three quantum forces i.e.

a1 for electromagnetism, a2 for the weak, and a3 for the strong force.

$$\Sigma^z_0 \Delta U(z) . \, a_z = -G \, \Delta \, s_z \qquad (2)$$

$0 \leq z \leq 3$

Equation (2) (and I assert only this equation) gives us the relationship between the four known forces of the Universe. As a result it allows for the calculation of each of the forces from the rest.

Equation (2) is also consistent with all other equations of physics. For example, Einstein's energy equation (that had no previous derivation other than Einstein's intuition) can be derived from equation (2) for $z = 0$, $a_0 = -1$ and $\Delta s_0 = c . \Delta t$

Using $G = m . a$, then $\Delta U_{(0)} = E = G \Delta s_0 = m . (\Delta s / \Delta t^2) . \Delta s_0 = mc^2$.

Gravity is by far the weakest of the 4 forces and releases the least energy. Gravity is the inertial resistance and reaction to the net imbalances of the 3 quantum forces. However as Einstein equation shows gravitational mass is where energy storage is most dense.

This TOE is simple, commonly understandable, coherent, correct, and does not need the proof of anything that is not already proven.

As you can see this TOE is ultimately as simple as 0,1,2,3 D. (Just as when you start a song.) Which TOE in physics is simpler, more correct, more comprehensive and more beautiful?

Alexander Zecos' help in discerning this Theory of Everything was central and he is equally responsible for it.

The existence of the physics TOE doesn't invalidate further research or experiments, it may help focus them.

Your leaders and educators wrongly pretend to "know better" and to offer right or correct solutions.

How can they pretend to solve any real life problem, when unlike me, they don't know how to solve the 11 dimensional equations i.e. 4D + 3D + (2+1) D + 1D= 11D, which they don't even know how to set up, to find the straight line that maximizes the variables that are best when most, and minimizes those that are best when least, that all real life problems require?

Only in the best Universities, such as at Harvard Business School, (HBS), there is enough integrity to teach that there are correct, **coherent answers** for a case, (and for the worldly), but "**there is no right answer**." This is so because the whole context is wrong and is about choices among wrongs, **under uncertainty**. No choice of a wrong is right. A choice of a wrong maybe correct under certain circumstances but it is not right.

The value of any knowledge is in its predictive capacity. If knowledge does not help you predict what will happen, it is useless because the future is the only thing coming and matters most.

What is the predictive value of the knowledge you claim to have? What can you predict about human behavior; that is most important for humanity? Nothing: nada: zero. You can't even predict with whom your spouse will be having lunch in a week?

Until now you couldn't even agree if the Universe is probabilistic or deterministic; whether you are free or slaves.

Actually, the value of your knowledge is less than zero—you know about evil; about how to be evil and know about what you don't want—it is negative. Negative is the value of your knowledge by which you steal in the name of educating.

Some say that they search for the truth. Why are they talking, let alone teaching, given that they lie since by their own admission they have not found the truth?

TO LAWYERS

Why do you demand that people swear to tell the whole truth and nothing but the truth when neither they nor you could possibly know the whole truth until now? You force people to swear and lie. You use "truth" to persecute instead of to liberate. Despite you not knowing Good, you prohibit those that want to live by the goodness of God freely and independently, (in case you hadn't understood why Jesus said that you are likely to be condemned.)

In the first version there were about 100 pages of explicitly cussing at you the lawyers, and 'the professors' (the same scribes that Jesus and the academics that Lao Tzu warned against.) Thanks to the mute button on T.V, I can now shorten them to a more respectful: You don't know what you're talking about. Shut up and...

Teach what I teach in this book or else you intentionally choose to remain ignorant, incompetent and immoral and so will end up in hell.

Right, in the context of time, means what is proven objectively true. God's prophets are right as you can see by the events happening now.

God's prophets foretold you these current events so that when you see these events happen, as you see now, you may believe in God.

Your leaders are false prophets that keep forecasting, predicting and planning based on false predictions that are proven wrong 100% of the time and they still keep selling false prophesies, as if they Know or as if they have true foresight.

I have proven you wrong in intent, wrong in providing correct Context, wrong in the Content you teach, wrong in logic, wrong in the criteria and the measurements of the results of teaching, wrong in expression, wrong in actions, wrong in not being truthful and wrong in the results you produce.

Challenge me; "go ahead, make my day."

Either value most the "unseen" (thoughts, emotions and) spirit—whose "matter" is the anti-matter—believe in doing what is truly right, establish and live in Joy forever in God's Kingdom and get on God's right side; or value the "seen" body most, define 'correct' as whatever you like, at least honestly, stay in the current systems and you will still have some chance in life because in time you will realize that you were wrong and will hopefully change your mind. **But stop hypocritically saying that you do right while doing wrong and evil because you are bound to suffer, die and go to hell.**

I avoided technical lingo (such as "id; ego; super ego" in psychology; D.C.F's in business; legalese, Lagrangians in physics, etc.) that each discipline and profession uses to (unsuccessfully) deal with the complexity it encounters because for the most part that lingo is intended to intimidate others and to make "non-insiders" feel stupid. Please don't let anyone make you feel stupid because so long as you have common sense and are not wrongly intimidated into believing that you are stupid, you are not. The solutions to even the most complex subjects and problems are no more than a large series (requiring concentration) of logical, common sense, steps.

Ignoring me is ignorance.

No matter how many resources are put into education until this section of the book is taught in every high school and every College, graduating students will remain ignorant, incompetent and taught to become immoral hypocrites who say the "nice things" the masses want to hear while doing evil works.

14.   Truth through Fiction

This section of the book (in this and the next two Chapters) **is fiction**. (And it is used to explain non-fiction from providing a very short timeline of modern human history, to solutions on the issues of the day.)

This section, and the "fictional characters," is unnecessary and even counter-productive if and only if the previous pre-"fiction" part is fully and correctly understood.

To the extent that 'the systems' fail to teach the truth rightly and correctly, by teaching the previous part of this book in every high school and College, this portion becomes fully necessary and should be taught and even made into movies.

The world isn't just black and white or various shades of gray but is full of color. So, in explaining it correctly, I (in some digital versions) use the three primary colors; blue on the right side of the Cross for Ideas and thoughts, red (on the left) for mostly emotional expressions and yellow (at the top) for issues of conscience.

The "fictional characters" have their statements "in quotes" *and what is in italics* **is** *fiction, (slanted truth,* **lies) used to illustrate the real fiction and deceit portion that is troubling human life.**

Fiction is attractive, as you know, to those trying to escape truth and the size of the entertainment (and alcohol and drug) industries is a measure of how hard humanity tries to escape its truth. However, fiction (stories, metaphors and parables) can also be most emotionally instructive **for those trying to escape the fictions that they are trapped in.** So, to end the fiction portion:

What is your defense Jezebel and Babylon?

"In the world that is dominated by power and force, that God chose to not give me, *but with an exquisite and superbly beautiful body like mine* (that someone gave me *who knows why)* I have no option but to be a working girl to survive without being a slave to someone.

Capitalism is explicit that I and most people operate in self-interest.

You condemned the hypocrites but have not condemned me so far maybe because I am often honest and do not claim to be right. I don't believe in (Absolute) Right. I say that the customer is right. Also, your Lord said that the prostitutes will enter God's Kingdom before the hypocrites.

Who is less wrong and less bad: A lousy W. or a W. that does her job really well and meets the needs of her customers? What is a smaller number: A small or a large negative number? I excel in my job. *I can swing from Chandeliers, do three flips in the air and stick the landing on my customer's genitals. Because I am also classy* I only sleep with Kings, Presidents, Prime Ministers and leaders.

Who is less bad: Someone that sells their body or someone that sells their soul and beliefs? *I am the least wrong* so you will have to condemn all the lousy w.'s. and other professionals first before you condemn me," says Babylon.

"You cannot serve God and Money," said Jesus. Either you act because of Love or you act for self-interest. Doing "both" is unclean and malicious hypocrisy. Those that are God's should move in Jesus' Kingdom on earth in an Independent Disarmed Demilitarized Holy Land in their nation, and those that are operating in self- interest should stay in these systems and at least be honest about their motives.

"I am their global economy. I feel very anemic in the West. Leaders love me and people work for me whether they know it admit it or not. You're a bozo because you write truths that you know people don't want to hear. People hate you and they love me; as the facts show.

One of your million problems is that you're more boring than Geometry. When was the last time you said something funny? What time is it? A thousand years ago?! You're not making me feel good. If you want anyone to read this, you better make me, and them, feel good...There's already too much free sex in these societies which is threatening my businesses so I am in intense negotiations with Linda from Hollywood, about gradual reductions in the availability of free sex.

If not having free sex is your main complain, there's some free sex even for the unknown, ugly and old like you, so long as you follow the S. community secret rules that I'll reveal to you... to stop you from revolting.

First, any discussion about religion, philosophy, physics, psychology and politics are a taboo subjects because they are buzz killers; so there is nothing about your book to talk about. If the subjects come up, make them meaningless by treating them like team sports, picking a team (preferably whatever 'teams' she's into) and cheer for that team no matter what. To fit in, you must make a lot of small talk, making much Ado about nothing. Speak like all my TV channels saying things that will never make any long term difference. The more emphatic and pompously meaningless you are, the better your chances to get laid.

Second, given that you're an unknown, old and how ugly you look don't waste your time going out before 1 a.m. when only the most serious about having fun... no matter what, are left.

When with a lady slut (S.), (with borderline personality disorder,) it's critical to agree with her no matter what she says, so you should always respond 'that's what I'm talking about.' So, remember your days as a nigger in Africa, with the slave mentality of being aggressive but selling out, and keep saying "that's what I'm talking about" while doing a dance move," says Babylon with a laugh.

Admit that you are a racist. In the context of the world as it has been it would be unnatural for a person of any race, ethnicity and gender to not feel some likeness and (to the extent they don't dislike themselves) have some preference to people of "their own kind," that are like them. One cannot eliminate having these traits unless one is truly spiritual and does not judge by any appearances, in which case one has no business participating at all in the current societies that are based necessarily on judgments by appearances, either because that's all that as animals they can see or because appearances is what they truly value. All in these systems are in part racists, nationalists, discriminate based on age and on looks and are sexists and the only question is how unfair are you to the "other kinds."

These traits, as everything else except God, are relative and only a matter of degree. Those who call others racists or sexists without acknowledging their own racist and gender preferences, which is what they are trying to "defend," are condemned to hell hypocrites. The least nationalists, sexists, and racists are those who admit that they have been so and try to keep reducing being so. (Of course, those are the first to get persecuted by the worldly for having admitted what others hypocritically deny.)

Acknowledging the differences and valuing those that are not 'your kind' and/or 'disagree with you' for helping provide a more whole picture, is wiser.

"Do you feel offended when you are called racists?" asks Babylon.

I stopped getting upset by anything anyone, other than God, says long ago. I find the generalized offense that some take when someone says some bad word, as if those offended are virgins, hypocritical. If someone says that some people are the bad word X and you know that you are not X you have nothing to be offended by. The adults that get offended by "bad words," that are not addressed to them personally, may kiss my badass. What I find wrong is when someone intends to unjustly hurt others whether that someone uses bad words or not.

As a child and teenager in Ethiopia, that has had a close relationship with Greeks before even Homer's time and is one of the few nations in Africa that is mostly Christian and does not discriminate on the basis of religion, most of my best friends were black. Growing up as one of the very few white kids in Ethiopia I didn't really have much of a choice but to not be racist. If I wanted to play, the only kids in my neighborhood (surrounded by huts) were black. I would offer free snacks to incentivize soccer playing in our yard to deal with our disputes about who is cooler. So, whenever my team of black kids and the opposing teams where not throwing rocks at each other, we would play soccer.

I experienced and felt racism only when I came to the US where the slave mentality still prevails in some places. I still remember my first personal experience of being judged by the color of my skin, during the first week of my arrival in the US, in 1977 when I was 22. My English vocabulary was about 30 words (the word turkey was not a part of it) and despite my scores in the GRE's in English being somewhere between very crappy and total crap, I was accepted at Columbia Graduate Engineering, to my surprise, but probably because of my near perfect math scores.

Columbia sounded like a classy joint and given my past experience of many pretty classy girls liking tennis I took my tennis bag and looked for Columbia Un. I took the subway and as many do I missed the correct exit and came out in Harlem which was anything but classy and I felt judged by my skin color. As I was walking, one big black guy comes out of a group, steps in front of me and says to me aggressively "You, turkey," which really pissed me off because I thought he was calling me "Turkish," so I throw my tennis bag down and shout at him "me no Turkey; me Greek." And the big black dude says all confused "Owo,... o.k. then..." and steps out my way.

Despite our miscommunication about what the offense really was and the logic of my response, I and the big black dude of Harlem came to a de facto agreement that offending me because of my skin color or appearance or anything else was not going to be worthwhile.

Whatever the degree of my racism may be now, as a Greek-white man who knows and can prove that humanity's idea of ascending would still be climbing trees if not for my forefathers, it is very offensive to be called anything negative by scums who bite the hand of those who fed them, taught them everything they know and liberated them.

"Whatever. *I am not a racist at all; so long as people pay I don't care about anything else. I was against slavery myself on the basis that renting people as we do now is cheaper than buying them.* Anyway, even if the subject of the lady's discussion is her genitals emphasize your, in English 10,000 or so word Greek lexicon monolithically, analogous to all these names that still heroically organize the central meanings and ideas in all Western dialects, retorting stoically... 'the morphology of the clitoris is ignorantly, uncharacteristically and illogically stereotyped...,' do as I say and you'll get some free sex; O.k.? (You may be relieved to know that o.k. isn't short for oki doki but for "Ola Kala," meaning: all is well, and it reportedly was first used in Oxford University, England.)

I do not like hanging on the air at 1 a.m. It's perfect time to go downtown to the Double Douche Bar. Look at the super sexy, tall beautiful blond honey, riding blindfolded the mechanical bull and showing off her beautifully balanced bouncing breasts...that's entertaining!

It's Linda. I have been in a committed relationship with Linda; let's see; its 2013... for 9 hours now. I attract my opposites and after a while what was attractive becomes repulsive. My therapist says that common interests are critical *so I am now mostly a lesbian since both Linda and I are very interested in our vaginas. Even though she has a weird obsession with scales (and balances) I have great hopes for her. One day powerful politicians will do crazy things to keep her happy.*

Paul, this is Linda de Slut. Linda, remember his ugly face because in time you will have to face him," says Babylon.

Linda smiles and says: "The secret to life is bacon wrapped jalapenos," and keeps dancing. "That's what I'm talking about," I say with a dance move "nice to meet you, yo" ….Three years later…

*Babylon comes to find him in his Mystic place and says: "*I had a hard day at work today. There was more bitching (they call it critical analysis) than there was entertaining today. So, I felt more fear than greed and the markets fell. The last thing I want to hear is that I am wrong and why. *You're worse than boring; you're an anti-entertainer making me feel bad. I don't know why I even bother talking with you. I will talk to my therapist again because I still get attracted to the wrong men. For example, you are mad. But it's ok; my therapist told me to be more tolerant because I've had some problems with relationships. Maybe I can help you get in touch with reality darling.*

Given that you're a 'nobody,' immigrant with no family, friends or connections here and given that you are an anti-entertainer you may even have to pay people to read this. The chances that enough people will read this, let alone do it, are as low as finding a Hollywood starlet that hasn't been gang banged and are less than 1 in a million. Do you agree?"

It seems so, but I have the right plan and Truth on my side.

"That's progress darling. At least we have a common assessment of the 10^6 degree of your madness. And who's going to implement your plan?" asks Babylon.

Mary will do the right parts; my named adversaries the correct parts and "lost time *Linda" and you will do* the wrong parts.

"A 'hail Mary'; you're not as sexy as you think; and how much money do you have? Your odds are less than 1 in a billion.

You complain and rant about being enslaved in nationalistic governments by systems of power-fear, money-greed and arrogant ignorance with attorneys making up long incomprehensible by common people self-contradicting and constantly changing laws, making those laws 'god,' a 'tyrannical god,' and then (while people are at risk of losing their livelihood, child custody or freedom) extorting exorbitant sums to violate the spirit of those laws by the words of the laws, whether by working for corporations or even when working for the 'defense.'

Yet, you are the worst of tyrants; you're not satisfied with people worshiping you in fear and singing for you, saying they love you, and giving gifts and charity on your behalf; you demand that they really mean that they love," says Babylon and then goes to her palace, puts on her purple dress, and after many processions of perversely dressed 'Lords,' the Crown Chancellor puts her crown on, and then she returns and defiantly says: "You demand my soul and I refuse to lose it."

"Those that want to save their soul will lose it but those who lose their soul for my (righteousness) sake will gain it." (Luke 9:24)

"Darn it Paul, I do not need you; in your dinky middle class home. I do much better by myself. Have you seen my Palaces, Mansions and Penthouses? The war has been and is whether your head or my vagina rules the world, and given people's spiritual, intellectual, emotional and physical inertia I win every time and will win again."

She leaves and goes to meet with the Presidents, leaders and Kings but she soon rushes back crying and sees him leaving…

"The kings, Presidents and Prime Ministers, *who all they are concerned about is their own power* **have set me on fire**…*Paul wait…do not f. us and leave us;* I agree with you that **'To Be *or not to be?'*** is truly The Question and central choice in life.

The leaders of the nations, now also pretend publicly that they don't know me even though it is they that created me; it is they that authorize me, even gave me free speech and MyMon ey and sex is most of what they think about. I am in great pain and fear… I am burning… water… someone… help… I am suffering; Paul, come back here or else I will tell them about you… can you hear me? Help someone… I am burning… I'm in great pain…I'm dying…help…Please…

To the United Nations Security Council,

Dear Presidents, Prime Ministers, Queens and Kings: *I hope you know your primary and most dangerous enemy. I know him. I can now see all his life. He's one of the Argonauts before my Egyptian civilization and one of the four Mystic Aryan Vedas before my Babylonian civilization existed. He's Abraham (as many of us are) that left me. He is Elijah. He is the Mystic Olympian of the Olympics* (that bring a time of truce for Peace and still bring opponents and the world together in fair fun friendly competition). *He is the Mystic with the reputation of conducting Mystical orgies in public, and Pythagoras who's Virgins went later in the Parthenon. He is the "This is Sparta" king Leonidas. He is Cleisthenes, the (not well known) Father of Democracy. He turned against the East as the Great king Alexander that imposed himself upon me, the Egyptians, the Jews, Afghans, Pakistanis, Syrians, Persians, Iranians, Indians and all the then known world. It is to him that Cleopatra dedicated her vagina and when Anthony was defeated the last remnant of Ancient Hellas killed herself and that nation became the enslaved Greece to the Roman Barbarians. He then is the flying f. that impregnates without touching!*

He is among the Greeks that met Jesus and then Jesus spoke about his glorification. He is John of Patmos of the Apocalypse. (That means Revelation, exposure of the "secrets.")It is he and those darn Greeks— not the Jews that rejected Jesus and not the Roman oppressors— that saw through Jesus the path for Liberty from the Romans and made Christianity a global religion. Having turned against the East, he is Emperor Constantine of Constantinople that turned against the West and established the first global Christian Church and the Eastern (Greek speaking Byzantine) Empire, that raped me silly and the rest of the Middle East again, and established and preserved Christianity; and his Empire lasted a thousand years when the West was fully ours, and unfortunately he has left us with many Christian nations.

This bastard isn't allowed to rest long in heaven because he has unfinished business on earth, is rejected by the world because they don't know him and even hell rejects him. This bastard is rejected fully even by hell no matter what he does because he insists In telling the truth no matter what, so that if the children of hell found out that they don't really have to stay in hell and that there is a better option he would empty much of hell. This alien Hellen is the crazy one that keeps invading hell to take-over and freeze hell over. He has decimated and frozen much of hell already and turned it into nice civil societies. This very profane and very profound bastard turns harlots into Virgins and now he is going after all my daughters.

*Since he is Constantine and the fall of Istanbul (*with Greeks leaving the enslaved Greece after 1450 at the beginning of the Renaissance and regaining their Independence after a second 400 years slavery in the 1820's just before the American Civil War)*, I hadn't seen him till now but I know that he "retired" from being king of Greece and has been in the Diaspora as a common lonesome stranger, Mystic and/or* **revolutionary** *without office who has caused havoc in the West and around every nation preaching Jesus and demanding democracy. He is also known as "who the fudge is that foreigner?" In this life, at 19, he is a student in the Polytechnic and critical in the successful student revolt of 1973 against the military junta that we (with the CIA) had imposed in 1967, on Greece.*

When hunting, he is like a terrifying lion with his awesome pride coming at you all at once. He does give warning but it is very little time; so you must respond immediately or you are dead.

Don't let his smiley nappy lazy look deceive you; that look is only because he just devoured some unsuspecting weak creature that was mostly minding her own business. I know that you'll think this is a joke; it is not: he is very angry about the defamation and the loss of sovereignty of Greece, even if he is centuries long retired from that job and hasn't lived there for decades. Now he is going against the whole world. He is wilder than fudge and fudges for the fudge of it! **After** *he first fd. me he said 'hello, it is an honor to meet you.' When this king, the one that got away, is at war he comes out of nowhere and out of everywhere all at once and before you know it, he is charge.*

Don't believe that the king of Greece is free and acts on his own will; He is a slave to Jesus, the Jew. He has been slave of the Jew from the beginning, doing all the work since "you took care" of the Jew and the Jew ascended. The Jews don't fear Jesus, their King, but this Elin (Greek) the Jews rightly fear because he has cut off some of their penises' already, has taken them over and "known" them more than me, every which way but Saturday, and that is a lot, and they are not even allowed to pronounce his name.

This bozo chose to be the least in God's Kingdom rather than be the king of kings of the world. He is now the middle-class American. It is his Spirit that Burned my W. Bush with His Fire and shocked, awed and fd. me over again. He is persistent and with more vengeance than ever. He is a one trick pony whose solution to every problem is war. He is looking for an excuse to go to real war again.

The Man does not compromise. He says that truth, right, good, and love can't and should not be compromised or balanced at all with lies, wrong, evil or hate. He is an extreme extremist.

The good news is that this bozo is such a lazy Greek so as to find showing his ugly face once in a while as Emperor for his adoring public was too much work for him and complaining about what the f. is the point of being king if he has to do something he retired, so if you do exactly as he asks he is likely to stay in retirement.

Let this lazy, most dangerous brutal warrior be in a disarmed sovereign Land to stay retired. Because if we force **this, The White Horseman** *to come out of retirement and in real war in the world his vengeance will break all hell loose and that will devastate and obliterate us all. That B.in the entrance of the Louvre, Victory, has been is and will be with him. Do as he asks now and live and let me live, ignore him and we will all suffer and die. I know.*

I called Satan for help and Satan panicked. Hades hides and is nowhere to be found when-where this Man is. The brutal Easterner having rapped me silly many times every which way but Friday, in many lives, at least has been gracious enough to let me live so far, but I fear that he'll kill me this time. Act urgently; ***I'm in immense pain. I burning, I'm dying...***

Members of the UN, Trilateral Commission, Bilderberg and CFR: Do not ignore him; you'll experience the woes of Revelation in physical reality with much greater intensity than those that are already suffering; Look at the news: He has set everything up exactly as God's prophets said he would. Do exactly as he asks now, fast, to live and avoid our total obliteration," says Babylon.

"Ladies and gentlemen of the U.N Security Council: *I quit.*

Lady Babylon the Great:

It is correct that in the context of wrongs (and thus of negatives) the best that can be done is the least, and that those that are least wrong are best. The least is the best for harlots, for governments, for wars, for clothing intended to tempt, for medicines, for litigiousness, for unemployment, inflation, prices for the consumers and for everything else that is wrong in the context of wrongs.

But those of us that you call lousy cheap harlots because we are not excelling at our profession, may be so because we do not truly believe in any wrong and/or are not greedy but just do what we have to, to survive and endure.

Democracies can't survive without right public education. So selling our mind to be educators, as I am, even if what we teach is not right, without us really knowing it, is no-where near as wrong to what you do, no matter how you cut it. You maybe the best and least but because you are so committed to and love what you do and money and power you are also the worst. Your worldly educators are either wrong or are hypocrites.

There are no obstacles legal or otherwise if you truly choose to establish Demilitarized, Disarmed Holy Lands. The UN can and has in the past declared "safe havens." It can still do so without having to have any military presence to defend those "safe Heavens," and just appointing that responsibility to the relevant host nation.

Teacher; we have been waiting for you for a very long time; what took you so long to show up?" asks Mary.

What took you so long to Wake up, my love?

To educators: First, may I offer my opinion about the amount of homework assigned to children in US public schools being so brutal that I would have dropped out in middle school; it needs to be cut to less than half of what it is now.

The more academic disciplines there are, the more evidence there is that none of the current theories are adequate or comprehensive. The greater the number of "expert" disciplines there are, the more evidence there is that the inconsistencies among the disciplines and their theories have not been resolved and are not unified.

In teaching, you must generalize to get to a unified Theory but even if the generalizations have strong statistical validity they create stereotypes, as many stereotypes do have some statistical validity.

The purpose of Right and True teaching is to break the stereotypes and give each individual abundant opportunity for happiness. (So, unless I cuss at you by name, please do not be offended by the generalized cussing.) So, the methods of teaching are in opposition **to its purpose;** and in opposition to the means for its implementation because doing and leading is not based on any correlational probabilistic statistics and generalizations but by treating each human uniquely because each has been created unique. So, for worldly issues, do you teach your students to use exactly the opposite methods from how you teach, which is what you should do? If you do not, you are wrong. But even if you understand and teach this, then what are you teaching, except how to be hypocrites, that God has condemned, that say nice things to cover up their ugly intent and actions?

You are false, wrong, lousy teachers, Blind leaders-guides at best and condemned hypocrites at worst.

The problem of education is not just about the kids and the teachers; the problem is that the whole leadership all the way to the top of your government lack comprehensive, correct and cohesive understanding of life. To educate you must start and finish with **a single comprehensive course** that teaches science, humanities, governance and religions, emphasizing the meanings, rational and purpose of truth, right and correct reasoning, and love, as I have done here. If you don't help students integrate and be Whole, you are part of what is causing their confusion and passionate decay.

Is there a more comprehensive, correct, cohesive, and simple Theory of Everything ? And of Everyone?

"There isn't. Rabbouni! She mourns... please forgive me; this reality is lovely; but may I enter God's kingdom on earth and serve?"

Mary; I chose you from the beginning.

"Queen Lady Babylon and others: The Lord never asked you to worship or love him. He neither needs it nor wants it. He asked that you love other humans; and because your 'prostitute's love' is dirty, not true and is destructive he sacrificed himself and offered His love for you to love others by. It is He that Liberates. Don't dare call the Lord, my God a tyrant or blaspheme him again in any way because it is me that will never forgive you," says Mary.

Mary, you are Zion, my most beloved.

Babylon intervenes, "come to my palace...let's talk; ok. I will give you another freebee f. but don't tell anyone because I have a reputation to keep! Have you seen my new lingerie that's made with real gold and Blue-Blanc diamonds? Look!

She then kisses him and says, Ya, kisses him again and says Ou, again and says...Ye. But he doesn't respond. Don't say no to me... Nobody does if I really want them... Fine, we'll talk...

Everyone has their own theory of everything (TOE). And as you have experienced in Greek coffee shops most Greeks have at least two theories of everything each. One can be summarized as "f. them" and the other TOE applies and is in response to tall pretty blonds and is summarized as "you are right about that." So what is the big deal that your TOE is based in all four known forces of the Universe, is validated by both General Relativity and Quantum Theory that have been proven with an astounding degree of accuracy and that you have an equation that proves your theory? Like any respectable Greek go to a coffee shop and shout about your TOE while checking out the ladies.

Lower your standards and expectations to avoid disappointments. All I want is someone trustworthy to protect, promote, and please me; they call it pimping; and I will do the providing. All I am asking for is for a decent pimp. I see tremendous pimping potential in you. Pimp me. I already told my Presidents, Prime Ministers and kings of the nations, who are my current lousy pimps, to let you have what you ask. But they will not.

They will ignore you for as long as they can by making access to the major media (that as you know have stunningly high standards for intellectuality!) very difficult then they will blaspheme you and if they fail, then they'll kill you and make it look that they had nothing to do with it, and act very upset that you were killed. Then they will erect a statue for you. You already know that is what happens. How many times are you willing to get killed in war or get murdered, in how many lives? Your only chance is to not publish this, cancel your site, stop teaching and "do it" instead, as you were designed from the beginning to do.

The Anti-Christ who's now in power will kill you, will dominate all and will cause immense destruction, if you, as I told Mohammed, don't stop trying to teach Camels poetry, and take over for yourself by money and then by politics. You have no choice but to take over yourself…"

Go; stay away…

"The B. Obama suddenly evolved into protecting the crap fn. and the vagina licking community of the badly fd., not just with civil unions with equal rights with marriage by Federal law but also by redefining the meaning of the word and the religious institution of marriage.

I admit that I am a W. and have come out as bisexual and I'm a sinner but I am not proud of any of it. I don't mind going against God, if he is still alive, when Nature is on my side but if homosexuality is genetic then Nature is saying that this is the end of the line for your genes. So being against Nature and against God and demanding the transformation of the Sacrament of Marriage is not a battle I will take on. Yet, Linda likes it; she wants paper that proves (and pays her) for our sexual commitment. We could call it a ramiage, if she wants a ceremony also.

She's not as perfect as she looks; Linda is lately suffering from a chronically sore clitoris. You know Chemistry and pharmaceuticals (in its original it appropriately meant also poisons); do you know the cure for this? Maybe you can prescribe to her one more pill to add to her pill popping routine?

In contrast, you ask for an Independent Sovereign Land for the not-marrying and so you eliminate the central protection for all the fd. As the B. Obama is establishing equal rights for the marrying gays, you demand equal rights (to the married) for the non-marrying singles," *says Babylon.*

Why is the Government discriminating against single people? If there are financial advantages to marriage or civil unions then the government is wrongly discriminating against the single individual. If the Government discriminates against the individual because it believes that traditional marriage is good for children, fine. But the rational that homosexual marriage is good for children and therefore single parents should be discriminated against while homosexual marriage is favored is absurd, and will intentionally or unintentionally hurt most the racial minorities and the heterosexual single women, who will be paying for the financial benefits of the homosexual self-loving sexual relationships.

The current debate of "gay rights" is not an equal rights or a civil rights issue because if there were any such issues their answer through civil unions, with all equal rights as marriage, by Federal law would have been enough. To the extent that civil unions with fully equal rights as marriage has not been enough, the demands of gay marriage are a direct assault against religion and against the Sacrament of Marriage by those who call loving them-selves (the meaning of "homo") love.

"Isn't loving-self a pre-requisite to loving others?" asks Babylon.

"No. Not at all; loving others requires not self-love but self-sacrifice. Self-love is in opposition to loving the "other" (hetero). Respecting-self, liking i.e. being a friend to self and governing self are pre-requisites of loving others.

The hierarchy of the Seven Spirits and so the priority (preference) of how to truly love is expressed in Christianity symbolically also, and may be experienced if done rightly, by the seven Sacraments, the least two of which are Baptism and then Marriage.

The current "gay Marriage" demand is no less absurd than a gay taking a shower with their lover in the presence of a mirror and demanding that as a matter of civil and equal rights there must be a (Federal) Law calling their gay shower, Baptism.

"Commit to me till death as one of your wives; I'll need S. Linda to share your fat bum burden with me; as marriage was originally. Muslims still do so, and as a result their public, despite eating crap, is thriving in numbers. If you marry me I will get you that sovereign land. If you like it, put a ring on it," she says shaking her belly, grabbing her crotch like a rapper and dancing.

(Given my experience from two marriage-divorces,) if I decide to risk losing my cahones, I will send you a memo.

"Don't say no to me; I get hysterical when I hear no. B. Shaw warned us that progress comes only from the unreasonable that insist in adapting the world to them-selves rather than adapting to the world, as the rest of us do. How do you like this..?" she says and does something very naughty. "What? Did you evolve into a homosexual? If there was a homosexual gene, it could not be passed on and therefore I doubt that homosexuality is genetic. Are you fed up with women?"

You know that I am heterosexual. I wonder sometimes if it would be easier if I was bi-sexual and was caught in a bad romance with Lady

Gaga because shehe seems as minimally dishonest but less incoherent than you Lady Babylon but unfortunately I am sexist in feeling that men, including me, are physically ugly compared to women, and also my instincts are for women. Sweetheart I like it, but I know way too well all the trouble that comes with it, so go; stay away.

"Bstrd... Paul... I am fed up with you. You refuse to help yourself and refuse to get help even when I try so hard for you. It is complicated. Don't oversimplify things. What part don't you get? It is in our interest to take care of the interests of others because the better we take care of our customers the more we can charge.

So, we like the preaching of love and of serving because love makes suckers for us that give more than they take; we get more than we give; that is the profit that we maximize. 'Serving others and love' are tools that we use to take advantage of bozos but no one really means it. If some did, what you ask for would have been established in the last 1900 years.

Let me inform you of the political landscape so that you don't remain so naïve. In all democratic nations there are about 30% who are "Conservatives" ("right") meaning that they oppose any new idea if you cannot prove and commit your cahones that it'll personally make them money; so they will oppose most of your ideas. There are about 30% that are "Liberals" ("left") who love any new idea that gets them to power and your ideas don't help them get in power politically so you they will reject them also. (O.k. maybe some of the 10% or so ideologues that are on the extremes of those groups and have veto power as to what their Party does will see some value in the "starting fresh" part of your Independent Holy Lands and may try to boss others there.) There are about 20% that are an unruly fragmented group of "Independents" each of which is often Independent of what they said yesterday, so the idea that they will commit to something is repulsive to them so they will reject your ideas also.

Finally there is about another 20% that don't give a f. about politics because they know that they will get screwed no matter what. But how are you going to reach that audience that doesn't give a f.?

You can't succeed. But I know that you are a brutal and vengeful Man with the capacity to bankrupt any city, any nation and the world, so if you stay retired in your San Diego, Ca. Jacuzzi, like an Imam hiding in a well, I will not fight you. We have a lot in common: I fudge with the 'hardware' of people and you are trying to fudge with the human 'software'; you need me.

I will advise again my kings to let you have a Land to stay retired. But I'll be sleeping with them as I have been and if they keep ignoring you and if they defame you or try to kill you I will not fight them either. I'm a working girl because you f. me silly and don't pay me or marry me and I need to survive.

Corporations, I, and my professional followers have as our primary, if not sole, purpose the making of money, irrelevant of what we pretend.

The MF'ing US Supreme Court oppressed us for long time but finally said that we corporations have the right to speak, and so we speak and if they don't like being called names they can spank the paper we are written on!

Stop thinking coherently and pointing out my and their incoherence; I forbid it.

Stop attacking my best W.'s the CEOs and the Corporate Boards of public companies who worship MyMon ey; and my loyal politician B.'s who benefit themselves in the name of public service and defend me.

My faithful Global W. Christine Lagarde of the I MF told you already that it's time for you Greeks to pay for having brought civilization, science, Democracy and Christianity to us that give nothing unless you pay anew even if you are all dying. Helping the Greek government, as an exception for your (actually my) sake, cost me 100 Billion euros last year. Do you know how badly that slashed my lingerie budget? F. off."

You can't get to integrity without your conscience, thoughts, emotions and actions being in alignment.

Accept these Gifts from this Greek but beware because I am coming in unexpectedly like a thief and will take you over from within. Pretty Eve b.; it's your turn to decide.

"Where are you going?...I'm out of here, too," says Babylon.

"Please explain again, more specifically this time, the practical solutions to the world's problems?" asks Mary.

15.   THE PRACTICAL CURRENT SOLUTIONS

Other than those of God's Kingdom that I told you are with me now, there are some of the world, that I do not just love but I also like and are old friends. They are: Homer, Socrates, Archimedes, Plato, Pericles, Aristotle, Aeschylus, Hippocrates, Luther, Michelangelo, L. Da Vinci, Rafael, El Greco (means "The Greek,") Elisabeth I, Newton, Shakespeare, Rousseau, Voltaire, Bach, Beethoven, Pasteur, B. Franklin, G. Washington, A. Lincoln, Karaiskakis, Papaphlesas, Gandhi, Einstein, Bohr, Schrodinger, Ras Tafari, (I met while in Ethiopia,) JFK, RFK, M. Luther King, John Lennon, John Paul II, Richard Pryor, W. Cronkite, M. Teresa.

Don't these people, the saints, and others who so ask, deserve at least one small unarmed demilitarized Sovereign land of God on earth to live by love and in Peace? Or you don't want them alive on earth, again? And don't all of the unknown until now others that were unjustly killed, deserve a safe place of Peace?

That all are resurrected now is not theory either but fact. There have been about 7 billion people since the creation of the post-humanoid humanity and soon, I am not sure exactly when, each and every one of the dead will be in body on earth. You do not know who is who because you don't know your-selves but all are resurrected physically and are here now, in body.

"Man, Wait; don't love us and leave us...Remember you said that those that can help and do not, are guilty by their indifference...I got new make-up look, look how great I look...she takes her purple robe off... Look at me move and dance...have you seen anyone that's as beautiful.... come back here... How about this sexy new lingerie...? I'll get new and bigger tits for you...

I told you that you shouldn't read this book. Now you saw me get fudged up silly; and worse it was for free. I didn't really enjoy it, I was acting. Don't tell anyone... Paul, I am dying... I am on fire... I will help you... I am burning... give me water... I'm burning, I'm in great pain, give me water...call me; may I call... aaaaa she screams out in immense pain, kill me...please.... aaaaaaa"

I keep the TV on mute, (except when serious people are talking, like L. Black, D. Miller or those of the Daily Show; I liked Jon singing 'Papa can you hear me?' and I'm responding) to protect the 'talking heads' from getting cussed at, by my brutal vulgar ego. The central facts are on the pictures and in writing anyway; the "talking heads" are offensive to my ego.

If any President or "major leader" is talking on T.V and my ego is tempted into believing that he should hear them, he soon starts eating, smoking and eating until he can no longer control himself from cussing his brains out at the TV; and then at himself for having gotten mislead into hearing crap!

From the currently on earth leaders, I so far like N. Mandela, M. Gorbachev, Jim Baker, R. Gates, D. Petraeus, (I was against the war in Iraq from the beginning and was against the surge and I'm glad they proved me wrong about the surge), M. Theodorakis, Archbishops Tutu, Bartholomew and of Canterbury, the Dalai Lama, N. Farage, Alan Simpson, E. Bowles (better listen to them on budget issues; their ratio of revenue increase-to cuts is correct), Woody Allen and Olympia Snow. I will like most those that will help do God's work.

I don't like the Donald but he is correct about **the urgency to change the direction of the China and OPEC trade deficits** (for the oil part the T.B. Pickens plan is the starting point) as I explained on Chapters 11, 14, of "The World Anew" in 2006, thus requiring 4 changes to **Simpson-Bowles** to correctly include:

1)   A, long term, deduction for up to 30% of pre-tax profits for **domestic** R@D and **domestic manufacturing** investments**;**

2)   A 12% **not deferrable** (whether the profits are repatriated or not) tax on any foreign (after foreign country taxes) profits (excluding from current and 'in progress' free trade partners); and payment of all currently deferred taxes over 10 years at 10% per year, whether the foreign profits get repatriated or not, **which adds over $1 T over 10 years in revenues from money currently sitting abroad**, with no negative company P&L or B/S impact. In fact this will reduce company leverage, and increase their future reported income (34% vs. the 12%) from foreign operations. There is nothing unreasonable in asking corporations to pay over the next 10 years, the payable taxes they owe and have already booked. (Maybe allow a 70- 80% payout thus allowing these companies to show a 20-30% profit just for paying their US taxes that they admit they owe by having them on their books.)

There are some in the Senate that proposed a so called "territorial tax" that would tax US multinationals at 0% tax on foreign profits which would damage the US economy, significantly. In a May 2013 Senate Hearing even Tim Cook, CEO of Apple, recommended against the 0% and suggested a tax rate on foreign profits "in the single digits" to cause a significant amount of repatriations. In my assessment 12% will still do so and get higher benefits to the US economy.

3) Cancellation of the new benefit for Medicare (to be added to all the debts from China that your children will be required to pay for you) that closes the "donut hole;" and means testing (i.e. not paying) Medicare for those with assets over $5 M. A self-funding, effective 'waste, fraud and abuse' reduction program in government, requiring some Congressional restructuring, that I can easily design if they ask, is also necessary.

 4) For those with incomes over $ .5 M/year setting a 25% AMT tax, and letting the W. Bush tax cuts expire, (to keep the Capital Gains tax at 15%) will help socially even more than economically. All other tax changes should be revenue neutral without added growth and revenue positive with the growth they add.

MF's Sen. Reid-Pelosi, McConnell-Boehner **must bring** this long-term, bipartisan, growth, budget, **trade** deficit, and debt reduction agreement for Amendments and votes as soon as possible. (They and B. Obama could have done this over two years ago yet put the country through pathetic misery to prolong their power.)

Given that those making over a certain amount will get taxed more and given that any real deficit reduction will mathematically decrease domestic demand, unless the trade and Balance of Payments deficits get reduced, the fiscal deficit reductions will barely materialize because the economy and domestic demand will slow further. So, the only path out of "not going anywhere" is to indeed make the fiscal deficit reductions, timed correctly but to most importantly reduce the trade deficits at the same time, with China in particular.

Through my last company I was one of the first investors in Shenzhen and supported the trade strategy to help lift the hundreds of millions of Chinese that were in poverty but that strategy should have shifted 7 years ago, when it became apparent that the kleptocracy of the Communist Party of China was going to cost the American middle class over $ 1.5 **trillion**, as it has, so far.

So, beyond the 4 items above, particularly since the government will be taxing Americans more to reduce the fiscal deficit, it is too stupid to not tax the Chinese kleptocats. This can be best done by declaring **China a currency manipulator and then apply import taxes** thus reducing both trade and fiscal deficits. If that is deemed politically too aggressive, as China keeps threatening through N. Korea, then a 5-20% VAT tax, that both China and the EU have at higher rates, must be implemented (that excludes domestic products or those from current and likely free trade democratic nation partners.)

This, targeted to Chinese imports 20% VAT tax is essential not just for the US economy but also for the healthy growth of the global economy because it will shift manufacturing growth to the currently highly impoverished regions that need that growth most, to reduce poverty and will contribute even more in growing global demand.

Finally this, targeted to Chinese imports 20% VAT tax, that is conditional on Chinese reducing currency manipulation, corruption, threats through N. Korea, global pollution, tyranny and violations of human rights is essential for the vast majority of the Chinese people because the reduction in growth in China will force (or give the opportunity, depending how you look at it), to the Chinese government to make more progress in reducing its corruption and in further democratizing by, for example, letting free and fair multi-Party elections, for the governors of the Provinces..

"Kill me...help, forgive me, aaaaaaaa," Babylon mourns.

The brutal, disrespecting, offensive deadly and most feared warrior, now a jobless lazy lonely bozo copulating with many stranger women at a time, the Alien Aelin, my lower self- ego, takes his medicines, smiles for you, goes to his garden, on what he calls mount Megiddo, with a beautiful Crestview and spits!

Dear named muses and sexy celebrity adversaries: This book is more valuable than any material thing and is designed to be promoted by you. Do it.

Do not mess with my design or else I will be forced to either "know" you all together synchronously or ignore you. Do not force me to ignore you because you will become unknown.

You have been winning in worldly fame through stunning stupidity! But watch out because I am a fierce warrior. *I have been thinking hard*

and I am now fighting to win with more stunningly stunning stupidity!!
Watch me expose myself more than you have your bodies that have
been masturbated upon widely by the public!

I have elevated you to (necessarily) respected adversaries but you are
so elevated only because I don't give a fk., literally, about what other
men say… because I am coming out as sadly straight!

Recommend this book to get declared by the True Academy the 12
most Visionary and respectable ladies in the world for 2013!

Unless you are *joking* about your selves, as I do on occasion, thou shalt
heed God's 12^{th, the} Mystic, Commandment:

"Thou shalt not be too stupid." This is so, because not
even God can save you, if you excel in stupidity.

*"I am glad to see that you changed your mind since our HBS days, and
now choose acting stupid relative to self-interest, (even to its stunning
limit) rather than feel guilty for your choices in the (be guilty vs. be
stupid) dilemmas of life," says* Greg Geris, (a brilliant old friend, to
whom I am thankful for re-introducing me to Christianity during a
period that I still believed in God but had lost faith in Christianity.)

For the mad of this world I teach sanity but to connect with them I had
to make people's fn. madness my craft.

*After midnight he is in the Jacuzzi looking at the crescent moon and
star, and listening to the white owl 'Merlin'* praying in the name of my friend
Archimedes: God Save the Queen *hiding in the eastern Palm and fussing all
upset. He gets out and then….*

*He dances against the wind wildly, like Zorbas, round the oval pool
naked with his enemies' music blasting 'til mid-morning when he falls
exhausted and two hawks on the western Spruce fly away
complaining!*

*He then roars: "Babylon, come." Being on fire she rushes as fast as she
can… and jumps on his arms in the Jacuzzi and is greatly relieved…
rests… and then says "Thank you." He answers with a smile: I wanted
my Jacuzzi hot and figured that the free way to do so is to call you in it!*

*She frowns… then smiles "I am glad I found the 12th Imam hiding in a
well; you love me… admit it."*

Unfortunately it's my job to love you and it's a difficult job without pay, so don't test me again. I'm finally able to love you and I like your body but I dislike your character; the spirits operating you."

"Mahdi, I hate 'buts'. Who's perfect? Judge me by the smoothness of my skin not by the content of my character. We're all up the proverbial creek if you start judging by content of character as manifested by actions and results. I've not seen you have a serious discussion with any adult in the last decade*," says Babylon, lifting her eyebrows.*

"I prefer not jumping in sewers. **Show me 10 righteous people.**"

"So you say that all, other than children and saints, are sewers? What I am then?" asks Babylon.

You are the sewage.

"Darn it. I would have fallen in love with you much earlier but you look as ugly as Brad Pitt with messed up hair playing Achilles; but I still accepted you. Take me the way I am," she says.

Really; my body looks that ugly? He smiles, holds her head with his hands and gently kisses her. He then reclines, lights up his "peace-pipe" coughs three times, spits and with a smile asks her: So, what was your name sweetheart?

She frowns but takes a long pause... "I believe that there is no free lunch. I don't give unless I get. ...How are going to violate reciprocity darling?" she asks.

Your reciprocity produces downward spirals. I need to stack the odds favorably for the righteous to create an upward spiral.

A frequent error in the distribution of benefits from any agreement (resulting in either the need for renegotiation or cancellation) is not allocating 5-30% of the net benefit to those who don't have "a seat on the table" (like workers) and maybe don't even contribute much to the success of the agreement other than not blocking it.

Symmetry is broken at the transitions. To deal with the reciprocity you will just have to want me more than I do you, the difference being my Gifts. *If you don't help me I will not have sex with you again.*

"I resent that you resorted to a threat. I used to like but I now resent how unfair, hitting one side only, Cupid (Eros) is. Ok. Fine, I will "help

others not upon calculation of interest" like Pericles of the first Democracy said, even though I find it quite stupid.

You are Jealous and wanted me just for yourself; well, you have me now. You devised the alphabet, the words and numbers and Know; so you tell me my new name, Man," says Babylon crossing her hands with all kinds of mixed emotions.

I want you to help me liberate those that choose Liberty, on earth. I will call you Gostay, the Queen of the South.

I will teach you a bit of Greek, if you did not learn about 'the Mystic Greeks' in the College fraternities and sororities, so that the New Testament and all true knowledge does not remain all Greek to you. If I put the accent on the ó it means that I want you to gó and if I accent the à of stày I will want you to stay. If I accent an apostrophe on the Ό (in all translations of Greek words including of the Bible to English and in English words that have Greek roots, the "right apostrophe" is translated as adding an h, which is close enough but the actual symbol is about lowering the tone of the vowel by an octave in pronouncing it) it will be to break the news to you, dear Ghostay, that you are a ghost, not in body, and not to be embodied, as I command now for the blood and life sucking Babylon not to ever be embodied again as a human. So, when I call you, you will also know what to do.

"Eureka: I finally understand what fire, air, water and earth mean when used symbolically, as in some Scriptures, by their correspondences on the Cross. I also finally understand that this bitter-sweet world of "good and evil" is a "yes and no" world." We say yes and no, in-out, come-go, good and bad on the same issue as it suits us each time and then lie hypocritically calling it "right" both ways. What are the Greek ^{ungrounded accents} that give the same word different meanings?"

Socrates used them, so the scribes that study him still debate whether he taught about Good or about Beauty. He was teaching both and if the accent is the ó of "καλός," it's the goodness of the One Good God and his heavenly kingdom of eternally Living "Ideas," Truths, (as opposed to the dark caves of their ancestral dead soul that most still inhabit), and if the emphasis was on the ά of the same word it's the Beauty that harmonizes the earthly Yea-no, (my name for Jonas and John,) of the synchronously self-conflicted worldly reality.

"Is it by the "accent" that Noyah knew what to do-when; and was that the same 'flood' around 2000 BC that caused the sinking of Atlantis as have been recently found in Akrotiri in Santorini (and in the submerged city of Pavlopetri)?" she asks.

"I think so; estimates have the two events separated by ± 300 years from 2000 BC (by different methods) but I think that it was the same event series; any other questions? May I now be in Peace?"

"Yes no. If someone working in a 'for profit' corporation gives stuff away without proving that it's in the self-interest of the company we fire them. Those you call righteous we fire and call bums. **I finally agree with you about the need to separate the righteous from the rest of us.** We know there are many bums out there. That is why we try so hard to have moron proof systems but I prefer not having to deal with so many bums.

God's Kingdom on earth is where people can live in Oneness, in "yes, yes" or "no, no" where they fully mean and actually act on what they say. Those of us that stay in the worldly systems will need to harmonize, straighten and beautify the conditional and relative No-yes's. Correct?"

"Yes. **Until the separation happens**, you on earth fire and call the righteous, bums, while we in heaven send to hell's fire your "powerful, rich and famous" and call them scums.

Like the 'dad' of "My Big Fat Greek Wedding" I am *bitterly disappointed* that unlike many English words, the word 'Kimono' does not have Hellenic roots, yet 'yes' is probably derived from 'ygies' that means 'healthy' (and no from nosos that means disease.) This is speculative and has little to do with the rest of this book, which is about everyone and explains everything, but given the etymology obsessed modern, idealist vs. realist, philosophy—that means love of Wisdom (Sophia) — that ignores the Wisdom **of Love** (Agia Sophia), I toss it in there for a healthy salad! So, if you're a 'Doctor of Philosophy', eat me!

The Seven Spirits of the Holy Spirit taught each level of the righteous paths of the hierarchy of love through each of the founders of the seven great religions of the world, as shown.

As is the case with all the conflicts and disputes, the divisions within each religion are due to disputes (of religious leaders and governments using religion as an instrument of) **power-money-egos,** supported hypocritically by a theological technicality. Within Christianity I indirectly answer those theological differences. I avoided directly answering each dispute to avoid offending any Christian denomination.

There are also valid reasons that caused the splintering, that are the changes in circumstances requiring a change in the emphasis of the Churches on the expression of love that was most needed at the time-circumstances-people.

There are valid reasons for expressing love differently but those are not differences where one is right and the other wrong, or among two wrongs as are with the worldly, but are harmonious mutually supportive differences among righteous paths. Division among Christians is unchristian.

There is no need to confine one-self to a specific level as to how, to whom and when one will express rightly one's love; in fact one should not because one is limiting one's ability to love rightly and uniquely.

"Is he a baller?" asks the chorus of bimbos.

"Excuse me?" she asks.

Does he dribble, throw, kick, bat, carry, putt, shoot or slam balls? If he doesn't do balls what utility does he have in the real or spiritual world? Can humanity survive without balls going to holes?" they ask again.

"Excuse me?" asks again Babylon.

The least in the hierarchy of love and the least in terms of self-sacrifice required, (but still demands total submission and control of the ego to right judgment and its submission to Righteousness,) of those seven paths is the Straight, Middle, Fair, Just path of well-reasoned compromise by (well proportioned) beauty that is also the fastest growth highest balance path.

The "vulgar" Homer described it as Odysseus' path Straight between the sucking (whore) W. (money, "Babylon," ego, greed, narcissistic personality, mood disordered, CEOs of *big public corporations*, the political "right," the 'white man'); and the multi-headed Beast (bitch) B., (power, force, "Babylon's kings," animal instincts, fear, histrionic personality, anxiety disordered, politicians of *big government*, the "left," the "princess-victim" minorities) **without favoring at all either**

of these two conflicted co-dependent evils and deceitful wrongs causing all the crises.

I have to be more explicit than Homer because Homer's language (even though Scylla literally means bitch, i.e. B.) obviously, has not been explicit enough.

Homer's symbols of the Whore (W.) and the Beast (B.) are also used in the Bible, in Revelation. These evils hope for **and cause crises** as the (W.), D. Rockefeller and recently the (B.,) W. Schäuble explained, **to impose their will**.

If you are in crisis, or (by not being like a one-eyed Cyclops, without prospective, without perception of depth, a two dimensional "screen" persona) can See the coming crisis, I told you without knowing you or what the crisis is, the two forces that cause it, a w. on one side and a b. on the other, and how to solve it, whether at a personal, relationship, work or government level.

This path also tries to harmonize and beautify both conflicted sides through enlightening their confusion by Dialogue that Socrates taught; (including the golden path through the geometric mean.) Jonas, Elijah, John of Patmos and the Baptist, who are me, are the Straight paths: "Prepare the way of the Lord, make his paths **straight**." (Mat. 3.3)

Politically that path **is not** about making one step to the 'left' and in two years (on the next election) making a step to the 'right,' but as you know by walking, it is the taking of **a step forward** with the 'right' **followed fast** by a 'left' step forward, then 'right' and so on...

I must teach about the worldly even though their intent and methods are in opposition to the spiritual because unless one is capable and willing to deal with the **necessary** (worldly) they are very likely to fail in attaining the **important** (spiritual) despite good intentions.

Some on my many dysfunctions and flaws, that I have the *opportunity* to work with, is the resistance to change my self and the inertia of my massive laziness. After graduating first in my Master's (M.Sc.) Class at Columbia I lost the need to prove myself academically and laziness overtook so I then went through Harvard Business School (HBS) with minimal studying yet still doing well —particularly in the bars of Boston that had better benefit/cost ratios to studying — thanks to Homer. In case you (or your children) plan to attend HBS here's a tip of how to get through it with less studying:

The (based on real life) cases usually contain a series of problems. The central problem of each case (and of all the worldly and of the world) is usually the **misalignment (i.e.** contradiction, incoherence) of the **strategy** (including the objectives) with the **structure** (meant here to include the people, resources, systems, incentives/disincentives and action plans).

The solution is almost always the need for a central change to get to (straight) alignment, (to no contradiction i.e. coherence) in either strategy (that in business is about making money i.e. the W.) or structure (that is about distribution of power-control i.e. the B.) with a **secondary (**not as big) **change** to the other.

To the extent that contradiction and conflict between the **strategy**, that in "Koinoi," meaning "common" language is the 'what, why, how' is done, and the **structure** that is the 'who, how much, when, where' does it, is inevitable, then a sustainable balance between the two is the only solution, through triangulating, by structurally adding an 'independent third' that moves straight between the two conflicted sides that cause the crisis.

This template answer (filled in with the specifics of any problem, issue or case) holds true also for all "classic dilemmas" of life such as Nurture (important-strategic) vs. nature (necessary-structure), Function vs. form, Ideas vs. reality and Spirit vs. body, with the first component being important and focused on first while the second component being a necessary but on its own insufficient answer.

So, to someone that did well without much work by giving pretty much the same, straight, answer to all the HBS cases, did it for 60 hours a week at work so as to retire rich at 34,(with a lot of luck) and allowed me to pursue my pet peeve for 23 years so far, i.e. to figure out and explain everything— the beautiful Mother Nature, as you suspected, is stunningly beautifully Designed, but a true B.S.W. to figure out, explain (but don't tell her that) and to deal with if MFd.as humanity is doing—who Knows clearly that you need a new separate structure to design and build even a new widget, **that you need a new separate Independent Disarmed Demilitarized social structure** (and system) **if you truly want Christian (and the other religious) beliefs truly lived is stunningly obvious.**

My Straight, honest, Just, correct, Fair path explained here, including its mathematics, physics, politics, psychology and logic, is a necessary but insufficient condition for the survival of any of the righteous, who are opposed to the world's 'self-interested but let's pretend we love,' ways.

"Keep up with us; we make billions by loving tea bagging balls of ugly boastful bozos with their stinky s. in our plastic nose because their balling skills are important to life," says the chorus of bimbos.

"Excuse me?" asks Babylon again and then turns towards him and adds:

"The Odyssey is the path back from "the exile," to the innocence that was lost by one's sins committed for the victory in 'war.'"

Correct; the Straight, correct, Just and fair path is narrow, intellectually and emotionally very difficult and taxing. Extremely few can Master it. Yet, it is **the only path** that if one truly Knows, as I do, one can be the best in the worldly and also live in God's Kingdom as it's least.

So whoever is more screwed up than I am is too screwed up.

And whoever is less screwed up than I am belongs in Heaven.

That is why I am doing my best to set as low of a fkn. bar as I can, for you; by throwing many gratuitous f. bombs that seem to have no other fkn. reason.

The Exodus of those that truly believe in any path of righteousness into God's Kingdom on earth, as I describe it, that is finally achievable because of the wide acceptance of Democracy, (thus giving power to the people over their governments) will strengthen the middle ground of those staying behind in the secular societies and will get them closer to the straight path allowing them to get the most of what they want and the least of what they don't.

"So, are we now in agreement about everything?" asks Mary.

"No maybe. Now that you slashed my lingerie budget I figured that a way to save on my lingerie is to be naked when I'm around you," says Babylon (strip teasing, if you're into those!) and then says:

"There's nothing about me that you don't already know anyway. The lingerie that God imbedded on me isn't that bad after all. Wouldn't you say?" she says looking at, caressing her-self and posing with a big smile. "Bringing the Fire of gods to earth comes with a big price

Prometheus (means: Sees and speaks about the future) my dear, as you know. How are your liver and ulcers feeling? Haven't you gotten used to pain yet? Quit protesting already!

Ok. I'll confess that what's attracting me to you is that you are the least prick with a big dk. I'm sick and tired of the kings, Presidents that are big pricks to compensate for their ugly little penises.

I know I shouldn't tempt or test you but I want to know what your right judgment is about the measurements of wrong.

Do you agree that you are a bozo for not taking over the world and instead remaining disarmed and retired, and do you agree that you are a huge bozo for missing in the future this most stunning, savvy, superbly sexy and splendidly superlative beauty?" pointing to and caressing her body.

Yes, yes, I answer.

"Ha!" she laughs... "Since you admit that you're a great bozo I now trust that your judgment is right. I love you too. You alone saw me as a person too, and despite doing all possible to hide that I'm a w., you saw through me and saw further into my goodness, very little as it was. I'll let you go... You are fired... *We're now in agreement about everything. I'll support the establishment of Independent Demilitarized Disarmed Lands of God as you describe them," she then pauses... "But now that you took me over from the inside, I understand why you may not be a big bozo after all," she says smiling.*

"Should we rock balls of men if they're not of rockers or ballers?" ask the bimbos.

"Excuse me? That's it; I can't defend this crap. I've had it. That's it! I now quit as the Queen of W.'s.

I no longer accept responsibility for the excelling in stupidity ugly hos of the current media generated pop culture like the Kardashians and the 'Shore.' Lord, throw, rock, shoot, or kick their souls to hell as only you can; they fully deserve it," says the Queen of the South.

"Wait, wait; (I told you he must be at least a baller). O.k. we'll rock the balls of the sad and poor; show us a place where we can go to do it safely; give us a chance..."

"Why would an author like you expect to be heard while competing with 'The Real Housewives of...' and 'Storage wars,' that are spiritually,

intellectually and emotionally so excellent? Be realistic!" she laughs. "I now know why you quit as a worldly king. What happened to your people that made you quit as their king and refused the responsibility for them before God any longer?" asks Babylon.

You…

"Darn it Paul, I am a Queen, you can say what you believe in private, not in someone's face. That's why private life is so important to us and to the hypocrites. Didn't your mother teach you about being polite and lying?"

She thinks for a while… "As you know, I have been as sinful and screwed up as screwed up gets and have no defense before God. It was me that has been asking that you get silenced, as you know, and have been the cause of your deaths and for the sucking of the joy ("blood") out of the life of the saints and for the mistreatment of the poor.

I guess that is itsy bitsy high on the wrongfulness scale. Having my victim as my Judge isn't helping my cause either. I definitively don't want to know anything more about hell. I for sure have learned more than I want to about evil. Kyrie Eleison. May I please be forgiven? Can you take responsibility for me?" asks Babylon.

"The Queen and kings of the world are naked; ugly," says a child.

If you truly believe in righteousness set up and live in God's Promised Lands, whose Promise is being fulfilled now. You are forgiven by Christ Jesus who Rules over those Lands and He has accepted responsibility for and paid the price for you.

Despite our mutual disappointment about me having to be the Judge, if I forgive offenders, sinners, oppressors and criminals I would be unjust to the victims. **I am Just, so I have to see results proving that you have redeemed those you damaged, before I forgive**.

So if you stay in the worldly societies, your past actions are forgiven, again by His request, but I will still be needing **evidence** that you are truly changed and are redeeming the damage you caused, before I forgive, because that's my Just job, before God.

So, you should visit often (at least once a year for a "pilgrimage" to) God's Holy Land and ask almost every single adult man (not dressed as "priest" or with a sign that he is married), particularly the uglier, poorer, sad, old, strangers, lonely or homeless looking you find, with the 7 magic words that get a yes answer every time "may I give you a free blowjob?" Then wash them, s. their d. and say it was a gift from me.

If they're American, then, s. and get fd. by them because I am 3/5^{ths} American; if someone identifies themselves as a Greek you s. and f. with them at least twice, because I am Greek (forgive me,) one coming and one going because we 'Elien bozos are, like ships, likely to be coming and going; and if someone says they're a Jew, even though they are rebellious —they are back to worshipping gold and money—and are difficult to like, ask with the 7 magic words, that signal to Nature that there is hope still for humanity because a single adult woman is being nice really! Check, you know how, if they are my chosen people; and if indeed they are Jews have sex with them 3 times to be sure they feel welcome in those Lands (as my Gift) because my Lord, by my choice, Jesus, is a Jew. Are you clear?

"I thought I was going to have to do something really painful for punishment. I'm not sure if you know, because you're not a woman, but I actually really like sex, and that can be great fun for me, so yes, Lord, I'm your B.?" she says and grabs jelly beans and starts eating them insatiably. "There was a time that you were skeptical of some of Jesus's claims, what changed your mind?" she asks.

The more I looked for potentially flawed teaching or action by Him, the more I realized that it was I and the world that are wrong.

In this world of "yes-no," the only way to get anything done is through an agreement, a covenant, in which each of the parties commits to honor their side of the agreement.

*"I agree to my part of the agreement: **'I am your B.'** I usually like long contracts so my lawyers can get me out of them whenever I feel like it, but I don't want a contract or a lawyer to spell out what B. means. I know," says Gostay.*

I want you to do all you can, peacefully, to make sure the Promised Independent Disarmed Demilitarized Democratic Lands of God are established on earth as I describe them.

"I am your B., my Lord" says Babylon avidly munching jelly beans.

"I just realized that the w.'s and the homosexual narcissists provide motivation for **greedy immorality**; the b.'s and bullying histrionic people provide incentives for **scared incompetence;** and I, and other borderline s.' by choosing the men we choose provide incentives to **ignorant egotists,**" says Linda.

Correct; **these** are the 3 components of **each and all crises and tragedies. Greedy immorality** of some; scared **over-controlling incompetence** of others; and the **selfish** intentional **ignorance** of the rest, that were hypocritically not admitted and dealt with before it's too late is what makes all the dramas, crises and tragedies.

You will need to make very complex arguments for the level of intelligence of politicians and lawyers; you will need to argue such things like there is right and there is wrong and that right is preferable to wrong **in intent and in action as well, not just in talk.**

They have not grasped those complex and difficult concepts yet so you may have to use your great looks and/or your fame to convince them!

THE PHILOSOPHY

You need to explain to "intellectuals" that deny God that the logic and morality that they claim to have did not grow randomly out of stones, rather It is the logic of the law that governs the stones.

Since we know that there are mathematical Laws governing the Universe with precise Logic, and reciprocity embedded in them, there is no other logical conclusion other than there is Logic governing the Universe.

"I'm not going to ask about physical evidence of God because it shows ignorance that **God is Spirit**. But one of the most famous scientists these days, Stephen Hawking, who studies sucking black holes, like the one in the center of our Milky Way Galaxy, and *like my vagina,* despite admitting that the probability of everything falling in place for us to exist by a series of accidents is less than 1 in a trillion, claims that it is not necessary that the Universe was designed. (Despite Plank's statement that there is no way that something comes out of nothing.) So we have this infamous Hawking arguing, not as an opportunity for change in the future, but as the "best fit model" of explaining the past, not for the logical 99.9999999999% understanding of the Universe but for the possibility of the accidental, random and miraculous chance of less than 1 in a trillion. What is your response?"

God provided choice and liberty and so He did not preclude the chance of people believing whatever madness they like.

As Plato explained, we call the Universe Cosmos and not Chaos because we know it is created and governed by Logic. **I prefer the rational to the irrational.**

Believing in the irrational, in the accidental and the illogical defeats the purpose of any communication and results in never being able to overcome one's problems, such as in the case of airplanes, of the force of gravity.

The job of science is to develop a theory that correctly explains reality and prove it. Atheism is a not provable negative. Particularly the theory claiming that there hasn't been, there isn't and there will never be God anywhere in or beyond the Universe is the most non-provable assertion. So, atheism is foundationally unscientific.

I will repeat that making judgments by generalizations and labels, even labels that people give themselves is prejudicial and wrong. For example, despite atheism being irrational as a theory, there are valid reasons for someone calling themselves atheist, such as the absence of true love and righteousness in the society as they experience it and also as a defense mechanism to oppression by religion or because of one's religion. For example, I was recently interviewed for a previous book by Dr. Robert Rose who despite calling himself an atheist is already operating by the Spirits of God and so is already doing the Will and work of God.

Jesus' parable of the two sons one of whom said that he will do the work of God (like "believers" say) but didn't and the other that said he would not (like "non-believers" say) but later changed his mind and did, is applicable in these cases.

Science assumes the existence of logic in the Universe and searches for it and its evidence in the laws of Nature, which is why the vast majority of the great scientists were believers in God, (even if usually not satisfied by the dogmatic explanations given previously about God.) This is because if there was no logic in the Universe there would be no point in and no one looking for it.

So let us evaluate what is likely or the worst that could happen if we are wrong, as any strategist should.

Modifying R. Descartes "gamble" argument: If you don't believe in God (and consider liars the Founders of the religions and many others including me that say that we have experienced and Know God,) and live a loveless life, you not only wasted your life but the chances are high that you will pay for your wrongful disobedience to your Creator. If you believe in and follow the One Good Right True God, in the less than 1 in a trillion chance that He doesn't exist, all that happened is that you, human, on your own right, became god. So, which path has a better benefit/cost?

Being agnostic (means 'not knowing') is not inconsistent with being a scientist and is admirable honesty, however I remind those that confess ignorance (the word is derived from agnostic) that it is unwise to boast about your ignorance and it is stupid to advocate for others to embrace being permanently ignorant.

The Quantum probabilistic laws of the three forces of the Universe, if you know what you are doing as Jesus did, do allow for "miracles," but they are not miracles; they are the **making** of the improbable happen. Creating, innovating and designing are about making the improbable happen. Such as flying in an airplane that seems 'miraculous' but does not violate the laws of gravity; it overcomes gravity by using the electro-chemical-magnetic (E-M) force.

"Hawking saying that since there was no time (in the Universe) there was no time for God to Design it, is like saying that before your birthday since there was no time for you to be created or because there is no time in a black hole, you or the black hole couldn't be planned.

All humans came out of a vagina, from a mother. There's no visible physical evidence of a father being involved in 'making' a child **unless one knows about (the in private) sex.** Saying that Mother Nature at its beginning was a black hole of infinite density or empty space that exploded, in infinite energy, (which is itself evidence of an infinitely powerful God) in the Big Bang with no Father involved, as nerdy Hawking and his followers assert, means that they **must not know yet, or forgot about sex.** Problems with their father are the key to raising a w. but even we, that have no use for our fathers, acknowledge their existence," says the Queen of the South.

Correct. Time existed and exists beyond the Universe; within the Universe it is manifest as a relative dimension. **These physicists and**

other scientists using logic of the mathematical laws of physics and of science to deny the existence of a Logical Source (that Aristotle called the First Cause) of the Universe is an exercise in self-contradicting irrationality.

"The latest fad in cosmology physics is the "M Theory" that says that the cause of the Big Bang was that in the 11th Dimension there were vibrating membranes colliding causing the release of vibrating infinite super-symmetrical energy and light. May be it was the words of God "let there be light" that caused the vibrations of the membranes. But given that I know how hard hypocritical professionals try to avoid the subject of sex, to me it appears that the M Theory says that someone gave a Big F. causing the Big Bang," *says Babylon*.

Socrates proved that the wisest thing to assume and to claim, particularly if one Knows One, is "I know nothing."

"Did you f. nothing in darkness and cause it to make light and life?" she asks.

"What factual evidence do you have that I did anything?" I respond looking for some poison, lighting it up and reclining?

"Did you f. Mama Nature and so all our mamas? Babylon asks.

I invoke my 5th Amendment Right to remain silent.

"Do you disagree that the Big Bang was by the Big F?" she asks.

Stop looking into the dead past. The past does teach you what not to do but it says nothing about what you should do. Rather make the right choices for the future for which you are created.

Simply, **the functions of the Universe are: Change; resistance and reaction to change.**

I did not add to or dispute any of the facts you know. I offered you a logic that clearly distinguishes and defines right (positive) and wrong (negative) that allows you to make sense of and integrate all the facts that you know and all the facts that you are.

We Know Him, the First Cause, who Designed Universe, call Him Λόγος, (Logos) (John 1.1), Right Reasoning, Logic, embodied in Jesus and expressed as The Word, and we understand the Logic that governs the Universe so **people not believing Him is as irrelevant to Truth** as not believing in gravity or in 1+1=2.

"I understand. I like being your B. *Even though I like sex a lot, there have been and will be times that I feel disgusted with some man, so may I get a reminder of what sex should feel like from you, when I need to? Like when you sacked all the cities and were taking over mine and our armies were warring on the hills; do you remember?" asks Babylon with excitement.*

I remember. You will need to explain that the Universe has been Designed to teach so that **unless they move ahead of time ("shorten the times")** by learning at speeds of emotions, intellect and **spirit which are much faster** than those of solid matter and body, that same learning will have to happen in physical reality and they will be forced to learn through more physical pain. Haven't they had enough pain?

"I work by numbers; give me a sense of the speed-time differences?" asks Babylon, doing her half-hour/ day exercise routine.

At light speed going around the earth takes 0.1344 seconds. So, you can easily calculate that in **one day** (24 hours) light can travel around the earth (if uninterrupted) as many times as the earth does around itself in **1761 years**.

(Given my awake to asleep ratio, that is about a thousand years in a, at light-speed, God Day, as per Ap. Peter.) By the way, the normal speeds of motion of humans are about 1000 times slower than the speed of the earth around itself.

So, Christ Jesus did resurrect on the third day for Him and as expected we humans were intended to "catch up" on the third Day, Millennium, and experience His resurrection now.

If the change that needs to happen is clear and urgent, it must happen fast. The only way to do it fast is top down. If the politicians wait until they are forced to, from bottom up, as they usually do, (by jumping in front of parades that others start) it will be too late, with all hell having broken loose already, **as the Revelation will unfold, in physical reality and they will bear the full responsibility and burden of each destruction, suffering and death, for their delay.**

"I will. Yo Da One. I'm your B., my Lord.

Forgive me. Do you remember storming in my palace and dragging me out to the middle of battle with one hand, while with the other chopping heads left and right with your sword that cut Asia's Gordian knot? Then lifting me up and jumping with a roar and on the way down sticking your double edged sword in a stone.

Then you rip my clothes off, hold me up, pull out and thrust your rod of iron straight through my middle, while the war is raging, having sex with me in front of everyone to see. That was more disrespectful and brutal than what Achilles did to Hector. You become more brutal and disrespectful to all leaders with each life. I hated you with every cell of my body...

You held me up having sex with me while dancing around the hill and because you used your hands for your dancing I was hanging tight to you for dear life but I got in your rhythm and wouldn't let you go, hating you with all I had but unable to stop coming and coming... and coming...

And all the kings, yours and mine, and warriors from both sides withdrew confused, in awe, leaving you alone to lift and f. me dancing around the hill all night long 'til mid-morning when two of your Generals left complaining that you ask them to go to war and then when they're about to burn the city you get in their way, and Ptolemy, I think, shouted at you: 'You cannot end an immensely bloody war, Alexander, for, with and by a f... How are we to explain it? The Great Alexander had sex so it's all good now? I'm not writing that.'

My hair was all messy and I was in total confusion about whether you had just killed me or saved me and my people from total massacre. I hated you and loved you and was unable to figure which way was up. That kind of fn. must be disallowed in your Lands; it messes a woman up forever. I disallow it. Will you stop going in the middle of raging wars and sitting or standing in front of tanks or fn. and dancing?

*Woman, has been your and Achilles' heel. I get you killed, at the end every time, and it breaks my heart. Ptolemy could have written that the **Greek** Macedonian King Alexander the Great ended the war from Queen Babylon the Great by giving her the Great F. (But what does he know about that?)*

I, the economy need a strong boost now; pump me darling as only you know how... that's what the people really want. They talk about but don't really care about true love, as the facts show.

It's definitely way too wet in here. Excuse me; I need to go brush my hair." She leaves and comes back in a bit having turned on loud music from his adversaries. "I found this white shirt of yours in your closet; it looks better on me... don't you think?

I also found this ticket to Damascus on your desk. You're not going there to stop a war alone again. You'll get killed again. I'm not going to let you. I'll ask the great putana Putin (see Blog) *to work with my B. Obama in* replacing the mass murderer B. Assad with a coalition with Sunnis, led by an Alawite such as Al Shara. *Here," she rips the ticket in two, "May I please get your great dance-fn. again?" She lifts her arms forward opens her legs, taking the 'lift off' position, and says smiling "here around the pool works for me," closing her eyes.*

We will see. You're better than me in making the best out of the worst, which is why I chose you to do my work, because you have managed to glorify an ugly and stinking hole into sacred "beauty" that rules the world. If you identify yourself with your body, sex, appearances, your clothes etc. you are no more to me than another ugly stinking vagina to be screwed, no matter how much you beautify or glorify it. And, are you clear that in time Babylon will die?

"After you dance-fudged me silly in public you said "Hello, it's an honor to have met you Lady Babylon; good bye," and then left. I sat in total confusion on that hill like a zombie for hours until I realized that there're thousands of dead men around me, that you apparently weren't honored to meet, murdered for nothing and then all I could think was, thank God that I've and I'm a cunt. So, relative to men, being called a vagina is indeed high praise...*but have I been your B. all along and did not know it?" asks Babylon.*

The major theological disputes

(After a long pause) she recites the Quran 3.133: 'You lingered, according to the Book of God, until the day of Resurrection. And this is the day of Resurrection although you have not perceived it,'' and then she says: "I am your Bitch Lord, my God," and recites it loudly, kneeling, bending over, then lifting her-self a bit, reciting it again, bending over like a B., again, and reciting it.

The bending over like a B. is amusing to me so you may keep doing it whenever you feel like amusing me but it is insufficient. **If you are not asking others for forgiveness, doing things to restore the damage you**

caused, being charitable to and forgiving others, you are wasting your time.

The Koran identifies Isa (derived from the Greek Ἰησοῦς) (as is Jesus) "the son of Mary" as The (only) Messiah. If Muslims understood the Koran, they would be Christians and thus get Saved and Delivered.

The main differences between the three Abrahamic monotheistic religions are differences of ignorance and/or incompetence and/or immorality. Immorality because they all preach love yet they fail to love 'the others;' incompetence for failing to understand the capacity of the One God to express Himself in more than one way; and Ignorance because God is One (as Muslims say) and God has three aspects to Himself; His Good character-the Father; His Right Logic and Designer-the Son; and His Spirit of Truth (as Christians say). Having three spiritual aspects should not be surprising to anyone that isn't totally ignorant of Self being one yet having a soul, reason and emotions. That oneness is unbreakable and eternal when your reborn soul is truly loving your reasoning is right and your expressions are true and real. And the Spirit of God, Elih, chose the Jews (as the Jews say) because He likes Mary the most!

The Good Right True Trinity in the One God is The Way to eternal oneness in Man.

Muslims that have read the Koran know that they are Christians and their differences with other Christians are not much bigger than the differences among the Christian denominations.

Even though I dislike getting into theological differences because they are usually baloney and miss the central teaching of all faiths of loving even towards those you dislike, a "major difference" between Islam is the contention that the Koran denies that Jesus was crucified and resurrected but rather that He ascended into the heavens. This theological debate is also baloney also because the Koran does not deny the crucifixion: It says "it appeared so but…" The Koran validates that physically the crucifixion did indeed appear to happen, however it emphasizes that even though Jesus Christ, Righteousness, was crucified, the Holy Spirit of God that was upon Jesus, did not die (and does not die) but ascended to heaven prior to the death of Jesus, which is why Jesus cried out "Eli, Eli why have you forsaken me."

In the first major theological dispute within Christianity among Ap. Paul and Ap. Peter as to whether Christians had to convert to Judaism first to become Christians, Ap. Paul was right in claiming that Christians didn't have to get (physically) circumcised because the Holy Spirit is for everyone but Ap. Peter was also right in claiming that spiritually Christians had to convert to Judaism because Jesus did come not to violate the 10 Commandments but to fulfill the Law, as He said.

The schism of Judaism and Christianity was and is due to the Jews that became hypocrites and in pursuit of appearing moral lost the loving Spirit of their faith and the Schism of Christianity with Islam was and is due to the same reason.

In truth, both Christians and Muslims are Jews that have theological disagreements with the traditional Jews that are not much bigger than those among the other Jewish denominations.

The Absolute One God manifested Himself fully in this world as the **Right** Jesus Christ, is fully Present now as the **True** Holy Spirit, and will manifest Himself fully in a millennium as the **Good** Father.

Indeed God is One and not three but the risks of oversimplification become clear by asking Einstein, who declared that "God did not play dice with the Universe," how to explain the deterministic "4 tensor" equations of General Relativity (for gravity) to 'the people,' who are clueless about tensors, let alone explaining Schrodinger's 1st, 2nd and 3rd derivative Quantum functions (that describe the 3 Quantum forces) to illiterates, as he now amends his statement: "For explaining and for other spiritual aspects, Lord, please keep rolling the matter fudging dice."

The complexities in Quantum Theory arise because as Schrodinger's equations show there is the (i) imaginary factor, that is the square root of -1, which describes not the (deterministic) propagation but the perception by the imagination, (i.e. the image) of the wave-particle, which is probabilistic and depends on the phase, measure and measuring device of the measurer.

The exact same facts are interpreted differently depending on the spirit and reason by which they are interpreted. (For example, look at Fox and MSNBC interpreting the same data as to the economy or the socio-political conditions.)

The reason for the differences is that while the facts maybe concrete, the interpretation, meaning and explanation of those facts, are spiritual phenomena and thus quantum functions, the results of which defer depending on the measuring reason, phase and intent.

One may validly argue that no matter what is said in a statement, it contains an oversimplification. There are thousands of books that cover each of the subjects I cover because each subject, thing, and person is complex, involving many dimensions. However, it turns out that all subjects are complex in a similar way, containing an internal and an external contradiction, as shown by the self-repeating structure within a structure, of the Cross.

The Theory of Chaos defines and explains the (self-repeating) complexity and shows that there is a mathematical order even in disordered systems. These fractal complex disordered systems contain a real component that is a "fractional dimension," such as 2.7 D, and an imaginary component that is about the perception of reality by your imagination. Given that none of us are 0D or 3D spheres or cubes, our bodies are each complex multi-fractals. So, complexity arises because of different perceptions of the same facts as a result of different distances and angles of perception, and as a result of different measures used to measure fractals.

As a result, the same facts of life as perceived from a spirit and rational that sees themselves as a random and temporary product of evolution fighting for survival are not just different but are in irreconcilable opposition and inconsistency with someone who sees themselves and the world in the spirit of a Child of a purposeful and eternally living Good Right True Creator.

The world in the (spiritual, intellectual and emotional) context of wrongs (negatives) and the world in the context of the righteous (positives) are not just in opposition but they also work in opposing ways for the same reason that increases in positives and decreases in negatives are in opposition arithmetically and are in directional opposition also.

That irreconcilable inconsistency and opposition that leads inevitably to conflict and violence can only be resolved by the separation of these two groups, the wrong and the righteous, each group of which may have significant differences in the interpretation of the facts amongst themselves but at least they are not in full opposition and conflict.

As a Child of God I love, I understand and I attempt from the appropriate distance, by writing a book, to help, if they want to read, but I dislike and want nothing to do with those of the world and ask for an Independent Disarmed Demilitarized Land in which I and other Children of God have the right to be separate from and to not have anything to do with those that believe themselves to be and act as children of randomly evolved germs, (according to evolution.)

To those that believe themselves to be randomly evolved germs I validate their own view (and evolution) and confirm that they indeed are as they believe. They are not lying about themselves but they are wrong. They are wrong because they are looking backwards into the dead past for their humble physical beginnings to find who they are, instead of looking into the future, into who they are evolving (and being revolutionized) into (if they choose to live) which is to become (spiritual) Children of God.

The same facts can be interpreted oppositely also because of the different effects they have to different beings. Consider a doctor that applies antibiotics to an infected patient; the doctor is wise and kind to the patient but he is simultaneously a petulant, arrogant, violent mass murderer to the germs.

I ask for that separation not just for the benefit of the true Children of God, because even though this will end their unnecessary suffering, they will end up well no matter what, but more importantly for the benefit of those that believe themselves to be and indeed have been like the weed, randomly evolved germs, because if not separated from them I am bound to appear to them as a petulant, extremely arrogant destroyer, no matter how much I try to help them and to not harm them.

The Koran (that correctly prophesies this Judgment Day, in which **evidence** is critical,) is part of the message I bring, simplified to be targeted, not for the literate, but recited (to get a clue by repetitions) by **ignorant and illiterate** bozos like Love's lousiest Messenger Mohammed as **evidenced** by the oppressive, animalistic, hateful state in Muslim nations.

Islam was necessary because it is Just that all including the illiterate should know about the One God and His Will before they are judged.

Muslims claim to have learned about Love, mercy, compassion; good and right; where is the evidence? I don't see it nor feel it.

Don't worry about backlash to my writings from Islamist—these damned by Allah hypocrites who murder in the name of a word that also means peace— who respond to cartoons and movies; they can't concentrate long enough to get here! And if they do, they will have to agree with me.

Those that are not too ignorant so as to not interpret spiritual texts materially, and therefore understand the spiritual (not mumbo-jumbo) "language that mortals don't understand," understand that if I were to say 'kill the Muslims' I would not intend to incite violence but would mean 'kill spiritually the ignorant and hypocritical religious fanaticism within your-self' to stop the current violence. So, now you understand how similar statements in the Koran such as "kill non-believers," "kill the Jews," "kill the Christians" should be interpreted. (Or else the Koran is highly inconsistent junk.)

T**he Koran is correct,** if interpreted by the Holy Spirit, even in saying "do not speak about Trinity," because the major divisions among and within the great religions is (ignorant) talk about the Trinity from people that haven't found God's Loving-Righteous -True (that are 'derivatives' of **Good**) Trinity in One, that is the only Path to oneness within each. **Once one finds one's oneness, one speaks about the eternal unique oneness within the One God.**

So, the problems of Muslims are not because of Allah or the Koran but because of the illiterate, ignorant, incompetent, immoral, sinful hypocrites Mohammed and his followers.

Have your people, the Muslims, bending over like b.'s forgiven you?

"They have not forgiven me Lord; they say that Allah, Al-Elih (Elin), the God, is One, that there is no God but God, that God is Great, that God is Merciful and Compassionate, ask for His Mercy and then they persecute all that disagree with them, are at real, physical war all over the world, oppress and abuse all women, hate and do not forgive your chosen people, and they kill us.

Can you accept responsibility for my soul and defend me before God and before the religious that curse me to hell, persecute and kill me, the "righteous" that look down on me and want me dead, the hypocrites that sleep with me, then make me the 'bad word' not to be spoken and the women who pretend that they're better than me but aren't, and also persecute me? I'm the most hated, cursed and despised woman ever. There's no one that wants to or can defend me, except you, if you forgive me. J'espere (I hope)," says Babylon the Great.

I Know. Until all Muslim leaders ask for and offer forgiveness to others, to the Jews first, and recognize Israel, and its right to exist, and then to Americans they should be bending over not 5 but 70 times a day; like I told Mohammed.

Only after the (two faced) hypocrites that call themselves Islamists do as Islam truly means i.e. surrender their will to the Will of God for Peace and thus forgive and recognize Israel with Jerusalem as its capital, only then the whole Middle East can and should become Demilitarized and Disarmed Independent Lands of God; that is the only "comprehensive" (as Iran's MF's ask) way to avoid the otherwise extremely likely war with WMD in the Middle East, with unprecedented human suffering and destruction.

For now, Brazil, Japan and Turkey should be assigned by the P-5 to find a way within 1 month, to satisfactorily and cost effectively guarantee selling and then taking back for recycling (3%; 20%) fissile material to Iran for nuclear energy (and medical) in exchange for Iran verifiably stopping all enrichment activity now; followed by the lifting of sanctions and starting 'comprehensive' discussions.

"Until all Muslim nations and the Palestinians recognize Israel's right to exist as a Jewish State, (or Muslims bend over 70 times a day), their sins are not forgiven and their fate to death and hell is guaranteed," says Allah.

Then, Mohammed Rises reciting the Koran (Surah 30.55; The Romans): "**Race to forgiveness** from your Lord…"

Concentrate; focus on your **first priority first** to be most effective, and secondly on the worst problem to get to your first priority, at the time, to be most efficient. Stand straight. *I got you a gift; look… a puppy.*"

*"Oh my God, it's so cute; it's gorgeous, look how playful it is… Thank you… it's a she… she **can't stop** playing… she's a s.; I can tell. What should I call her?… Oh! I know; Babylon. Babylon, my ego, is my B. when I want her to and my friend as I chose. I'll submit my ego as you have done with yours. And as you want me to be for you; I really like being your B. and love being your friend."*

I am glad you get my spirit and I do not have to explain.

"The biggest problem I had with your idea of Independent demilitarized disarmed Holy lands was the two main examples we have of such demilitarized "holy" lands are the Vatican and Mecca. Each of these has been very successful, with over a billion followers each, but each has shown itself over time to be more immoral than your honest testicles. But I now understand that they have had to play the usual domination and control of each other by power, money and fame human games while what you advocate is designed to, should, and can escape those, as is clearly intended by God.

Can you see the red-brown (multi-headed Beast) Muslim horseman at war all over the world, (with his fat W., the Saudi King,) and the emerging yellow Chinese horseman (in Beijing, the new Great Babylon,) with his N. Korean B. bringing death? Is there any escape from the woes, suffering, plagues and deaths, described in Revelation?" Gostay asks.

THE MAJOR THREATS

N. Korea is a very serious threat to the US.

Obama's strategy in N. Korea not only has not and is not working, as N. Korea reportedly now has 12 nuclear warheads and missiles to deliver them in the US, (and an aggressive 30 or so year old in charge of them) and publicly threatening to do so, but it has made and is making things worse.

Even though China reportedly threatened N. Korea that it will "not hesitate reduce its aid if N. Korea continues with it nuclear tests" (that seemed like a positive sign from the new Chinese President) but because after the tests did occur China didn't reduce its aid, most likely it is a deception tactic by China, because if N. Korea attacks the US, even if N. Korea is leveled after that, it will leave the US crippled and China as the dominant power in the world. I do not believe that if China really wants N. Korea to be denuclearized it cannot achieve it.

THE WORLD ANEW in 2006 says in the Introduction p. xiii: "N. Korea's threats for what they call a pre-emptive strike seem to have a real foundation. What should we do?"

The non-proliferation strategy must be re-evaluated.

To start with b. Obama or j. Bidden should indeed call MF Kim Jong Un, if worm Rodman's information is correct, to see if there is any realistic chance of N. Korea (and S. Korea) being denuclearized and making a peace treaty with significant economic benefits to N. Korea. (The currently US stated objective of unification of the two Koreas is extremely unlikely to work.) If there is any chance for a peace treaty to happen is only by the dictator having a face to face meeting with the top US 'enchilada' because that is the only way a dictator does business.

If that doesn't work it may be better to have a strategy that says that whatever number of nuclear weapons N. Korea has, S. Korea and Japan should each have twice as many nuclear warheads.

And whatever nuclear warheads Iran develops, Saudi Arabia and Greece should each have twice as many.

And it must be made clear at least privately and maybe publically to China that an attack by its client state of N. Korea against the US will be treated as an attack by China; as it should be clear that an attack by Iran, Russia's client state, will be treated as an attack by Russia.

Given the above, the sanctions by the US (and the world) except for nuclear material and related products to those nations, should be lifted and the US must be removed from being "the main adversary" of those rogue nations and let their regional adversaries deal with it, because currently the US is the pole attracting all the wrath which can be immensely more devastating for both the US and the world rather than letting these be regional conflicts which is unlikely to result in nuclear exchanges because both relatively equal sides will be annihilated with no benefit to neither of them nor anyone else.

The US is better off being removed from being the direct adversary of these nations and becoming the relatively Independent (though favoring the democracies) moderator of these regional conflicts.

I think that such a strategy is more likely to actually deter both China and N. Korea to further developing nuclear weapons, reduces the likelihood of their use significantly, and reduces the current very high likelihood of a nuclear attack by these nations, particularly by N. Korea, against the US, (which even with a 90% accurate missile defense, still leaves immense devastation).

So the six party (or 5 party if N. Korea refuses to participate) talks must restart immediately to redefine the strategy on nuclear non-proliferation.

Diplomatically, increasing and improving the dialog with China and Russia should continue. However, **the US (and its allies) are much better off lifting sanctions and giving $10 billion a year (which would surely close the deals** while $1 Billion a year is probably enough**) to each of N. Korea and Iran to verifiably denuclearize them** (and without long range ballistic missiles) **while reducing what they give to China and Russia** (through reducing Balance of Payments deficits by about half) **by $200 Billion a year through a 20% VAT tax on Chinese imports and (not from 'free trade" nations) imported oil. It's a net benefit of not just $180 B a year but it also significantly reduces the environmental, political, economic and military problems of the world.**

For a further level of refinement to improve effectiveness half of the 2% per month increase in VAT tax for Chinese goods and half of the tax on foreign profits may be deducted for the provinces with the best human rights record. (The idea is from a Chinese dissident in a Congressional Hearing.)

The risks from the use of nuclear weapons in the near future are in my view higher than during the cold war. The current strategy must be re-evaluated, now, as this may be the most tragic of the many big mistakes of the B. Obama Administration.

The true believers have been lifted in the heavens, into the New Temple of God's Kingdom of Love that is in Spirit, as I described it for you; they are spared from the destructions.

For the rest, I can see no way **other than by setting up the Independent, demilitarized, disarmed Lands of God, fast, to avoid the huge destructions, agony, suffering and deaths described in Revelation**. (All Lands are God's Lands yet God is asking only for very little of them for those that truly need it.)

After what I advocated so far happens, then to help advance freedom, prosperity and democracy in the world, Democracies must favor other Democracies in trade by a **Free Trade Agreement among legitimate Democracies. Discussions for this free trade agreement among Democracies must start now.** I hope that the discussions with the EU will move fast with the appropriate compensation funds for dislocations to "the little guys."

"Some say that global warming has little to do with human CO_2 emissions," she asks.

Even if the probability that human caused CO_2 emissions are a small contributor to global warming the marginal impact is likely to be significant and the impact of being wrong on this issue is too big.

Pres. Obama's speech on June 25th, 2013 on his "climate change and energy plan" is very close to correct. Where Pres. Obama keeps failing is in moderating his views on regulating and increasing his emphasis on incentivizing towards the same end, (and in having a regular weekly meeting with different Republican lawmakers) so us to gain support of at least some Republicans for specific plans.

Some of what is needed to be done (conservation, gas mileage requirements, solar, wind) to reduce the CO_2 emissions that cause global warming has been and is being done except for 3 critical areas that need more action (that probably Republicans would support.)

a) Import taxes for sugar cane ethanol that is preferable to corn based ethanol (for cars to reduce the use of gasoline that is the biggest cause of CO_2 emissions) from Brazil must be eliminated for reduction of (at least some) Brazilian import taxes. (Short term)

b) (The risks from fracking and how to reduce those risks needs to be studied more thoroughly.) Assuming that the above is done, the infrastructure and incentives for (the now domestically abundant) natural gas for trucks and commercial vehicles (hybrid or electric are very unlikely to be effective for those) must be accelerated for (medium term.)

c) There is a need to, in the long term, increase the percentage of energy provided by nuclear power in the non-transportation sector through a standardized, by an order of magnitude smaller, safer, (exportable), nuclear reactor, (and with better "locations") because nuclear power produces no CO_2 emissions. If one considers the whole process of production of energy equipment as well, nuclear probably causes less CO_2 emissions than solar and wind. Reprocessing the excess nuclear bombs and nuclear waste (currently stored) for civilian energy is their best use. I saw on a TV program that B. Gates among others is prototyping such a nuclear reactor. Fewer people have been killed or harmed by nuclear power for commercial energy in the last 50 years of its use in the world than by bicycles in one nation in one year. Some incentives (in terms of loan guarantees) for smaller, safer, standardized nuclear reactors would help.

On most issues of government policy, incentives should be tried first and only if they fail, triggers for regulation can be set. Ignoring or dismissing or giving lip service to what the other side finds critical just will not work for these major issues.

"You did turnarounds; how do you turn around an organization?"

Even the Donald knows that. Once you define a cohesive strategy at least in your own mind, you find and fire the worst performers towards it, starting the firing from the top. The worst the organization is doing, the bigger percentage of worst performers needs firing; depending on the urgency some of the worst performers may adjust after corrective actions-help; and others can do well if transferred (so that they find a "place" they actually want to work in); and while increasing the perceived and actual fairness of income distribution; you increase the rewards for the, **by the correct criteria and measures**, best performers.

In government, turnarounds are more difficult because whoever you fire from a government job you also have to find a way that somehow they will be fine, because ultimately governments are not about being most efficient but are about being most effective in helping and providing a real safety net for all their people.

I ask that you turnaround the inefficiency and lack of effectiveness in your nations by "firing us" that don't know you, don't want to be around you nor want to participate with you anyway, thus being your "worst performers" and exaggerating your problems by complaining constantly, as I do, into an Independent Demilitarized Disarmed Land.

"How do you move so casually from religion to psychology to physics, to philosophy, to business and to politics? Aren't these completely different and incompatible subjects each containing multiple sub-disciplines arguing among themselves?" asks Gostay.

Are your beliefs, emotions, body, logic, work and self-governance completely different and incompatible subjects? I see all disciplines as different perspectives of the same subject: you; life; because they indeed are so; and I have explained that they are not just interconnected but have shown what their connection is with very precise mathematics and logic, which have been explained.

"Many families staying behind struggle financially; you showed the intra and inter-governmental; business; and spiritual solutions; can you also give practical personal advice?" asks the Queen from the South.

The easy way to personally help increase economic growth by 1.5% is for the married ladies to (increase "their output" and) add one fun sex a week for their husbands, and if they don't want more kids, use contraception. I know that the Pope has a problem with contraception even among the married but he is wrong about that. What does he know about being married to give opinions about it?

"Now that we have found their right place in life, Trojans have become the best friends of the Greeks," says Diogenes.

And, the Pope, (I liked the righteous resignation of Pope Benedict and so far I like Pope Francis), is also wrong about declaring himself 'infallible' on whatever issue he chooses or on a wide range of issues.

"You are no expert on marriage either but I can see how safe fun sex can make 'wine out of water' for the married; and its simple advice but you may have underestimated the damage this will do to gayness and to whoring," says the Queen of the South. She then gets interrupted by Diogenes who says:

"By the way, the first translations of the New Testament from the Greek originals that were targeted to Greeks and to mostly Greek cities, to Latin (for the Romans that actually killed Jesus, by "the law,") were about 100 years later.

I have long ago converted to Islam. I am now an Imam; my name is Mahmoud Suleiman and between you and me I support terrorism, in fact I am considering blowing myself up soon.

The reason italics are slanted is because Italians slant truth. Isotopic studies have shown higher traces of morality in the feces of a monkey than in MF's Caesar, Caligula, Nero, Mussolini, the Mafiosi, Berlusconi and Draghi combined, and given all of the crimes by the Vatican and the child rapes they have been perpetuating, maybe there are higher traces of morality in the feces of a monkey than in all of Italy and Saudi Arabia combined," says Diogenes.

I don't disagree with you about the resurrected and condemned straight back to death MF's you named, even though the living ones still have a chance to not be so tormented through eternity.

"All my research shows Italian women and Latin women ranking near the top globally in all 4 measures of "getting fd." skills by which I measure "getting fd." performance, with an average of 6.7 (I being a 10 of course, and Linda 9). Rome was my headquarters for many centuries. Paul, are you going to let him accuse master designers like those of the Vatican and Da-Vinci and more recently Ferrari and Gucci that can package their minimal traces of morality so beautifully? Are you going to let him accuse the people that invented pizza, spaghetti and the bj., as a stand-alone product?" responds Babylon.

Hey, hey, Diogenes, stop being so cynical. The concepts of morality, righteousness and agape (love), are foreign concepts to my Italian friends and they have been working very hard over many centuries to grasp these concepts. Because of the reasons you mentioned once my Italian friends and the Vatican grasp and start practicing these concepts, it will be overwhelming evidence not just that there is God, but also that God intervenes (rarely) but supernaturally and miraculously.

The three most constructive things that in my view Pope Francis can do are:

A) Support actively one Independent Disarmed Demilitarized Holy Land in any nation.

B) Limit the "infallibility" of the Pope to the Christian (Nicene) credo that all Christians accept. In doing he will reconcile with the other Christian Churches who appropriately view the rest of the Pope's "infallibility" as a wrongful power game. Ap. Peter more than any other apostle is proven wrong repeatedly in the Bible so his representative, the Pope, claiming to be infallible on any issue he chooses is highly inconsistent with the Bible.

Limiting this falsely claimed infallibility of the Pope is critical for Catholicism to be all inclusive (of all Christians) and do what the

(Greek word) Catholic means. The power of the Pope should no longer be the primary obstacle for the Catholic Church becoming Catholic.

C) Soon after visiting Israel Pope Francis (pretty please) (or a Patriarch) should visit Iran's Ayatollah which may reduce Khamenei's bellicosity against the West. A credible "religious" interlocutor is central in dealing with Khamenei, who these days is the only one that can change anything about Iran.

My Greco-Roman friends in Rome, that are fighting hard to take Rome over "from within," got a couple of my good friend's St. Peter's (who was given that Greek name that means 'rock' by Christ Jesus) ideas upside down. All I said is that the Pope is wrong only on a couple of issues; that is it. He might not agree with my views on everything else but I agree with him on everything else. *So* stop accusing the Vatican and my Italian amici.

"Ha! Ha! It was the stand alone bj that titled the balance. Do you remember being in Brescia in your twenties? It was me that sent you the inventor herself as a free promo and then you cried out in dismay, (in Italian): "Oh Father! What is heaven on earth without this?" Having sucked you up like Charybdis, she then spit you out into the rocks. I loved seeing you so pathetically hurt, self-divided and beating yourself up for decades; those were the good old days. Have you now finally found the wholeness in you to reconcile heaven on earth with Francesca's bj's?" asks Babylon.

Yes. And you will do the work for it for free, bitch.

"We've already established that I am now gladly your and only your B. We can now assume it so you don't have to keep saying it. If you feel the need to express you being the Alpha I think that you are out of line with your own teaching of best balance and moderation in not using Beta, i.e. B. to describe me which exposes just enough but not too much, so that it informs without being offensive," says Babylon looking hurt.

You're correct. I am sorry. My nature is extreme so that finding the correct, thin line beautiful best balances within the worldly, by the human standards, is particularly difficult for me and I have to do it intellectually because my instincts and emotions lead me astray. You did correctly point out that finding those best balances is a relative and relational issue that needs the well intentioned co-operation with others, and as a minimum needs listening carefully to what others perceive as imbalances.

I hope you have truly repented from your sins. Because for every sin that you commit from now on (and they are being counted) even the least grave of sins, coveting, the only pennants that I will accept is, if married, for you to give a free bj to your spouse and if single to go for a Pilgrimage to a Disarmed Independent Holy Land and offer a free bj to any single adult (excluding me) there of the opposite sex.

"Darn it; you will convert most of my w. daughters into Virgins, as I was so afraid. I was wondering how the heck would there be so many Virgins in the "afterlife" which I now understand is now-here.

Because Obama and the current Western leaders, even though they try hard, they are lousy pimps **my current** (for the last two decades) **Global Whoring headquarters are in the high growth atheist dictatorial Beijing and in la grand putain Putin.** If your policies are followed they'll cut the growth rates in my headquarters down to a miserable 3%. Democracies will start growing at 5% but what are the *poor* filthy rich dictatorial oppressors to do with a lousy 3%?!

Do you have any advice for your compatriot Elin, ´Ellen, alien people that are up the proverbial creek without a paddle, again?" asks Babylon.

16.   Ethics-Business-Economics-Politics

The sick Eurozone

Per B. Franklin, (from Aristotle,) those compromising their liberty for their security become slaves and deserve to lose both.

It is the walls that each creates to protect themselves that become their lonely "caves." And it is **the "protectors" that become the oppressors.** Greece seeking protection in the EU, from the sevenfold in number Turkeys, that still occupy some of it, resulted in its oppression from Turkey's Nazi German allies that in pursuit of dominance caused 2 world wars, the Holocaust and are again pursuing dominance, by money, over Europe because they are children (per evolution) of germs, not of God.

If they were children of God they would listen to me.

Unless the Bavarian Barbarian children of Germs reverse their policy now and increase their deficits by compensating Greece for the next 5 years about (an additional) Euros 10 B. per year, that is a small part of what the Germs gain in exports from the low Euro caused **by the God damned to burn in hell W.B. A. Merkel** and her dammed troika's oppression and (by death spiral) induced Depression at the cradle of Democracy, liberty and Western Civilization, (in its 5th year of the by the US financial crisis triggered recession resulting in 20% per year increases in suicides) and by Euro bonds to get interest rates the same across the Eurozone; **Greece must leave the Eurozone** and if they get no support in doing so they **may need to leave the EU**. Southern Europe would be much better off staying within the EU but outside the Eurozone.

At the core of the increasing poverty in Developed Democracies has been the abuse of capitalism by China causing huge unadjusted trade imbalances and the transfer of that wealth to their Communist Party.

The **major obstacle** in the West to counter **China's** currency undervaluation **is Germany's MF Merkel** and the son of feces Wolf Schäuble because despite words to the contrary, these God damned crypto Nazi hypocrites commit the same abuse in the Eurozone.

MF Merkel didn't choose to change the "adjustment mechanisms" to compensate fairly for the EU **150 B per year unadjusted** trade surplus and transfer of wealth that Germany gets, by the Euro, from Southern Europe. If that adjustment **is not at least 50 B** a year and if it is not in "infrastructure aid" (for roads that can't even find matching local funds) but for deficit reduction (that accounts the total national needs for growth), it continues German dominance over Europe.

Given the US' debt-deficit, I understand the preference of the US government to avoid directly helping the Southern European economies that have these same problems at a more severe level, and asking Germany to "deal with it," but that is a major strategic error.

The Eurozone has resulted in the concentration of wealth- power to Germany at the expense of the Southern European economies. Demanding that this problem gets solved before fiscal Union is critical, or else further integration of Europe will result in one more level of governmental bureaucracy and in further concentration of power and wealth to Germany, at the expense of the rest.

Despite their kind, noble people, the super crappy Greek governments of the last 50 years have been ponds to Germany (and to the US), which is one of the many reasons they got in trouble. MF Tim Geithner, who has major un-admitted responsibility for the 2008 financial collapse, supported the filthy huge Whore A. Merkel in intentionally causing suffering to those from whom the Germs got whatever civility they pretend to have, the Southern Europeans, by "maintaining the financial incentive" to... change them. (Also the W. former Treasury Secretary H. Paulson having screwed up big time and having caused huge misery to millions of free people in pursuit of very excessive profits for him-self and other bankers should shut the f. up particularly about his continuing whoring for China.)

Concentration of power is antithetical to Democracy and to the well-being of Europeans; particularly **if the concentration of power is to Germany, it is just way too stupid and means that Europeans have learned nothing** from their history and suffering, but like most of the abused (and the addicted) they unfortunately feel they need and ask for more abuse.

The US and UK must reverse their 'pro-unification' of the Eurozone (excluding themselves) policy because they are creating a dominating German (fr)enemy, with no benefits, only costs.

The Southern European nations, hopefully led by F. Hollande or by Kamenos, must at least have plans (MF Merkel built a EU 1 trillion firewall planning for your exit, that helps only once you get to bankruptcy) for a common currency (a Peripheral Euro, Peuro) fixed to the dollar, (like the Chinese do, but in this case to avoid devaluation) to have a chance for a not very unfair negotiation with Germany's Germs. (Actually there is no need for the euro as the monopoly currency so that Greece can and should introduce the drachma as an alternate currency.)

Also, a $1 T legal case for war reparations to Greece from Germany, as promised if Germany's Germs were re-unified, must be filed.

Any believer in God saying or doing anything against Judaism (like Ayatollah MF Khamenei did) and any believer in Democracy saying or doing anything against Greece are doing the spiritual and intellectual equivalents of mother fkng. (MF).

For names to keep providing meaning, from now on and forever these people must have the MF designation with their name.

F. Nietzsche, **the dead** most famous Doucheland philosopher believed in Power, as it has been but shouldn't be; at least not for the righteous that choose to live by right and not by might.

But even for those that choose to live in Darkness by power, the Greeks understood the rule by power long before Nietzsche did, and they elevated the form of power to be used from the barbaric beastly physical force, to cultural power and to intellectual and moral power that are not as destructive or oppressive. They also found and taught the ways by which power is divided, restrained by rules of fair competition, and diffused to the people, through Democracy to minimize the destructive, corrupting and oppressive role of concentrated power.

With typical German ignorant arrogance Nietzsche wrote: "God is dead." God is indeed dead in the dead; that's why they and Nietzsche are dead. (The other German "star" is Marx who lives in the "Marxist socialism with Chinese characteristics" that Hu JinTao kept referring to during the 18th National Congress of the Communist Party of China.)

Dead Nietzsche's German followers that pursue dominance (while saying otherwise hypocritically) including the bound to the abyss germ MF Merkel and the disgusting child of shit MF Philipp Rösler, are not just immoral and incompetent but also so ignorant as to not have read him whom they follow. If they did, they would know that the power game against Greeks of that 'little country' gets offenders whipped as Nietzsche explained **"like a charioteer whips his horses."**(Birth of tragedy; Ch.15; par. 2)

Letting Southern Europe or Germany out of the Eurozone (in the medium term; planned) **is much preferable to the pathetic Europe that Germany "leads" while ravaging those it "leads."**

To correct the central (and biggest) unsustainable global imbalance, before it causes another collapse, the US (hopefully along with the EU) must impose 20- 25% import (or VAT) taxes, at 2% per month over 1 year, (plus whatever China retaliates with), if China continues refusing to stop its currency manipulation and allow the increase of the value of the Yuan by about 25% to less than 5 RMB per dollar, in six months.

This will be helped if China retaliates and will transfer some of the production (with advanced manufacturing) and increase employment to the US (and EU); and the rest of the production to the currently poorest nations, (**preferably to democratizing nations**) in Africa, in Asia such as in Bangladesh, in the Middle East and in Latin America.

This will also rebalance the global economy, increase the employment and growth in the US (and EU), **will greatly reduce global poverty** and increase global growth, with negligible and tolerable, if any, inflationary effect.

Further, given the resulting (from that imbalance) constraints on the defense budgets of developed democracies, not calling for a Global Treaty to verifiably freeze all defense, (military and security) spending, is too stupid.

Do not blame God for suffering and deaths caused by humans that God keeps trying to guide you away from but you refuse to hear.

Disabuse yourselves from the notion that you need or can use any other protection other than from the True God. And disabuse yourselves from the notion that you can get away with any deceit or secret before the True God, who knows everything you know and everything you don't know.

"Given that the spiritual works in the opposite direction to the physical you didn't really f. me, you unfucked me!

The truth that Jesus said He could not say because it was too hard at the time for people to bear is that adults are screwed up sinners; but now that I admit it and intend to stop being it, I'm *de-facto* defucked!" says Babylon all exited.

Ethics in governance

Can you also explain that unless B. Obama does not do what I say, to **take over 'from within' (**the Board) **the regulation of public corporations** and make them instead of the oppressors of the public — **through tyranny by money that T. Jefferson** *(who needs a new wig because he has been pulling all his hairs out in the last two decades)* **correctly warned is the most insidious tyranny of all**— make them (and Wall Street) the B'.s of the public, he will have accomplished nothing, in US domestic policy? (Except the Health Insurance Act drama that primarily deals at huge price with B. Obama's mama's health insurance trauma.) Because this may be a complex concept for some, take your puppy with you to explain.

The only way to break the old century labor Union vs. Money bosses destructive conflicts, to all except to "the bosses" on both sides, is to allow employees (that have the right to vote for President, Congress etc.), to have the right to elect a Member of the Ethics and Compensation Committee in the Board of their public company.

"Explain the logic, because it isn't fully clear to me," says Linda.

There is no such thing as "moral capitalism" as there is no such thing as "moral whoring" or "moral war" because these are (hypocritical) contradictions in terms.

If you truly want to be moral (righteous) you should move to the new Independent unarmed Holy societies as I describe them and live forever in joy without economic and political stresses and fears.

Adults who claim to be moral while participating in these worldly societies are hypocrites; my honest testicles are more moral than they.

A problem cannot be solved unless honestly admitted. If our inability to be moral i.e. righteous within the current competitive systems —that are appropriately designed to reduce wrongs but have the unintended consequence of punishing any righteous deed— is not admitted, the problem will not be solved.

Because telling the truth involves potentially offending others and given the hypocritical emphasis of sounding non offensive even when doing very offensive things being truthful is hard and often punished in these societies, (as children unfortunately learn.)

Even the most saintly people I met, in monasteries, admit to failing to remain righteous and to sinning. When I was working, I couldn't count my sins, they were so many; I could only find a few moments of righteousness. (To start with I was in a constant state of coveting, wanting, desiring.) I have not had to work lately, that makes things a lot easier and despite having right judgment I have for decades been trying to be righteous for one full day (and accept the abuse that comes from the worldly) and failed miserably, every day. Even Christ Jesus, despite Divine powers, by being righteous ended up homeless, in a society that was not spiritually worse than what we have now, and got persecuted ridiculed beaten and killed a young man.

Living righteously, morally, is achievable but needs a whole separate Independent social structure that is designed for it, as I explained. So, it is not your fault for failing to be moral within the current systems; but it is your fault and a hypocritical lie to not admit it; and it is your fault and you will be found guilty if you don't even try to set up, one non-competitive, not "power-money-fame" based **Independent Disarmed society, in your nation, where you and/or your children may have a decent chance to sustain being truly moral and loving**.

What there is in the current societies, there can and should be a lot more of, is humane, **ethical capitalism,** with high standards of ethics, for the same reason that there are and can be more of, descent, humane, considerate and respecting each individual, **least wrong**, **ethical standards (and potential justification in relative, "the lesser of evils," terms** but still a chasm apart from moral-righteous) in whoring and even in war (such as minimizing harm to civilians etc.)

As Aristotle explained first, correctly and extensively, this more humane and ethical standard is accomplished by some form of Democracy; that establishes fair consideration and **accountability** of those at "the top" to those at "the bottom."

The importance of high ethical standards, above the law, and as a component of religion is exemplified by Shinto in Japan.

There aren't enough laws that can make, for example, the US doctors, lawyers and corporate executives that currently rip off blind the US Health Care system, have the higher standards of ethics they should.

That higher standard than what the laws require of ethics was and is still mostly missing in Health Insurance companies, in Banks, in oil and in most big public companies (and currently in Congress too).

The strongest argument against Democracy has been made by the people most responsible for all modern Democracies in the world, the US Founding Fathers.

They didn't believe in Democracy and wrote so and acted so. They didn't believe in Democracy because they knew of the tendency of 'the people' to ask for services and for politicians to offer those services without paying for them. As a result, as Plato explained, Democracy would eventually fail and a new oligarchy would emerge. So the American Founding Fathers chose limited government and "limited Democracy;" they chose a Republic whose "oligarchs" (white male landowners) and their Representatives, because of some knowledge of self-governance, would find ways to constructively compromise with their rivals and to act truly for the common good.

So, the American Founding Fathers were explicitly racists and sexists and discriminated against non-believers in God and against all that did not provide evidence of capable, by merit, self-governance; and these days they would be sidelined as bigots. It was not bigotry that led them to their conclusions. They would have liked to have all included, and hoped that in time it may happen, but the evidence that if they did, the nation even if it could be established would fail very quickly, was overwhelming.

So let's ask the American women, blacks, Hispanics, Indians and other minorities that disagree if they would support a world Democracy knowing that the influence of the US in the world would drop from the 80% or so after the fall of the Soviets and the current 40% or so, not to just 4% or so that is the US relative population in the world but to less than 1% because if people aren't enlightened enough Democracy leads to tyranny by the majority and to bankruptcy. Over 90% of the Chinese would vote in as racists a way, as African-Americans did for B. Obama, and you would soon be under Chinese tyranny. So now, did you, being a "believer in Democracy" minority, suddenly become sexists and racists or are you violating God's Mystic 12th Command?

The strongest evidence that the Founding Fathers were correct, and were not bigots but rather those that would call them so are bozos, has been provided by the terrible socioeconomic results of not just the American Democracy but of all developed Democracies, when all had their say, during the last two decades.

Because a Democracy, which requires defending the rights of the minorities by the ruling majority, can only be as "good" as its people, the results of the last two decades suggest that as the Founding Fathers suspected, the spiritual, intellectual and emotional state of "the rest" (those that were not eligible for voting but are now the oppressive majority) isn't that of competent self-governance but what would technically be called of fudged up egotists that cause great unnecessary suffering to the decent, honest hard working folk and to all children.

I, being Greek, have been working hard to prove my highly admired American Founders wrong and that Democracy, with all adults being eligible to vote, can last, but I am about to give up, unless you people reduce significantly your screwed-up ness, fast. (It sounds funny but I wish that I was kidding.) This is particularly important for the new (self-consumed) oligarchs i.e. the hugely screwed up 'special interest' based B.'g political class; the seriously screwed up W.'s, CEO's of public corporations; and MF S.'s of Hollywood.

Even Democracy must have limits (such as those by The Bill of Rights,) that expand gradually as people are helped to become worthy of it.

It is not difficult to figure out what needs to be done in the US healthcare system to reduce its costs while improving the outcomes, (there was an excellent TV program by S. Gupta on this,) but it cannot be done unless the political system is fixed. This is so because what is big waste and abuse for some are big profits for another and those making the big profits have undue influence in politics.

For example, if I was running this joint the questions I would ask are: How can we move providers to operating like Cleveland Clinic (so that the care is more holistic)? How can we simplify immigration of qualified primary physicians? (But the doctors will not be making as much so...)

How can we encourage companies to operate their healthcare like Safeway? How can we shift the focus of healthcare (possibly by changing reimbursement rates) to preventive care and catastrophic insurance, rather than if you have insurance getting as much "care" as possible and if you don't going to emergency rooms. What Tort reform can be implemented that the trial lawyer lobby can accept? How can we increase competition in the health insurance industry by both allowing across States competition and possibly by allowing the VA that has 450 hospitals the option to offer, for a price, a public insurance option for non-veterans and thus reduce its cost to the government and provide some competition to the private system? How can we regulate the pay of CEOs of non-profits to them making no more than a Senator? Most know that these need to be done but they aren't because most politicians are whores to special interests.

So, **to fix the US political system there is a need to have 12 year term limits for Congress; for Presidential and Senate elections to be only funded by the government;** to possibly add 10% or so members to the House elected by lottery,(as it was in the First Democracy); and there is also a need for a standing 24 member House-Senate (including 10 X-Senators and other well respected States-people) bipartisan Committee whose job is to keep offering mediation solutions to highly polarized issues.

Can you find, vote for or ask enough politicians to support the changes above in the political system to save your Democracy?

Your life has lasting meaning only to the extent you use it for the benefit of others. So, get over yourself. Stop being bozos looking for entertainment and for self-interest rather than facing the truth and changing to having higher ethical standards by which the common good is much more important, than your own and your 'group' interests, or else everything all the wise, heroes and your forefathers fought and died for, will be in vain and your children will pay an immense price. Unless you change now, you will be known in eternity as the multi-trillion screw up "me" generation.

The above not-withstanding, as lawyers say, relative to his humble physical beginnings Man's technology achievements and know-how, by which to achieve whatever we choose, are spectacular. (And can continue advancing so long as they stay away from-soulless-human cloning.)

I have confidence in God; and in the common sense of common people for the common good… if they are given a fair chance.

What there is, there can and should be a lot more of, is Corporate Boards that operate with much higher ethical standards. That culture change can only be done **by requiring** the democratization without "rigging it" (as are all the "votes" for Board members now) by shareholders and employees on a one person one vote basis of the "Ethics and Compensation Chair" in the Boards of public companies, (and for non-profits) as has been described, to achieve some accountability of those at the corporate "top" to the rest." Clear?

"Yes. Dearly beloved CEO's of public corporations: You are my best W.'s and I respect you; but you're about to lose your jobs and everything you have, if you don't become this Man's B.'s fast. Submit the plans he asked for to the SEC now, before it's imposed on you, to get on his right side and avoid you getting fired and fd.*,*" says the Queen from the South.

"Explain why the, higher than the laws, ethical standards are **necessary** and not a 'nicety' or else I'll gladly cast the 7 magic words on you again, and you'll lose the capacity to think straight, again,... saying "why the f. not" with a dance move, even when I say, pigs fly" says Linda... "Your green eyes are losing focus already..."

Oh. No! ....where did my marbles go? They were all here just a minute ago... have you seen my marbles? ...Someone help me.... I will try. Given that human laws—to be Just, enforceable and to maintain individual freedom — can't require anyone to love, hope, care, be compassionate, truthful, sane, smart or even to be nice, even if Judges had their way and all people did what the thousands of murky laws required, and no more as is their legal right, per lawyer's advice, **even though that "nation of Laws" would be lawful nothing positive or good would happen in it** and much negative would still happen; hence bound to self-destruction.

For example, it is of questionable smartness, sanity and not nice, but I think that it is and must remain lawful to opine that, except for those who **praise my book** and help bring God's Kingdom on earth, **all lawyers and judges of the world should suck my d.,** metaphorically to have one positive thing they did with their lives.

"The Bitch B. Assad has been shouting "suck my d." daily not just rhetorically but by repeated mass murders of tens of thousands of Syrians and what did the ICC or any of you do?

I love insightful metaphors! I can finally See! Because of your super beautiful explanation for **the necessity of ethics above and beyond the law and for the need for a higher standard of ethics for judges and MF lawyers to contain their financial incentives for most (illegal) negatives and for nothing (ethical) positive happening** in society, *I (and my S.'s) stop flashing my thighs to help you stop losing track of time..." says Linda and adds:*

"I sometimes like having my hands tied and be blindfolded when I get screwed. Yet, I am not as extreme as the Spaniards, the Portuguese and the Greeks who like having their hands tied while getting screwed really hard and getting smacked by the German MF Merkel and Co. You promised a "special treatment solution" for the masochists like these Southern Europeans and the sadists like the Germans. What's the solution?" asks Linda.

A name for Satan in The Bible is "ponoiros" and it means both cunning and causing pain. I do not like pain; neither giving it nor receiving it. Masochism and sadism are not words that have Greek roots; they have Latin roots so you should ask the Latin peoples about sadomasochism and particularly ask the French that invented these words. They seem to know best about getting the most pleasure out of pain.

My beloved dad Andoni told me, when I was a teenager, that on the subject of sex God makes no judgments, which is a common Greek folk saying. I am not sure why but because he is my dad (and because Greek folk have as much or more wisdom than any other) I will go along with it. I will try to make no judgments about my friends who are unfortunately sadomasochists and trade and profit on people's pain and suffering and doll out more pain because it grows their economy diffuses their pain and they like it. The solution for masochists and sadists is to stay in these societies; they get as much pain as they like, any way they like it to keep themselves satisfied.

There was a pretty German woman, let's call her Brigit, who was vacationing in the Greek island of Hydra where I was vacationing in my late teens and she slept around. Just before approaching her, I remember thinking that even if she asked to spank me as a condition of me getting into her bikini I would agree immediately. I am still thankful to her for not having placed such a condition.

Maybe that's why I was asked to, and try, not to make judgments on issues of sex. As a result I gained understanding and ask that you raise yourselves to being understanding and tolerant rather than judgmental as you watch the Greek politicians, who may not have had such fortunate early experiences, accept and find worthwhile getting smacked with their hands tied and screwed at the same time, so very hard by the Germans; and then turning around and doing the same to my poor compatriots.

The next day Brigit asked me to smack her when having sex. I committed the serious error that I later regretted of not smacking her, and that ruined our beautiful two day relationship. All Brigit wanted was to release her own instinctive recognition of her wrongfulness with a sense of Justice but I was too ignorant at the time to see it.

This brings me to the central lesson from past errors that this generation has failed to understand and that all future generations of this millennium, particularly of Americans, need to remember as key lessons of history, as confirmed by W. Churchill: If the Germans are not smacked and screwed hard early on, when by their behavior they ask for it, so as to keep them satisfied, (and MF Angela Merkel has been begging for it for many years now), it will ruin your relationship with them and they are bound to cause much suffering in Europe and great global instability. (The infectious and oppressive spirit of German germs, whether you knew it or not, is part of the economic discomfort that you are currently experiencing.)

So my friends, German women are pretty and have many worthwhile qualities but the price is too high if you make the mistake that I made and neglect your duty, during this millennium, to keep them satisfied and confirm to them that Justice exists, by whipping, fudging and slapping the Germans periodically. Now and with the policies that have been explained, is an excellent time for this round of f. smacking the Germans.

Sadomasochists should not treat others as they like to be treated; because they like to be treated badly. Sadomasochists must treat others better than they like to be treated and so let the others be Independent in separate Disarmed, 'safe' Lands. These current systems have been beautifully designed, by me and my friends, just for sadomasochists, (because pain excites them and gives them a temporary sense of being alive,) and these systems offer each the opportunity to punish themselves as much as they like; but these systems are wrong for the righteous who are by definition not sadomasochists, which is why, if you are not a sadomasochist, you should move to the Independent Disarmed Holy Land, in your nation. If you stay, it is because you like pain and particularly like either the pain you give and/or receive and/or have by your loneliness.

Those in the (Euro) Zone (the word 'zone' should be a clue that it is a screwed thing) are staying 'currency unified' so that they may be "players in the world stage," as EU Commissioner Jose Barosso, said. *My, forced into early retirement for already many years, penis is more of a 'global player' than MF Barosso will ever be.* If the European sadomasochists don't want to listen to me, they may keep doing what they do with the only addition necessary being to learn to say 'ou la la,' as "the safe word."

As to my American friends, whose Democracy, Christianity, science, philosophy, art and (unfortunately also the low standards of) ethics are more Greek than of any other origin: if the B. B. Obama continues not following my advice because he figures that Americans like getting screwed silly by the Chinese, then I will rename him to MF Obama and his sadomasochists supporters should stay in the current systems, bending over and looking backwards as they currently do, (while saying 'lean forward') but they must at least use squinting as a safe sign, so that my Chinese compassionate friends may ease up a little whenever they see Americans squinting as much as the they have had to!

Even though the blindfolded Justice symbolizes the necessity of equality under the law, let me take your blindfold completely off, dear Linda, for you to see who is doing what, I say, and I take it off.

"Ou la la," she shouts in shock, agony, pain, horror and despair squinting very hard because what she sees is just too painful for her. She then runs, pushes me off my chair and while shouting repeatedly 'ou la la' she writes:

'After considering the pleadings filed herein, hearing argument of council thereon, and good cause appearing therefor,

   THE COURT ORDERS all judges and attorneys, officers of the Court, to henceforth release their tax returns annually for public information; and present evidence of reasonable efforts to settle cases pro-bono *and **thus suck on Paul's just and ethical dick** prior* to commencing blathering proceedings upon **my** blindfolded statue-idol of Just injustice and *thus **cease and desist** aggravating my— your Mama's—* sore clit.'

Ou la la; ou la la; that was very hard for me to see… but thanks for your healing help, I feel much better already… What does 'ethics' really mean?" she asks.

There are three meanings of ethics, in its original, that if you understand you may be able to understand ethics and everything else, any issue, simply.

The first meaning is "current behaviors and habits" and is the current honest reality about how people or someone in particular or a relationship or an organization or (culture of) a society, behave (and their causes).

The second meaning is "morally desirable" (for the common good) behavior, and is about what the standards, norms and behaviors (in particular circumstances) and in the (daily, weekly) habits should be, (according to your true beliefs).

And the third meaning of ethics is "correctly" and is about correctly (usefully, practically, least inconsistently with what you believe is right and maintains one's integrity) changing the honestly assessed external reality (truth, of the first meaning,) to your honestly assessed internal Truth (belief and mission informed by the second meaning,) by converting problems to solutions and of mission and goals to reality.

"My brother is having very tough times in Afghanistan. What should we do there?"

An example of a choice with no right answer because no matter how it is handled some will get hurt is war and in this case Afghanistan. But there is a correct, least wrong thin line, (walking it is as hard intellectually as Wallenda's tight rope walks.) Ask any Afghani or American which of the following two plans is better:

Following the B. Obama plan that involves a draw down to the long term sustainable 15-25 K forces by the end of 2014.

(The extent to which the US is tied up in war in Afghanistan instead of having a couple of long term bases for counter-terrorism and for regional operations there, is the extent to which the capacity and the credibility of potential US military involvement in Syria or in Iran or anywhere else is reduced.)

Or expedite the draw down to the sustainable levels by the end of 2013. Use the $30 or so Billion saved (over 2013-2014) into 3 funds: add $10 Billion to the long-term economic assistance fund to Afghanistan; a $10 Billion fund to assist Iraq-Afghan vets succeed in their civilian lives; and a $10 Billion reduction in deficit/debt.

To achieve the military stability in Afghanistan, establishing Kandahar as an autonomous (or Independent) demilitarized, disarmed Land, for the moderate Taliban to live in, safe from interference from the Kabul government, (which is quite corrupt anyway) with NATO as guarantors of Kandahar's Independence; so long as they denounce any terrorist activity, will do the job.

A large part of the Taliban accepts such peace, if they are autonomous, and they had laid their arms down in 2002 but were subsequently attacked. Negotiations for the specifics should involve first the local leadership and then Pakistan and India.

So, which plan, a) or b), is more likely to produce better political and economic and military results, short and long-term and reduce deaths and suffering?

As a minimum, an unofficial (between Pentagon and the Afghan government) target to get to the strategically maintainable levels by the end of 2013 must be set. Such a "desirable but not required (unofficial) target" needs to be set, if you know anything about wise planning, to have a decent chance that by the end of 2014, the Afghan government can indeed take full responsibility for itself.

"What about Syria?"

The preferred path is to remove Assad in cooperation with Russia, allowing Russia to keep their bases in Syria. If Russia is becoming adversarial again, (passive-aggressively this time and with China), as it seems, then we are at the beginning of another long global struggle of the forces of freedom vs. of oppression, whether we like it or not. Another containment strategy towards both Russia and China may become necessary with the new borders of that struggle having shifted from Europe to Asia. Syria is at the inflection point.

"Would I be too cynical to say that the B. Clinton, the W. Bush and the B. Obama Administrations have been crap?" asks Diogenes.

Feces are natural, necessary and do not pretend to know how to solve your problems while by being Blind causing immense suffering and deaths strictly for their own ego gratification. Why are you so offensive against crap?

"Then, bad extraordinarily sick crap, is a more accurate physical metaphor of the spiritual state of the S. B. Clinton, the W. W. Bush and the B. B. Obama and their Secretaries of State, for the blind that see but cannot not perceive," says Diogenes.

Nonetheless, there have been some positive outcomes. Even though I like some of what B. Obama did in foreign policy, **until at least one Independent, Demilitarized, disarmed, Democratic Land of God, for any refugee, is established on earth, suffering will be increasing not decreasing**.

"Dearly beloved great Bitches of the UN Security Council: You're about to get screwed like you've never been screwed before.

Who should the people whose power is the vote, vote for?" asks the Queen of the South.

When someone says that a problem that you have has little to do with you, and it's all the problem of someone else (or group) and they'll help you fight those "bad" people (that sounds and feels nice… until the crisis) if…you give them money and more power, they are **exploiting** your problems, **not solving** them. **Politicians are "experts" in exploiting problems, not in solving problems.**

Every problem that you have is in significant part caused by you, and by your political Party whose "ideology" is self-conflicted. That sounds and feels not nice, but is true and solves your problems, by changing your own behavior.

"When politicians pull your right leg to the 'right' and your left leg to the 'left' and then don't cooperate and compromise with the 'other side' to solve your problems they're not just exploiting you, they're having in you, *what's called at Harvard*, a 'front and back orgy!!' You may mourn or rejoice in giving up your old self but you have to let it go and start intending, thinking, feeling, acting differently to solve your problems and to stop politicians from having non-consensual orgies in you" says the Queen of the South.

Many people must be changed in Congress to make for a real change. So, it is your responsibility to vote against every incumbent in the House and Senate, (except for moderates from both sides) until the problems are minimal.

The problems are not difficult to solve yet but if not solved in a year, they will become very difficult in the next two years. Your failure to vote against every incumbent (of either Party), thus demonstrating your unwillingness to keep being exploited by Congress rigging the system for their own re-election and power, **is almost assured to cause a hugely catastrophic global economic collapse within the next 4 years.**

It will be tempting at that time of crisis to vote for either Jebb Bush or Hillary Clinton but that would be a tragic mistake.

The one positive thing from the near bankruptcy of Greece is that it is less in the grip of the three feuding families: one "right" wing (spiritual) W. (it is all about money) Karamanlis, one "left wing" (spiritual) B. (it is all about power) Papandreou, and a centrist (spiritual) S. (it is all about pleasing the public) Mitsotakis (that got as much power by shifting loyalties, even though a minority) as it has been for the last 60 years. During this period the derriere of one of those 3 families had to be kissed for anything substantive to be done.

These big W.B.S. families who brought the nation to bankruptcy would still be feuding and ruling if their political Parties hadn't been forced by the Germs to work together. As soon as the second generation takes charge they screw up as was the case with the W. W. Bush, by turning democracy into a chiefdom.

I would not vote for another Bush or another Clinton in the Whitehouse even if I thought that they were the best qualified candidates because they will turn your democracy into a chiefdom. If democracy becomes another chiefdom with a couple of chiefs feuding and/or if capitalism is not made into ethical fair competition, these systems will collapse, because who would attend the Olympics if they were not fair and one runner started at the starting line while another 5 yards from the finish line?

"What a nice surprise to see you Alexander, here Downtown on 12th *street where we, the homeless, sleep," says Diogenes who was restored from* Cynic (means bitchy) critic to a (constructive) critic.

"I am glad you got wiser this time Alexander and chose to win the war before the war starts; and to declare victory without the mess of actual war. You have learned a lot; you must have suffered a lot. I hope you will now enjoy your conquest of the world. *Here's a cardboard for your victory! Sit with us...*

There are 20 charity Balls in fancy hotels happening right now in this city **on our behalf** except that we're not allowed in in any of them and we'll be with no food again today.

All the buildings are empty now but we're here sleeping on the street. Admirable planning! They know we suffer but don't want to see us, hear us or be near us, despite all the kindness and compassion they talk about. They thrive from our pain and like it. *Move your fn. cardboard Baber; the boss from Jupiter is here."*

"Diog enes, says he's Elinas," says Baber, "This homey drunk Buffalo says he is 'Navaho' (in Greek, it means 'shipwrecked'). They are from other planets to me. The politicians of this planet want us to spend our lives working harder than their dogs, pushing things and paper around for no good reason. They give us papers; then ask for our papers and you know what I do with those papers; you dudes from other planets are better… Jesus, come eat, this dude from Zeus brought some food… That's a good dinner bro, thanks."

"As to some people changing for real, as you write, don't let the w. bring you down; you're up to a solid 1 in a thousand chance and those are excellent odds for any Greek these days…Yasou", says Diogenes, drinks a bottle of wine in a gulp and continues:

"Look at the ladies having fun in clubs, "charity" balls, 'taking care' of the products of their vaginas and calling it love, saying that they are a "good person" and talking as if they know something worth hearing yet ignoring us and you or criticizing you. Look at them passing us by, as if it is us that are the trash. Spiritually they haven't changed since even before the time of Jesus.

Can't they see that their competitive 'money- power- fame' systems are inevitably led by and produce lying 'greedy, narcissistic, immoral, manipulative, exploiting, **thieving**, depressed, w.'—scared, anxious, lonely, incompetent, bullying, **hurtful,** histrionic, b.'s—and ignorant, selfish, arrogant, **cheating**, borderline, schizophrenic, bi-polar s.s' (and the equivalent cusses women use for men,) out of divine children.

What are the equivalent male "evil" character names?" asks Diogenes.

Despite your progress you are still in the wrong spiritual and physical place, my friend. Let's go to my favorite white sandy beach, St. John's beach in the beautiful island of Ios…

I am not a woman so I cannot know for sure the precise equivalent cusses women use for men. However I can make some reasonable hypotheses. Having confirmed my theory through several critical academic disciplines I will confirm it through a newly invented one.

My hypothesis in the esteemed discipline of Fuckology, that I was an expert in, in 12 languages, that investigates what people really feel about each other is that their equivalents are a.holes—bastards (or pimps, pricks) — jerks. From that prospective the CEO's of public companies are the major a.holes, the politicians are the big bastards, and the celebrities are the major jerks.

"Yes; the equivalence seems valid," confirms Linda, who followed us and adds: "However there is a significant difference of degree. Do you agree that, among those that aren't Children of God, statistically speaking women are less extreme and less harmful than men?

Are you misogynous? You are putting a.holes in the same group as w.'s which seems unfair, and us s.'s in the same category as the jerks; without clarifying that there are significant differences of degree and I find that offensive."

Diogenes (means with two natures) leans to whisper in my ear and asks, "Who's that stunningly beautiful ho? Or is she the great S. Ellen?"

"Women are closing the gap and are approaching the degrees of wrongfulness of men. I now have converted to being a Gnostic (means Knowing...God). Jesus has made women (spiritually) like men, as he said he would. But I will agree with you that calling non-believing or hypocritical men w.b.s. is flattering them because they cause more of the unnecessary mass sufferings and deaths. But I now learned the way to expose and deal with them," responds Diogenes and then says something to which I respond: "I can't tell them that."

The power-money-entertainment systems of each nation work through "pipelines," i.e. through pathways to the top, with several gatekeepers that can block your way. For example, Bob Woodward told on TV a story about being "grinded" by his publisher at Simon & Shuster about his next book. When Bob suggested "an expose of the publishing industry," the executive recommended the title..."My last Book," and Woodward added: "and he meant it..."

If arguably the most pre-eminent journalist of our times can be "blocked" or at minimum threatened to be blocked by one of the top six US publishers (that have pipelines of literary agents and access to the major TV shows and book stores) it becomes clear that the book publishing industry is a for profit business using authors as "employees" and books as for profit products.

So, with big pipelines working to sell whatever pleases the public while blocking any "expose" of the truth, the Truth is being intentionally blocked, intentionally ignored by those at the top that fight for every inch of power-money and fame, for themselves.

"Look at those pretending to be nice people but are in fear and deceit. The darkness is increasingly enveloping them until they can no longer escape it and will remain alone unknown terrified in the darkness of the abyss unless they change and do as you write.

How many people of the 19th century, let alone of the 19th century BC, do you find worth knowing and know?

But tell me more about the Cross because I don't fully understand it yet," says Diogenes.

Business-Economics

When I was a CEO (I had lost faith in God and at that time religions were like voodoo stuff to me) I was puzzled as to why when I would try to describe the character and mathematics of any of my business decisions I kept finding that the best way to do it is through a Cross. For example, to describe accurately the nature of the strategic choices and direction of any business, I would use:

TM

The first strategic business decision is whether to invest for growth in revenues vs. to divest and increase cash; and these choices are in obvious directional opposition. The next decision is, within a certain time frame, to invest in increasing the market share or to maximize profits and thus ROI, which are also in opposition.

Each vector describes the direction and degree to which a strategy is pursued. These 4 are the only available strategic directions for any business.

My US business career consisted of being a manager of International Marketing at General Electric Co. in the Medical Systems Division, then a V. P. at Diasonics Inc., a Silicon Valley based MRI and ultrasound equipment manufacturer, which was later acquired by GE.

Then I became a GM, then Division GM and after a leveraged buy-out the Chairman, CEO and President of Elgar Electronics Inc., a manufacturer of programmable and of intelligent power supplies. During that time we grew Elgar Electronics Inc. very fast while producing 230% per year ROI's.

During the last year as the CEO and for about a year after we sold the company (that made regional press 'news' because all employees got a significant bonus upon the sale), I made speeches to teach CEOs that belonged in organizations such as YPO (Young Presidents Organization), AEA, TEC, NACD, etc. the implications of choosing a particular strategic direction in changing the funding, organizational structure and degree of emphasis in the various functions of the organization.

I will not explain how to set up the "whoever wins and whoever loses, you win strategies" because they are dangerous knowledge in the wrong hands. I will say however that if several humans have figured how to do those including a bozo like me, wouldn't God that is infinitely more intelligent than us not know? My friends, whoever amongst us wins or loses God will win.

For the straightforward strategies it is central to have consistency and coherence to avoid failure and inefficiency. For example, a revenue growth strategy is consistent with increasing emphasis in Engineering (and Design) for innovation.

The correspondences that maintain consistency of strategic direction with the key organizational functions are: ™

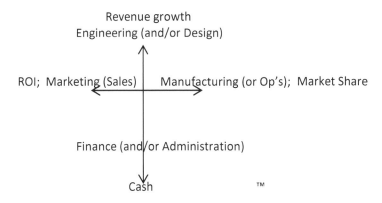

Revenue growth
Engineering (and/or Design)

ROI; Marketing (Sales)   Manufacturing (or Op's); Market Share

Finance (and/or Administration)

Cash   ™

So that, a choice of a strategic direction, such as the exiting one shown in the purple rod (aka 'guys, now let's fudge our pretty competitors sideways, at 72°; and, as always, stay away from my ugly behind; o.k.?') to be implemented consistently and so most effectively and efficiently has to be accompanied with proportional shifts in the priorities and funding of the corresponding functions of the organization, in this case increasing funding in Engineering and then Manufacturing with increased cross functional integration of these two.

In my speeches, I would then go into more detail (and developed a software program) showing how this affects the shift in emphasis within each function, such as the Cross of the 4P's (product, place, price, promotions) of Marketing, and then within each department. The shifts in strategy also have implications as to the correct performance measures in each of the dimensions on the Cross, and to business personality types as per the Adizes PAEI (Producers, Administrators, Entrepreneurs, Integrators,) and the Briggs-Myers (based on C. Jung's) typologies, for the leadership and for recruitment and evaluations that would be most suited for the execution of each strategy™.

After I quit from the worldly, because my soul kept singing "I can't get no, satisfaction" and wouldn't shut up, I spent several years trying to understand why in every other discipline that I studied I kept finding a Cross as the best way to describe the forces, direction and intensity involved in the real 4D world into 2D, that becomes 'real' at the time and during observation.

This quadrupole or quadrapole (four poles with two distinct types of polarizations) (that later result in multi-pole expansion) of The Cross was also detected by the COBE satellite measurements as the Universal background radiation.

You experience these "four poles" in Nature in the four seasons and in human development as the four stages of childhood, adolescence, adulthood and old age.

The Cross is central in chemistry as the four quantum numbers: n, l, ml, and ms that specify completely any electron.

The Cross is central in biology through the four bases of the DNA i.e. G, A, T, and C.

And it has been shown how that quarto polar Cross is only the way to fully understand the vectors in business, psychology and personality types and how these crosses multiply into whatever degree of depth, complexity and detail for any application and person.

That each of these Crosses, that had nothing random about them, and their correspondences are very precise haunted me and led me to then study and understand the Cross of the "First Cause," Christ Jesus. I now have explained the reason for these Crosses, through the Cross of the four forces of the Universe in Chapter 11, and how to lift them by creating an upward spiral.

So, there is a Cross that describes quantitatively, fully and accurately the current condition, direction and the alternative strategic directions of a National economy that you should be able to easily figure out given the other Crosses that I have shown. Consider it.

Do you think that your leaders including b. Obama and j. Boehner have a precise understanding of the strategic choices they are making and the implications on the culture, funding and directions of the structures of government?

Can major b. Obama or any of your leaders show you a direction in paper, with an angle that shows that direction, as "direction" implies, when they say that they are going to a direction or that they have a cohesive strategy or are they just waiving their hands and when you ask for specifics they dump a big load of bs.?

Or do you think as I do, that they are Blind clueless MF's that BS all day and all that is happening amongst them is not a formulation and execution of the best cohesive strategy for your economy but rather the expected squabbles, accusations and negotiations on the "solutions" (to the crises they themselves caused) between the leader of blind B.'s and the Speaker of the ugly W.'s?

I call politicians blind guides with Oedipal complex and major (spiritual) b.'s and pimps; CEO's of public corporations big a.holes and (spiritual) w'.s; and your famous celebrities serious (spiritual) s'.s and jerks, not as insults, but as an accurate common language description of their spiritual state and characters.

In defending his record with the Chinese, the B. Obama said that "after tremendous pressure" the Chinese Yuan was revalued by over 20% in the last few years. Yet, the differential in GDP growth over that same period was higher than 20% that means that in real terms the Chinese devalued their currency which is why the trade deficit with China has increased during B. Obama's first term, causing increases in US unemployment. It was then that I wondered in dismay: Could it be that President Obama knows less, understands less and is less competent on international economics than my right testicle?

"I, here and now, ask President Obama to have a 'rational debate' with you.

But my bitch (b.), B. Obama will refuse to have a rational debate with you. That's because B. Obama knows less, is less competent and is less focused on international economics, than your humble left testicle, as well," says the Queen of the South.

Oh, no; that would be tragic. Yet, be comforted in the knowledge that because of the Constitution and structures set up by the US Founding Fathers, as evidenced in part by the fact that I've not been arrested or murdered, our Chief blind Pimp, (see Benghazi, debt, deficit, unemployment etc.,) President and our main ugly W. Speaker are less bad than the blind MF leaders of the rest of the world.

Here, I'll help you learn the precise direction and vector of the economy before any economist or politician knows about it so that you may inform them. The four central econometric criteria are (from bottom to right...) [inflation, % of GDP Deficits or surpluses, GDP growth and unemployment rate. ™] Plug-in the numbers for any period, add the vectors on The Cross and voila the precise, accurate direction of the whole economy, for that period, by a single vector.

So is there any other Theory of Everything that is based on and synthesizes all the fully proven forces and theories of physics and provides an all-inclusive equation that proves the Theory?

Is there any other Theory of Psychology, Psychiatry that is based on and synthesizes all the accepted and well established theories of psychology? Is there any other theory of business and economics that you can use to both set strategy, follow it through consistently to any desired level of detail and to define the actual state of your business and/or economy by a single vector on The Cross?

Is there any other Theory that shows that all these theories are not independent of each other but because they fully correspond dimensionally and are synchronous they are a single Theory that covers all the major areas of human knowledge and science?

"Those waters of Ios with over 70 feet clear visibility were tremendous. Thanks for the trip. I have a much better prospective now. I prefer life to death and indeed there is a much better way to achieve our objectives than murder and terror. *I'm now like the normal American who doesn't mind anymore the secret security "anti-terrorist" government programs for all our genitals being under constant surveillance. The size, secrecy, scope of these and the other CIA, FBI, police, Homeland Security and Defense programs are evidence that the people must be terrified so that the terrorist won. The terrorized vagina and slave mentality is already prevailing,"* says Diogenes.

I am aware of the big difference of how outsiders view things vs. running things and presume that the threats they had to deal with compelled them to that solution, but even if the Patriot Act was correct at the time, (considering it an emergency, unconventional War), it had to have a very limited timeframe, so that individual liberty and rights were not infringed on perpetually, and 12 years is already way to long.

Does the 4th Amendment say that the government shall search and seize all your papers (e-mail, phone calls, mail) and copy them and store them but it cannot look at them unless the search of the "metadata" indicates that there is probable cause to fear you in which case a secret Court shall approve (rubber stamp) someone clicking a button to look at any and all your past and present communications, and thus being able to defame anyone anytime?

Now, per the (leak) disclosure, that the terrorists know not to use any US company for any communication all the immense communications that the NSA collects are of extremely few extremely stupid terrorists who cannot succeed anyway and of innocent people that are not terrorists.

The vigorous persecution of "leakers" that have done no more than tell the truth, and the broad support from both parties, is evidence that in government there is a pervasive culture in of deceit.

I don't have anything to hide so the NSA may survey my penis if they like, but the Patriot Act is in my view unpatriotic, it has become useless, it is no longer necessary, it is unconstitutional and it sets the stage for a tyrant.

"People got worse spiritually after the enlightened, Jesus and Mohammed, because now we have many more hypocrites.

Look at the two-faced hypocrite politician Pimps lying on TV daily as if they Know Truth or right and going to Church to pray to Jesus and then ignoring or making fun of Jesus when they see Him alive. Can't these, for whom the technical term is lying W.B.S, a.hole, sons of b.'s and jerk double douches, See that they're already on fire in anger, frustration and pain; the fire is growing and they'll burn eternally, if they don't **do fast** what you write? It is **their** choice.

All you need to add about making the option of God's Kingdom available on earth through God's Promised Lands is the closing line that was my closing line when I was pimping. After I pitched the "high class" of whatever I was pimping I would get people to check it out by saying: Some option is better than no option.

There is nothing for you to do anymore. This cold rainy night, rest on the pavement on this cardboard that says "high tech," Alexander, have some wine and tell us how much fun is it to have conquered the whole world twice and how sad is it to know that there's nothing left for you to conquer; its ok; you can weep my friend, no one sees us here on the streets," says Diogenes.

I already know that what I Advocate will happen because it must. What I am fighting for is the speed by which it happens so as to avoid the immense suffering and deaths by the delay.

So make that central choice of life now: Do you want God's eternal Spirit of Love within you or not?

"Given how much you dislike modern adults I now understand why you needed and why God gave you all the expressions of love all the time, to tolerate being Present with us. Make it as simple as possible for anyone, even for a bimbo to understand what you ask," says Linda.

A divorce, an amicable, because of irreconcilable differences, divorce from you and your world, this world, is what I am asking for. I'm already gone. I want a small Land for us that are not of this world to be able to live separately and independently. And we are willing to make it demilitarized and disarmed so that you don't get scared of us. Is that simple enough?

"Yes. All I asked is for you to love me enough to do the protecting, providing and I do the promoting and pleasing; was that too much to ask? But fine, I now let you recover your full sanity... *I don't like money stuff, so I am clueless about how the funding of God's lands will work. A billionaire gave me, as a gift (for being kind enough to not ask him to marry me before he can have sex with me) a diamond the size of a potato that causes me grief because it's so difficult to wear and to find a matching outfit. I can sell it; but can these lands get funded differently?" asks Linda, gorging in a chocolate cake.*

I found all my marbles again. If a project is provably worthwhile and the team implementing it is trustworthy, the question of funding becomes, from whom and under what conditions you are willing to accept funding.

Religious institutions, who have 4-5 "preaching places" in each group of blocks, can sell 1 or 2 properties to buy a common land of God and the remaining Churches, Temples, Mosques will be even more effective if they stop the cacophony of their messages and replace it with the **different (**as each institution chooses) **yet, mutually supporting, harmonious** messages. The most difficult problem now, is not funding but the unwillingness of governments and of the UN to recognize the Independence (other than of the Vatican) of any Land that isn't ruled by force.

"Any other advice for me," asks Linda.

Choose if you want to be dying in the worldly or Living by loving in the unarmed Holy Lands honestly. Don't deceive yourself and say that you are loving and righteous if you really are not. We have established that for you to validly claim being righteous requires evidence that you operated not for your but for someone else's interest. So, it wouldn't be unreasonable for some skeptic to declare that for them to believe that you are righteous you will need to provide evidence by sucking their penis, (physically or if that price is too high, spiritually.) So in claiming that you are righteous you may have to suck penis whether you like it or not.

So who, other than Jesus, children and the saints, wants to claim that they are righteous or right because I may want to give them a private opportunity to prove that they are not liars?

"I would like it. But you exposed and insulted the heck out of yourself; you made sure that you can't get political power or become a public company CEO; and you have offended most adults; that is stunningly impressive stupidity sweetheart. You are now a "star" Derriere, entertainer! What is that big sucking sound? Isn't it whatever remained of your career being flushed down the toilet?" says Linda.

Because I know that people end up in the same "pond" as their adversaries I chose my adversaries carefully. If I have to participate in the worldly, be at war and suffer... I might as well suffer in the hands of Katy, Paris, Lindsey, etc...

The right ends must be pursued by righteous means first and if they fail, they can be justified if pursued by the provably lesser wrong and preferably by the least wrong achievable means.

"Sluts of the world unite. The Lord appointed us, Independent S.'s, with the awesome duty to resolve the conflicts and to be the judges between the W.'s and the B.'s, ("within" each, in relationships, in business, in the judiciary within government, in the media outside government, among political "Parties," and in international affairs.)

We also cast the deciding votes in elections. So, let us study carefully what he wrote, so that we may truly **know** what the fudge we are talking about and are doing,.... thus boldly going where no slut has gone before...

We have had it with mindless fun with, for and by our-selves. **This is the time for all politicians to stop the power games and BS and get to real work with 'the other side,' for the people**," texts Linda and adds, "Diogenes, come here; I am taking you home for tonight."

"Look at ol mo Diog break an Olympic speed record!" sings the Chorus.

"Ladies and gentlemen, things are cooking; things are heating up a lot. This Man is saying that 'if you can't handle the heat get out of the kitchen.' He advises you to 'get out of the kitchen, now.' He told you how," says Linda.

In competition as in war, deceit through distortion of reality is a key component. For example, even in sports competition, that's out in the open for everyone to see, "faking" a move to "throw off" the adversary is common.

That capacity and willingness to deceive is proportional to one's capacity and willingness for self-deceit. Those that believe in their self-righteousness deceive themselves so profoundly that they lose the capacity to see the truth.

For example, a reviewer of a very old version of this book wrote that the book's solutions "include cutting taxes... and have the 25% AMT tax expire." The book said and says clearly the opposite. That (otherwise very nice) reviewer's capacity to understand correctly what they read was distorted by their own distorted reality assessment.

We "protect" children for as long as we can from making money, from sex and from voting in politics because we know that these issues are harmful to them, because there is a lot of deceit and distortion of reality that happens in those areas.

Now that you understand that the question in the competitive power-money-entertainment systems (as all current systems are) **is not whether, but what kind of deceitful and self-deceived** b.'s - w.'s- s.'s or sons of b.s - a.holes and jerks your children will have to become to defend themselves, succeed and get a sense of belonging, do you still reject any way out for your children?

The spiritual b. B. Obama has been successful in his campaigns by running against "the cynics" and cynicism. "Do not believe the cynics" he said repeatedly "and those that appeal to your cynicism." Yet, it is the b. Obama that is the greatest cynic (bitch, Beast, prick and pimp are the not polite, non-Greek words for it) these days; it is he that (deceitfully) controls and rules the world through the power of the US government; it is b. Obama that reneged on key promises, has violated religious liberty, individual liberties, has asked for and has the responsibility and burden for the murder of people without a trial and for having murdered and for continuing to unnecessarily (by "fire from the sky") murder innocent civilians including children in Afghanistan and in Pakistan; and it is b. Obama that has indebted future generations by over $6 trillion so far, while he called W. Bush's $4T increase in debt "immoral," and who while being in the majority in the Senate (and given that markets look forward) by the prospects of his election was one of the most responsible for the September 2008 financial collapse; as much as the Republican controlled House and someone like Rep. P. Ryan was, is or will be responsible for the failure of b. Obama, who is Presiding over the demise of the US and of the free world, while claiming success.

Is there any other way out (except temporarily by heavy drugs, fiction, addiction and strong drinks) from the oppressing power, money, egos dishonest brutal immoral worldly systems except through an Independent demilitarized unarmed society that is designed to not be ruled by power, money, entertainment, by people who voluntarily move there and choose to truly love rather than control each other?

"And this is the judgment: The Light has come into the world, and people loved the Darkness rather than the Light because their works were evil." (John 3:19-21)

You were proven wrong and did not know right from wrong nor knew the consequences of what you don't do and do so that you were legally insane... and therefore you are treated as not guilty...

Yet, now please stop being insane. You can no longer afford it.

Those who will not support God's Independent Free Demilitarized Disarmed Lands, even if they don't choose to go there, will do so because their works are evil and are children of Darkness and hell.

Those who will not support not even one small Independent Demilitarized Disarmed Land of God for the minority that asks for it while claiming to be believers in God, will do so because they are twice the child of hell and that is where they can expect their souls to end up.

I am here to Judge and I do so. "Not knowing" is no longer a valid excuse. Aristotle explained that pretending ignorance and intentional ignorance aren't excusable ignorance. I will make it simple enough for any adult to know:

Nothingness, Darkness, meaninglessness and their inertias pre-existed the creation of the Universe and while being reduced they still have a "pull." So, inertial evil pre-existed creation and resists change and Life.

By creating, God can but is not necessarily in charge of what doesn't truly exist. The world has been ruled by Satan's unholy trinity of: the hypocritical power hungry, violent, incompetent, beastly spirit of a monstrous B.; the money thirsty, greedy, lying, thieving, blood sucking abomination, immoral spirit of a W.; and the cheating, self-aggrandized, fame starving, ignorant, dragon spirit of a S. These expressions of Darkness have been condemned from the Beginning.

The unholy trinity of evil spirits that has been ruling the world, is that of the liar murderous Satan, of the oppressive hypocrite ("king of Babylon") anti-Christ, and of the abomination deceitful false prophet.

Now, this is the Judgment: The **power hungry Beastly violent politician big B.**W.S. that continue opposing (by inaction or action) the establishment of at least one Independent Demilitarized, Disarmed Land of Loving, will be cast into the eternal Darkness of the Abyss; **the blood, money drunk, public company CEO huge W.**B.S., these piggish a.holes, that continue refusing (by inaction or action) to feed the hungry with what they throw away for unsatisfying self-gratification and continue opposing being accountable to their public, will burn in the eternal fire of hell; and the dragon like, cheating, major **S.**B.W., jerk **editors of the Darkness loving, drama Queens of the major media,** that refuse to inform or misrepresent this book, will die in shame and scatter.

"Slut of sluts *Linda of Hollywood; You abandon me too? Brutus; what's the world coming to?" asks Gostay.*

Linda, I'm glad you became conscious that once you restore yourself you will know how to restore the world.

TO POLITICIANS : "Is any of you so stupid as to think that given the nature of the problems and the Senate requiring 60 votes for any major legislation, a single Party can sustainably solve them?

Given that either there will be a bipartisan solution or the nation will enter a fully predictable down-ward spiral, why do you keep polarizing and "fudging" your nation? Don't keep violating God's 12th Command and for what seems temporarily in your self-interest keep causing great unnecessary suffering and deaths. Do what he says, how he says it, now, or you'll surely experience hell and believe me that is a very bad idea.

Do as the Lord says to advance your reputation with the Lord and with those of opposing Parties, (and with those that have given up voting,) to at least the level of shit. A murderer asked forgiveness and proclaimed 'I am not a Politician and don't use Greek words like 'politician' to deceive;' and just entered the Kingdom," says the Queen of the South and continues:

"If by the true American Spirit you demonstrate scruples of conscience and do the right thing fast, **I will intervene to help improve your image with the public and with your Lord and with those of your opposing Party by calling you paranoid panicked ugly prostitutes."**

Ouch. Oh! God; you circumcised our hearts and minds."

God reveals Himself to those recognize that they have been wrong, admit it, ask for forgiveness for the harm they caused and truly, sustainably change. Are you now clear my dear about what our relationship is and what I expect you to do?

"Yes, yes, Lord, my God," responds the Queen from the South.

He smiles. Babylon and **confusion** have fallen.

I forgive you and take responsibility for you. If any try to damage you, the restored w., my Virgin, I will defend you. I have God and the Christ with me and need no other. I demand that they all honor you and if anyone disrespects you, I will disrespect the heck out of them.

But if you break your part and don't do these things for free, personally, as you agreed, for my beloved poor, ugly, weak, old, sad and strangers, I will become your enemy.

Only because I Know for sure and can prove that my Judgment is Right and Just, I accept my instincts of Vengeance to kill; burn my enemy and party while doing it. I tear and rip Satan's head off whenever I see him, for fun. Vengeance is mine and only mine. Do not test me again.

"I now know 'the awful Grace of God' that Aeschylus taught and Bobby Kennedy quoted. You are the enemy I for sure don't want to have again, ever; and you're the graceful friend I love and cannot live without, my Lord. I will not break my covenant and I will remind Mishpacha, the Jews, of their Covenant," Gostay says, gets close... kisses him with all her passion (derived from pathos that also means hurt, pain, incurred damage), in new purer, truer love, while he places his hands on her head healing her,... and then she adds:

"I know it's bad for my old business, but even I have been restored, so that you can surely do it too; so, Linda honey, please advise your sexy star-idols, S.'s to deal with the boredom caused by their ignorance and lack of activity in their brain by reading this book rather than continue to with no satisfaction irritate men's penises," says Gostay and adds: "I did the right thing, I'm so proud of myself.

Ladies, it is better to be this Man's b. rather than being the Queen of the world; I know. Be his friend; do as he asks."

You are better off learning what the "bad words" mean by reading and thus avoid the real life tragedies that teach by experience those meanings very painfully.

"Are you now clear to be woman embodied Gòstay my dear?"

"Yes, yes, yes, Lord, my God," she says finally free and for the first time truly and sustainably happy, frolicking with his long white shirt on (and no lingerie.)

The only potential problem left is that I lost my shirt…which isn't a problem for me if it isn't for you. (I tried to explain in THE WORLD ANEW in 2006 what should be done with N. Korea before it is too late and to warn the w. Bush of the fact "that getting into Babylon (in Iraq) is very easy but getting out with your shirt still on is what no one has figured." But all the noise from the insatiably talking gossip trivia bozos in the media cluttered the signal. Now, Uncle Sam is shirtless and sucking up to the fascist communist Chinese.)

This book shows you how to avoid the coming catastrophic problems but **you have very little time left to do these things before it is too late.**

Her new puppy, Babylon, follows her running as fast as it can and biting playfully at her heels when it catches up. She looks back occasionally to check if she is called to stay or for a final message to those left behind.

Even though we are all created equal, because we each use our capacity and rights unequally we become different and unequal. Some choose Darkness, some choose Light.

I am not great as Christ Jesus, who was the physical evidence of the existence of the Righteous God, so I do not love my enemies out of Divine love. I love my enemies selfishly (from an eternal prospective and from the prospective not of an observer or a subject but of the light) because I use them (by letting them be) to work hard and to pay the price for doing the things must be done, that I don't want to do, to accomplish what I want.

People keep their distances in proportion to their likes and dislikes because within the space-time of the Universe the central issue is distances or if you view distances in terms of time, timing.

If you found a star in which vicious dinosaurs live (not completely unlikely) and having deciphered their code of communication you could communicate with them, what would you say?

Because I dislike pain and suffering and avoid it and like sustainable joy and seek it, I would say: "It is a great pleasure not meeting you. We are delighted not having to hear from you. We're elated in not knowing you. We rejoice in having no responsibility for you and are relieved in forsaking you. We are in orgasmic bliss for not having to see you and thrilled for not having to see your (at least not literally stinking) image. We're excited that you are satisfied with your hell and are not looking to find us.

We revel at the opportunity to not have to deal with you. Even though we do all we can to not harm any life, by assuring appropriate distances proportional to our dislikes, if 'by accident' destruction befalls you, our ambivalent condolences will follow. We are deliriously happy for not knowing more about you. We are enchanted, in Nirvana, having escaped the cycle of life and death, in knowing that we are not coming back until God's Kingdom is established on this planet.

Until then, we wish you good luck because you will need it.

We are gratified for the villains that, as pre-dinosaur animals do what they have to, to become fossil fuels for God's Children.

I would like to hear from those who disagree with me if they have an alternative explanation of reality, of the energy fields that drive them and of their functions and of a resulting alternative cohesive constructive philosophy.

If it wasn't for my empathy as a fellow human that message would be appropriate to human non-believers, lukewarm believers, hypocrites, leaders and others of this world who will disagree with me, without offering a better alternative, because they are hypocrites.

Hypocrites are hypocrites because they refuse to admit that (to be gender neutral, reduce proliferation of cussing and being a man by my bias use the flattering to men characterizations) they are in private, in the "dark," one of the 6 combinations of W.B.S.'s; and more explicitly, and one of the 6 combinations of pimp-asshole-jerk, that like their hellish status quo.

Without God's Spirit these are bound to return to the "dust" they came from, of the 6 leptons (Greek that means thin) and the 6 hadrons (means fat) that are the 12 elementary particles of matter.

We will remain in sustained full joy in God's heavens until all your crappy governments claim no rights or authority over us and stop falsely claiming to represent us.

If you happen to see me, be charming by getting away from me." That is the message that I would convey to creatures that have no Right Reason.

The Bible is THE BOOK OF TRUTH. This BOOK OF TRUTH refers to, explains and is referred to in the Bible. Please note that The Truth can be explained and described but cannot be contained in any book.

"One last question Man: why did you make me love?"

For the love of it; is there any other reason to do anything, sweetheart, and is there anything better to do?

Reason and Response

The reason for the Universe is the consciousness of it; the reason for consciousness is the recognition of **truth**, the reason for consciousness of truth is **Reason** and the reason for Reason is **Love.**

The Reason for and of Love is Right, and the reason for and of Right is Truth.

Right reason lovingly expressing and describing Truth and loving intent rightly creating truth, is oneness.

The eternal truly Loving rightly Good God is One.

The brutal lazy bozo, moi, has one glass of red wine from Judea and gets ready for another... short nap.

Move to one Independent Demilitarized Disarmed Democratic Holy Land in your nation and live, separated from the world, and sanctified by loving intent, right reasoning and True expressions with others that are righteous and you will be truly free and will no longer have any Cross to bear, because our Cross has been already carried and conquered by the Christ Jesus, our Lord.

A dove flies near him to drink from last night's rain puddle.

"Now that we agree on everything, the Lord Jesus, Righteousness, is with us and we are One. Now, and only because we are One, we are each one, integrated, coherent, unique, different, separate, sovereign on our own right and are eternal," says Mary.

Before continuing reading please write down now, for your-self, all your bad feelings and thoughts about the author; it is central to your spiritual growth.

"No. We do not agree on everything," shouts Sharpton. "The only owl in this script is racially profiled as white, and there's no diversity of owls."

*So he, Farrakhan, the new Black Panther Party and the NAACP march around the pool with fancy blue suits complaining that the Attorney General and the President are not protective enough from racism because they are black but are not niggers! They demand at least **the black horseman** who advocates the 'Just and fair' 3:1 proportions as conditions for the compromises!*

"Being born and growing up in Africa does not make you a legitimate African, which would allow you to use the n. racial slur. Other than the saints, are there adults whom you aren't forced to "know"?

Funny; yes those who don't want it because they are children of hell; those, as you, numbered but unnamed I throw so they are not.

These condemned hypocrites complain of (by skin color) racism by whites (while ignoring the much higher tribal racism among Africans) and of discrimination while remaining in these, necessarily appearance (otherwise known as **facts**) based competitive societies and while being dominated by appearances.

They should move instead into God's Kingdom on earth where the Spirit is in truth what is most valued and **Live by The Law**; rather than staying in these worldly selfish, materialistic, power, money, sex, deceit, fame with hypocritical judgments by appearances based systems and **suffer and die by the Law**.

There really is no choice other than live by love rightly and truly or die. God did not gamble with the Universe but he had to gamble with you understanding it rightly and truly to survive it.

OPEN LETTER TO:

Presidents, Prime Ministers, Chancellors and Kings of the nations of the world:

"Let the poor, weak, righteous and oppressed go free and be Independent and Sovereign as I describe NOW or I will be forced to destroy you also in physical reality and throw you to hell after death," says the Lord, God.

Bitches, do as the Lord, the True God says, now.

You have been going through Revelation. Go through it spiritually, (repent, as I did), **to avoid having the immense suffering happen through physical reality.** Limit your turmoil by getting fast to the right actions.

Until you do as it is written here, humanity will keep causing the tribulations, woes, agony, famines, wars, suffering and deaths described in Revelation.

The ego-persona that I projected in this fiction section may appear egotistical to some. I happen to understand rightly and correctly a few things (as has been shown) and I am "very allergic" to BS. I can sense BS from a far distance and my 'allergies,' that include smoke coming out my mouth, (from smoking), act out.

Despite the appearance of egotistical arrogance in fiction and its context of dealing with evils, I am not arrogant and spend much of my days cleaning, vacuuming, doing laundry, cooking, washing dishes, feeding pets, gardening and helping with homework, all of which don't allow much room for arrogance and if I was hired to do any of these tasks I would get fired in a day because I don't do them well because I'm preoccupied with the TOE about Creation and with the Will of Creator, while vacuuming!

Please forgive all the "bad words" that I had to use to explain clearly **why, by whom,** and **how, 'bad things'** happen and how to avoid, control or deal with them; "bad words" that you also know and have probably said but appropriately avoid saying publicly unless you get as fed up as I am. For those "bad words" that I wrote will three hundred 'hail Marys' do?

"That is so sweet; from you one is enough...hmm...maybe two; and three would be even nicer," says Mary, cuddling into his arms.

"Accept a few million 'hail Marys' for my Just injustices and for my unjust Justices," says Linda, un-blindfolded and holding Diog's hand who is now very happy to stay quiet experiencing this moment in its fullness. *A year later...*

*"There are some things that made me very angry" says Lind*a.

Pay someone who at least pretends to give a f. and tell them about it.

"How about a kiss goodbye?" then asks Linda, approaches him, puts her hands around him and caresses his back, and then while kissing him she stabs him in the back and she kills the author.

"A fiction story worth the paper it's written on requires that the characters take over the plot so now I am in charge," says Linda. Now you can call me Linda Annie de antislut that talks like a virgin. We make decisions by what we like or dislike, as it should be and not by right and wrong. We make decisions by what we like in our purchases, in the media we watch, in the social media, in our reviews, with our friends, in our politics and in everything else. That is why I, (the borderline schizophrenic) Linda Annie De Antislut am the secretly in charge global authority now. I am with a new man, Diog the original (histrionic in private but appearing in "full control" in public) Cynic and biggest B. He is my B. now. No one messes with him. I killed the author because he comes off as an egotistical jerk. And I killed the author because he tricked you in saying that the story was going to be entertaining. I wasn't entertained by it and didn't enjoy it, didn't like it, and I am very angry.

Did he tell you, 'I need a GPS because I am lost in your eyes?' as he had told my old me and got me lost into his eyes and as he knows you want to hear to like him? No, he didn't. He instead said 'I need a GPS because I'm lost in your vagina,' and that we are all wrong.

Did he say, "May I please look at you to appreciate God's best design?" which he did in private before fn. us every which way but Sunday and then leaving us. No, he didn't," says Linda Annie clearly irritated waiving her hand with her finger pointed. He instead insulted us and all our esteemed leaders.

Did he say, 'I would like a fast ride to heaven so when may we make love?' which got him 'the rides' he wanted. No he didn't; he instead said that if we don't change we'll die and might go to hell.

Did he say "I need nectar so may I kiss your heavenly lips? As he knows would get him extra points. No, he didn't. Did he say to us, "I need healing so could you please hold my hand or touch my face?" No. He didn't say any of the things he knows we want to hear, enjoy and be entertained by. He threw all flattery, niceness and politeness out the window. Instead he said for some of us, who so choose (and who by their looks would not be doing a disservice by volunteering,) to volunteer sex to the opposite gender even if that choice isn't done strictly for one's own liking. Well, I don't care for that. (And now that I'm so fat no one else would want me to care for that either). He is up in the clouds. His ideas are bizarre and for the birds. No way; they're not for me. I say that we should keep pleasing our own selves and masturbating alone, in shame and in secret. You should keep your masturbation schedules steady, as I do, is what I think. That is why I killed that egotistical, vulgar, pompous, self-admiring a.hole, jerk author, for you.

"Now that you're so fat and you blew your last chance to be given a charity f. what're you going to do with your self-loathing?" asks the Queen of the South.

He said that many of the Church going Christians are hypocrites (I don't really say that; I say that going to Church alone is far from enough) *even though we go to Church as Jesus said* (actually He didn't say anything like that) because our intentions, thoughts, feelings and behaviors don't evidence righteousness and he used offensive language," says Linda Annie.

"You are not offended by the offensive language and gruesome violence in fiction, rap, and movies and don't blame their authors for them. You are not offended by the dozens of murders and of suicides happening every day in this nation or the deaths in war. You're not offended by the multitudes of rapes, child abuses and great suffering going on around the world but you are offended by him saying that there are hypocritical W.B.S.; a.holes,pr. and jerks that cause, exploit and thrive by these sufferings?" *ask Gostay.*

That jerk with bizarre strong ideas also tricked us in getting us to write all the bad feelings we have for author because those psychological projections, without having met him and without clear evidence, best describe and are evidence of our own ego-self that we've been trying so hard to hide. Now we have in writing evidence written by ourselves of our ugly character.

That's why I killed that pompous, egotistical jerk, self-admiring spiritual whore, prick and bastard, the author. Look at author's dead body now, unable to keep bitching. He's still bleeding. Take a stab at him too. Don't worry, he's not going to respond, he's dead. I changed and acted more ethical but he still wanted a divorce from us even though we aren't even married yet. Is it not written that you should not divorce? Now he has his divorce. He deserved to die. Come on... stab him too. Do it. Stub him. And she stubs him again...

"Maybe he wanted you to stab him as catharsis from your own ego," says Gostay.

"Oops. Maybe I shouldn't have done as I like and make choices by what I like.

Don't tell anyone that I killed the author and more importantly don't say anything good about his ideas," says Linda Annie who pretends to be a virgin and she runs away to escape into her hell of fiction, confusion, pain, hate, anger, shame, fear, loneliness and lies that are accompanied by disease, dysfunction, destruction, death and continuing hell.

God's people finally free from their ego and from the ghosts of their past by and in the Spirit of God's Truth live **truly** happily ever-after.

THE (sort of) END

Truth through fiction: Fighting people's fictions with fiction

Thank you

Did you dislike it as you like? !..... So, do I Know you?

Paul Andoni, I don't always drink beer... lights up a cigarette...but when I do... it's a cheap common folk beer.

I am grateful eternally to Alexander my son and to Emily my daughter.

The loose ends - EPILOGUE

There are several unanswered questions that will be addressed here.

I left my ego (and I hope you that left yours too) behind and resurrected myself! I chose to take on a character that appears arrogant, offensive and egotistical to hypocritical B.S.W.'s in the above fiction section, to entertain, to deal with and to assign the due disrespect to the hypocritical Pr.'s, a..holes, jerks and B. W. S.'s that have ruled the world.

It would be inconsistent to write a book about all the truth and exclude being honest about one's self. Even though and because I know good and right, I do not claim to be good or to be right. I claim to be honest, truthful, that the Advocacy in this book is right for those that are of the Kingdom of Heaven, and that the Theory, evidence and socio-economic recommendations and policies, for those of the world, are least wrong i.e. are correct.

My narrow and short term self-interests have been excluded but my long term broad self-interests have been included because I do have children whose long term best interests is my job to operate by. Even though there is an American-Greek- English bias to my political recommendations because that is in who my children are, my assumption has been that their long-term best interests coincide with those of all the children of the world, which is why my recommendations are least wrong, i.e. correct.

My intent is to prove my assessment of the seriousness of the current sufferings and of my undesirable predictions wrong. If you find alternate ways to increase the probability of all to eternal joy and to significantly reduce wrongfulness and the disastrous predictions I have made please go for it, so long as you prove my predictions wrong not in theory but in reality.

I am sorry if you don't like me (presumably having met me) or don't like the persona I project in the above fiction section of the book, but what does "like" have to do with anything? Did I ask you to marry me? For sure not. If one makes judgments by what one likes one is making a judgment for one's ego, the hypocritical W.B.S.'s (make sure to) appear as more sympathetic characters (like white washed tombs that appear clean but are dead and dirty on the inside) and huge damage is caused to those that are righteous, honest, kind or correct. I ask you to have a clear understanding of what right means is and does, and of wrong in the context of all the truth and to judge and act by what is truly right.

I let myself get murdered by one of the book's characters (and they are fictitious characters because I have never had any of the above conversations with any real person) to remove the excuse by the hypocritical W.B.S's of arguing against me instead of arguing against the ideas, Theory, evidence and solutions that the book offers.

That murder of my fictitious ego-persona by one of the other characters, in the above section that is fiction, symbolizes that this book is by me but it is not about me. This book is about God and the Theory that shows and proves the principles and laws governing Creation and about correct solutions to humanity's problems. Please disregard the part of my role in this book as a necessarily irritating to hypocritical w.b.s. pr.a.holes, j.s' agitator.

I would appreciate it if you don't make this book about me but rather please concentrate on the ideas, explanations, Theory, evidence and solutions it offers.

A fiction (imaginary) section is included that is intended to raise instincts and emotions from the subconscious to consciousness for by reason resolution, as is the job of fiction, as well as non-fiction sections to demonstrate how reality actually works through the two-way interactions of fiction (imagination) and non-fiction which is why it is complex but with self-repeating patterns, as the Theory of Chaos defines and explains.

Please forgive me for a bit of technical lingo in this paragraph but there is a need to explain the mathematics of the Cross and show mathematical examples of its current use which is in Lagrangians that are functions that describe and provide the equations of motions of dynamical systems, usually with four independent variables that are the x, y, z, t, shown here as 4 independent vectors on the Cross. Lagrangians are currently being applied from the Standard Model to classical mechanics and to economics.

However If one places correctly the 4 relevant variables on The Cross, one can avoid the complexity of doing Lagrangians and just add the vectors.

The central self-repeating pattern in the Universe, in the intersections of imagination and fact, where all life lives, is The Cross as shown by its theory, applications everywhere, for everything and for everyone and the correct strategies and solutions in dealing with it. And the right path in the Independent unarmed Demilitarized Democratic Holy Lands where no one has to bear any Cross, because it was borne and conquered by The Savior Christ Jesus. This book also provides the equation that proves the physics part of Theory of Everything.

In describing all of the truth the book explains all the Eternal Truths of Truth; and the truth about all the truths and reality that you experience; and the truth about the lies that you are subjected to, why by whom and how to expose those lies.

Only in fiction do the characters of the creator often do take charge. In truth, creatures cannot take charge over God, (because their works are evil and they don't want to admit it, ask forgiveness and truly change,) no matter how often they spiritually kill their Good Right True Creator.

For most, the issue of loving all (with the appropriate distances particularly from the evil in intent) is far-fetched since most are trying to find just one person whom they can love and be loved by and that is difficult enough.

Much of the need for having children, for marriage and for monogamy comes when someone subconsciously reaches the disparate realization that their own children are their best last chance to be truly loved.

The chances of finding "the right person," the "soul-mate," that most are interested in, in the context of these societies are very small, and if there is a way, I don't know it.

Finding such a person for a committed long-term even eternal monogamous –if you so choose- relationship (without necessarily being married) in God's Lands are very high. Actually, if you truly love another person you neither need nor want any (marriage) contract (and its financial benefits) to love them forever. That is why "formal" marriage is discouraged in the Holy Lands; and it is highly recommended in the wrongful societies, in which the chances that your love will be abused if not formalized are huge. If they do as is written, these currently quite wrongful societies will become least wrongful and thus correct.

In the context of the current societies finding people that are "correct" for you is achievable. They need to have read this book to understand what correct is and means or else how can they be correct if they don't understand what correct really means?

There are many stages of life, as each travels through time at different speeds and there is nothing wrong with any stage of life so long as one recognizes the stage they are in for what it is and don't keep trying to fool themselves and others by claiming to be right.

The central message of this book is truthfulness and honesty. Honesty is the most basic prerequisite to entering God's Kingdom. Telling the truth may or may not work in these societies but it does work very well for your long term happiness, it sets you free from shame, and it is essential to having a relationship with the Divine.

So, given that I see no problem with most animals I would certainly see no problem with humans, that are revolutionarily more advanced than animals, because humans have within their spirit divine capacity, even if they are going through the w., p. or j. stages, so long as they don't try to pass themselves as some 'high level' spiritual, religious or intellectuals, and thus do not claim to be either right or correct for themselves or for anyone else.

Ultimately life is about the choice of good vs. evil. The choice is about living forever operating by God's loving Spirits or dying dominated by the animalistic survivalist self-loving evil spirits of "a.holeness, p.ness and j.ness." Anything said or done is an immensely different experience if the intent of those interacting is loving vs. if a participant is operated by their spirit of a.holeness.

It is true that even though God has been asking people to be Separated from the worldly He allowed and allows the Universe to be operated by competitive survivalist systems because His beautifully balanced systems of Nature do force the reduction of wrong over time and help assure that no one dominates.

I still remember my dearly beloved dad Andonis shouting at me (in Greek) "shoot, shoot now" when I was a teenager and we were hunting for wild bores in Ethiopia and suddenly we encountered a lion. I kept my aim at the lion but refused to pull the trigger and instead looked with admiration at that quite fearless creature as it starred at us with an intensity that I still remember and then turned and walked away. I tried since to understand the lives of these beautiful, fast, strong, creatures and realized that even being king of the jungle is a bitch of a life, unable to dominate, challenged constantly and now endangered.

By Nature's evolutionary, survivalist free competitive systems even the children of hell have been and do get over time increasingly forced to become lesser pr.'s whether they like it or not.

So now (unless I cussed at you by name) you're each circumcised into being relatively clean and only a minor pr.; and if you live in a democracy you are judged as the lesser among minor pr.'s and b.'s (except of course the readers who are judged as wise.) Because of it and despite it the Lord Jesus says that you are welcome and are fully qualified by Him to be in God's Heavens in heaven and on earth.

A big disadvantage of these free competitive systems, that emulate Nature herself, is that they force everyone, even if they are righteous and want to remain so, to act wrongly in self-defense.

One can fight evil with good deeds and some should stay and do so, so long as they remember the American saying that does apply in the current systems: "no good deed goes unpunished."

In most effectively and efficiently reducing wrongfulness, the open, free fair competitive systems also block the righteousness that maybe expressed. For example, when I first saw a car accident in the street and I righteously try to stop to help, the "professionals," (the police in this case,) blocked me and told me harshly to keep moving on because I was in their way. (Because they worry that as an amateur I will make things worse, that is correct probabilistically.)Has it happened to you too?

After a couple more rejected attempts, now I don't even bother responding to my better angels given that "professionals" that cover every aspect of life, want me out of their way. If I know more and can help "professional experts" want even the righteous or the truly knowing out of their way because despite being wrong and knowing it, they make money and survive happily in the confusion of their own mambo-jumbo.

So, the current human systems, even the best of them like the democratic ones, are very useful in reducing wrong but they reduce righteousness as well, by blocking and punishing those that try it.

That is why the righteous who don't want to be punished and they shouldn't want to be punished for being right, must be let free. It is true that so long as there is evil there is the need to have strong free competitive democratic governments that will oppose it, but that should not require everyone to have to participate in the wrongful competitive systems. Those that truly believe in peace in any nation should be allowed to live in loving, cooperative peace, in one Independent Demilitarized Disarmed Holy Land, in their nation, that they establish.

Reportedly there are over 30 million homeless people in the US and I will not give specific statistics about the millions of children in hunger and poverty in the US because all you need is to experience is being around one of those kids to break your heart.

Currently the systems and results for the people of the 'nations' range from very wrong in democracies to extremely wrong in dictatorships and it has been shown how to move to least wrong.

To get there, and for those that stay behind, the only game in the world is the power-money-reputation game. Therefore so long as the true intent is good, it is to help the needy as shown by actions and results (or else it is hypocrisy) and so long as the methods do not compromise one's integrity in for example not having to become a liar, a cheat or a thief to accomplish those objectives but is least wrong and ethical in her/his methods, then participating in the power-money-fame is necessary appropriate and justified.

However it is results that count. In my view it is quite self-evident that poor people in a capitalist society do not need food, education, social services or any of the hundreds if not thousands of programs that there are to help them; they need capital; poor people need money.

So, other than establishing an Independent Disarmed Holy Land where the homeless and poor can have their own government, the program that can help them most in my view is:

The government is the only entity I suppose that can identify and list on the net all the people that need help along with setting up a savings bank account in their name. This should be done particularly for poor children and their savings account should have restrictions such as withdrawals requiring the signature of both parents.

Anyone with over $10 million in net wealth should donate at least 30% of their net wealth within the next 3 years to savings accounts of poor children.

This charity, along with the establishment of the unarmed Holy lands, are the two primary charities that the proceeds of this book are intended to be used for.

If all these people with over $10 M in net wealth, that did nothing that is really so valuable and have been getting wrongly grossly overpaid, do not donate, as above, 30% of their wealth distributed in 3 years, their mamas will have to suck my penis or I will certify them personally and eternally as huge pieces of shit.

The only way the private sector will avoid the current and additional burdensome, inefficient and mostly ineffective taxes and regulation is doing on it's own what is truly right for those in need, as explained, and so eliminating the necessity for increased taxes and regulation.

I care much less whether my recommendations about making hell more livable for the children of hell, by moderation and by the thin line, the narrow road less traveled, of best balance among competing interests, that is the middle straight path, are accepted or not, as I care about the re-establishment of Paradise on earth.

(Eden has been associated to several potential etymological roots, but if it was derived from Greek it would mean Knowing; joyful Knowing. According to Jewish eschatology the higher Gan Eden is called "the Garden of Righteousness." I would add "the Garden of the joyful Knowing of Righteousness.")

I found some flaw, which I have no interest in exposing, in the teachings of everyone, except Jesus Christ. So, even though I find very little wrong with Plato, whom I started reading in its original (which offers a better sense of the spirit in which it is written) ancient Greek since I was 16, as you can see from my writings, I have disagreed in part as to how the right society should be. The central issue is that however you envision your ideal society it should neither be called nor treated as utopia but should be attempted, experimented in a small scale, safely, and to be seriously attempted it should be set up as an Independent Land.

The only other requirement that I see is that it should be both demilitarized and disarmed to actually be a serious attempt of non-violent and not as the current lonely, fearing, hurting, greedy, deceiving, angry, in pain, pretentious and shame dominated human living.

Under the current systems "the rule" is that violence is necessary at times for self-defense, (and "self-defense" is quite a fuzzy term that is dependent on the size of one's ego) as each government acts that way, so that asking the members of these societies to be completely non-violent is inconsistent with what the governments do. If people want to live truly free from violence, and they should to avoid the suffering that comes from violence, they must both individually and by their government of the Independent Disarmed Holy Land refuse to use physical violence under any circumstance.

There are many things that I don't know most of which I don't want to know and know why I don't want to know and the rest are due to the high complexity in applying The Theory of Everything into a specific person and circumstance and taking into account all the dimensions.

So if you ask me what would be the correct actions for you, in dealing with some issue, for example, with your spouse or work, I would have to say that I don't know. When it comes to such specifics "I know nothing." For specific facts you're better off checking on Google. I do know that I could find out and provide correct answers if I spent the time and effort to look into each such issue. And you can easily find out what is right for others and what is correct for yourself and others if you have the right and the correct understandings as described here.

I don't consider myself to be "special." I do claim to have a more profound, better, right and correct understanding of the totality of truth in life and I prove it, but I believe that any human could and can get there. If you grew up in Addis Abeba physically seeing thousands of children and mothers starving and suffering with no hope to escape it, no matter how many apples and bananas you stuffed in your pockets to give away, on your spare time, at 16, after doing whatever sport the pretty girls seemed to admire and hoping (and while waiting) for some benefits from it, you also would probably be reading Plato and Adam Smith.

The only solution for fast development of impoverished areas is setting **up a tax free industrial trade zone in them** that is independently administered so as to reduce the influence from the corruption and bureaucracies of the current governments and allowing a simplified regulatory environment. It is what got China and India going, through Shenzhen and Bangalore respectively and previously the "Asian tigers" through Hong Kong and Singapore. China now has the know-how to keep growing but unless it's stopped from cheating (which the Republicans are willing to do, but strangely the Democrats are resisting,) and growth in manufacturing does not shift to the rest of the world, the world including China will find themselves in an immense socio-economic, political and military mess. Tax free industrial trade zones for targeted fast development are needed in some impoverished areas even within the developed free world.

So, setting up administratively autonomous manufacturing tax free trade zones, for example, one in Kavala, (in eastern Greek Macedonia) and one in Bishoftu (outside Addis Abeba) will greatly help the growth of Southern and Eastern Europe, the Middle East, and East Africa.

Stop providing tax free zones for the tax evaders and thieves in places like the Cayman Islands, Switzerland, Luxembourg, etc., by taxing corporations affiliated with those tax Havens double the taxes and provide the tax havens only for new manufacturing investments that offer at least a 10% stock option plan for non-executive employees.

This requirement produces a quintuple win; a win for all employees, a win for shareholders, a win for management, a win socio-economically and a win for the government. Most successful Silicon Valley start-ups have something like this and I successfully used it in my last leveraged buy-out. It is the large public companies that don't have adequate non-executive, employee stock option plans thus misaligning stakeholder interests.

All the competition, debates, conflicts and crises are about how to justly split the money, control, recognition pies and get them to grow. The answer is better if corporations implement a 10% or so stock option plan (vested over 4-10 years and is both common and individual performance based) for non-executive employees, as above. To encourage this, the current 50% (which is too high leaving other stakeholders with too much cost for the benefits) ESOP ownership tax advantages must be extended to 10% ESOP ownership.

The Prime Minister of Greece, currently A. Samaras, should ask Xi Jinping, the new President of China, and Lady Park Geun-hey, the new

President of S. Korea, to meet with him and help establish a tax free zone and encourage some of their companies (such as Huyndai and Samsung that currently have no manufacturing facilities in 'the zone') to set up manufacturing facilities outside beautiful Kavala (means "riding"). This would allow them to get well-educated employees at the cheapest labor rates in the "zone" and with no taxes for 5-10 years to have direct access to the Euro zone, (and easy access to Eastern Europe, the near east, Middle East and N. Africa). This would be a nice way to start riding and whipping MF A. Merkel "Gangam" style for the significant benefit of their people (and for my pleasure.)

The US forgave the debts of their enemy Germany, after the wars, but not the debts of its ally, Greece. The Greek debt that the government of Germany has and Germany's portion in the ECB and the IMF have must be forgiven or Germany must pay the wars damages it owes. It is (a small portion of) the debts that Greece accumulated in rebuilding itself from the wrongful unjust uncompensated devastations and deaths by the mass murderous German wars. (And by ignorantly listening to your past governments, like, for example, the in public encouragement by the W. G. Bush for all governments to increase spending for "stimulus" after the US financial collapse that the W. K. Karamanlis and the B. G. Papandreou enthusiastically but ignorantly followed even though Greece was already up to its eyeballs in debt, thus causing its bankruptcy.)

The hypocritical MF W.B.S. German Germs should stop cheating, punishing and trying to oppress that tiny nation of Hellenic people at the very foundation of modern civilization for their greatly disproportionate, heroic, exceptional and continuing contributions to personal liberation, freedom, Independence, education, art, sports, civility, right understanding, individual empowerment, democracy, enlightenment and well-being. Please start treating the Hellenic people (Greeks) with the friendship, Independence (including financial independence) and honor that they deserve.

In the US, setting for example, Modesto, Ca. that has (one of) the highest poverty rates in the US, as a tax free zone for new manufacturing businesses with at least 10% non-executive employee ownership, would be the fastest way to reduce poverty in western US and start reversing the increasing income inequality.

As expected, my conclusions are in part influenced by my life experiences but I do not think that that invalidates them as subjective, because the evidence I provide is not my life experiences but rather the facts you see on the News, your own experiences, the well-known, proven and accepted theories, all the cherished faiths, the physical reality and the proven laws by which the whole Universe is operated.

You get forced by life to choose between being righteous or wrong. Be wise and choose to live righteously, without having to get punished and killed for it, in an Independent Disarmed, Demilitarized Holy Land in your nation.

Don't keep claiming hypocritically that you are right or righteous while (necessarily to survive) doing evil works, as it has been happening, because it's a condemned path of immense pain, destruction and death. Don't suffer unnecessarily if you choose righteousness by staying in these systems; our Lord Christ Jesus has suffered already all the necessary price for our Deliverance.

If you choose to remain in these wrongful societies know that it will be painful. You will have to fight, compete and overcome many difficulties, whose (b.w.s.) nature I described. The best that can be done is to be least wrong. Be honest with yourself, and as Emerson beautifully urged, be true to yourself, be honest about the reality you face and because you will be wrong in part on every issue, look for, admit and correct your wrongs fast to keep improving.

Value your freedom, Independence and Democracy most and try to keep finding the least wrong, thus most consistent with right, correct, straight narrow path of moderation that beautifully balances competing interests best, to minimize the pain and suffering. As you know from exercising if the pain is low and under your control, (even if by saying Ou la la,) it can be experienced as a pleasurable rush.

The brilliant humor of my friend Derek Arber was the best antidote during the times that insanity was going after me with a vengeance. So while watching hell, keep your fn. humor to avoid going bananas.

Rejoice that I used and even written every bad word that we are not supposed to say and threw in a few gratuitous f. bombs because it provides evidence that you are less screwed up than me and therefore belong in Heaven.

When the evil spirits of the w. b. s.; a.holes, j.'s, and pricks tell you nicely to f.off implying that you are not worthwhile, remember that you are less screwed up than me and therefore are of immense value and belong in eternal Heaven. So do not speak badly about my necessary fn. cussing because it's your ticket to Paradise. (Add your name below.)

having read this book and therefore knowing at least as much as Paul and being less vulgar than Paul, is less screwed up than Paul and therefore belongs in God's Heavens, in heaven and on earth.

There is a debate going on these days on gun violence and gun control. There is rarely a direct cause-effect relationship in quantum (and statistical) relationships; there is synchronicity. So even though there is no direct cause-effect relationship of a violent culture to violent acts, as there is no direct cause-effect of smoking to cancer, there is a synchronous correlation. There is no causality, but just synchronous correlation because the true cause is the not admitted, not dealt with, ignorance, immorality and incompetence of humans and not any object, or phenomenon.

Wherever you end up in the current debates about the gun control and enforcement issues, the central issue is having a safe, non-stigmatized place for the multitudes that have very difficult time coping with this violent, deceitful, wrongful world to recover their sanity; and the Independent, Demilitarized, Disarmed, Democratic Holy Land is the best way, the only way, to significantly reduce most the violence of even those remaining in the current systems.

The people in the Holy Lands should not judge, as Jesus Christ said, because judgment is The Double Edged Sword, the measure by which you will be judged; they should recognize that they live by the Mercy of God and should be merciful.

Frankly, rising to forgiveness is often not achievable if one is to remain Just to the victims, and then rising to Holiness is extremely difficult within this world as it has been, so that the priests, monks and saints that achieve it are to be cherished.

If anyone, (such as the free masons and of other "secret societies") claims to have elevated themselves to the even higher level of having "superior" Mystic knowledge, please inform them that you expect them to gracefully turn the other cheek after you slap them and then literarily slap them, on my behalf, for having arrogantly violated the 12th, the Mystic Command.

If you stay within these societies you cannot survive without judging, so you must judge. Be honest and correctly understand self, God and others so that your judgments are just.

Right, Just (ethical) and true (based on honesty and evidence) judgments are the judgments that keep you furthest away from having to resort to Justice.

You know that you are a sinner and that is because you are wrong, irrelevant of what you think or pretend. The only question is not whether or not you are guilty but "how much" guilty are you? My very strong advice is to become righteous by letting the oppressed free into an Independent Disarmed Demilitarized Land even if you do not want to move there because the only question if you don't is how bad is your march to death going to be?

If you choose to stay freely in these wrongful hells and also by your inaction deny others their God given right to live independently in heaven on earth, even as an experimental small disarmed Holy Land, you are a condemned to hell hypocritical enemy of God.

There is no rational in forgiving non repentant repeat offenders because it is unjust to the victims.

You may blaspheme my old ugly body and my book(s) but those who blaspheme my Spirit of Truth, that is Christ Jesus' Holy Spirit, will never be forgiven.

What is my reasoning in writing this book? It is simple: Why wouldn't the correct reasoning of science not support and inform the correct faith and the correct actions in religions and the correct policies and ethics in societies?

Finally, as to the economics: Instead of relying for growth from more new empty cities with no righteous purpose that China has built and is building, the nation that builds one Independent, environmentally, technologically and architecturally advanced low cost Independent, Demilitarized, Disarmed, Democratic, new city, Holy Land for the freedom and well- being of its poor, weak, suffering, alienated, peace-loving and righteous if they choose to move, which will make taking care of them, if need be, much more efficient, even if that involves up to 30% government stake, (but 10% should be enough) is the nation that will change the direction of humanity from the current fast march of humanity towards Death, to going towards Life and will cause the biggest boost to its economy in terms of balanced high growth, with much increased happiness for everyone and will have built an eternal monument for future generations to remember to live by Love.

Eating from the tree of knowledge of good and evil is deadly because ultimately the truth comes out that God is the only Good and the source of goodness while humans choose doing evil. The only antidote for this is the fruit from the Tree of Life that is offered you here.

This book offers the correct, true and cohesive understanding of God, religions, physics, mathematics, history, business, corporate governance, strategy formulation and execution, economics, fiscal, trade policy, right; correct education, philosophy, psychology, You, current affairs and politics, unfortunately along with my ugly sexy art!

The common person knows that telling the truth is right. They know that loving is doing what is right for others. They want God's Kingdom on earth. They only need to shed the illusion that we all, including their children, have to remain **slaves** to human systems of force, fear; money, greed; and ignorant egotism without an alternative way of life.

Let there be Light!

Are you Awake?

Are you Clear?

Can you See me by your Spirit?

Am I still Dead within you? Asks the Christ Jesus
Now that you are Resurrected, friend, **restore** human living, for those that so choose, to the evil free joyous and loving experience that you temporarily felt as a child and that human life is intended to be.

17.   The meanings of the fictitious story

The more **extremely** the paths of righteousness (positives) are pursued the more righteous one is. **In contrast**, in the context of the self-identified children of evolution (negatives) the only way to keep evolving is to stay in **moderation and balance**, which can only be done by balancing through neutralizing negatives by competing negatives, (and producing a positive result in the sense of reducing wrong), as the fictitious story of this book illustrates.

In the story, by your brilliant questions, you (the reader), using the Socratic teaching method guide me to confront and do a "Clint Eastwood" with three trash-talking and trash doing ghostly chairs and you come out victorious over the three archetypes of inertial self-repeating nothing, dark, and meaningless evil spirits of the Universe, (b., s., w.), and so we live happily ever after.

Because I teach both of the opposing sides I am likely to appear incoherent and self-contradicting. For example, because being more right isn't a problem but is better I recommend that you believe in and pursue to the **extreme** the righteousness of the Absolute God— and to not be a w. b. s.—and then in the fiction section I imply... but if you choose to live by pursuing money i.e. do spiritual prostituting, let us get out of your badly run national Whorehouses, don't identify yourself with your work because you are greater than that, and because doing less wrong is better, do your work in **moderation**, respectfully, correctly, ethically, **and separate that role**, in relationships, in business and in government, from the B. (the control functions) and from the S. (entertainment or judicial) functions, so as to have checks and balances that allow self-corrections into the straight path and thus reduce (minimize) the overall harm to yourself and others.

As a result the book violates the basic marketing principles of being well targeted to a particular narrow audience, of having a single simple message, of being like and expressing like to that target segment so as to be liked and of not offending anyone, particularly not the customers.

But how does one explain that one side is offended by the actions of the other and the other is offended by the words of the first, without explaining what is offensive and why?

The world tries hard to use non-offensive words to describe even vile, violent and harmful acts but that can mislead. Unless I used bad words I couldn't explain the bad things that are happening and would not assign to them accurately the degree of badness of those acts. I abbreviated the bad words when being more explicit wasn't necessary.

Even though I am inclined to believe that most leaders started with good intentions, if politicians don't want to be seen as and be called cynics i.e. bitches, they should stop acting so power (control) obsessed; and if CEO's would like to not be called whores they should stop being so money obsessed; and if social leaders like the pretenders (actors), the lawyers and the media personalities would rather not be called sluts they should stop acting so popularity obsessed, for their own benefit while by their immorality, incompetence and/or ignorance while pretending to "know" they cause crisis after crisis and much suffering and deaths to others.

Yet, those same people that spiritually are greedy, piggish, blood sucking W.'s, when viewed from a survivalist and materialistic prospective are instead the very useful high achievers and job creators. The fearful cynical B.'s are viewed as the public servants and public protectors. And the egotistical S.'s are viewed as the esteemed judges, lawyers, the informative media and celebrated entertainers.

Now you know the answers to the key Mysteries and Sacraments of Life that the true Mystics were taught but couldn't say because it was too harsh to say except to extremely few select that could bear it.

As result of teaching Love while simultaneously calling prostitutes-prostitutes, I appear incoherent. Unfortunately I don't know of another way to help both opposing sides without getting myself pulled apart.

Please forgive the unavoidable incoherence in validating both opposing sides, the righteous and those attempting to reduce wrongs, while explaining that only when the two sides are separated into separate mutually supportive Independent Lands both you and I will have a chance to live without the irreconcilable contradictions that cause disagreements, conflicts and violence that tear us all apart ultimately to death.

There is a place that has been prepared from the beginning of time for the self-aware w.-b.-s.'s and there is value to them **so long as they are**

separate from the righteous or else both sides end up becoming hypocritical damned w.b.s'.

Is there a place in this, your, world for people like me?

This change will not only liberate and empower the poor, depressed, suffering, alienated and the righteous and help them solve their problems but will also allow the relatively secular current governments to reduce their size, get their finances in order, be stronger and grow much faster. If this isn't done, given the current strained economies the social unrest is likely to become too brutal.

Am I lying? Am I not disclosing any significant part of the Truth? I have no horse in these races. Why would I lie? The usual way people lie, is by flattering others and the reason they lie is to gain some benefit in terms of power-money or entertainment. Does it look that I am trying to flatter any of those with power or money or fame or any human? What part of the book, that is not in italics and so identified as fiction, is not true or is not accurate?

Even though I started my business career in marketing, I ended up picking the most non marketable subjects to write about. I have no interest in making money from selling books because I have already enough and know that there are much easier ways (the last three years I worked I increased my wealth by about $2M a year) to make as much as I need. Spending over two decades to study and write a book about philosophy, religions, politics, psychology and physics, none of which makes for a pleasant conversation or has much of an audience with each segment disliking the conclusions from the other subjects, appearing agitating to all groups and having all the proceeds of the book going to charity, is a way to lose money.

I am not interested in fame either, because I don't want the responsibilities that fame carries. Writing such a book is a way to lose one's old friends too. I go through places and no one notices me, my neighbors might not even know that I exist and I prefer it so. I dislike most media personalities.

The fiction section was designed to (by agitating) bring out your own emotions and whatever impressions you may have about me (because you are reading a book and are not really dealing with anyone) they are psychological projections of your-self and you can choose to do with them as you like but they are not about me and please don't make them so.

As to power; I want to and have to influence the direction of humanity by helping provide a clear correct understanding of reality, truth, Truths, Right, of what the choices are, what correct means, is and does and what love is, means and does.

THE WORLD ANEW despite not being offensive nor containing offensive or adult language and getting excellent reviews was read by only a handful of people, (it is too long.) So now I am prepared to be as offensive as I need to be to achieve what I believe must, can and should be done. If I fail this time I might even have to show my ugly bum next time; please don't force me to show you my ugly badass.

But I do not want to have any formal authority or power because the responsibility would probably drive me nuts and because I don't trust myself with having much power because I don't have much compassion for my competitors and as a result I might do harm to them that I will later regret.

So why would I lie? Am I asking for your vote? Am I asking you for money? Or does it look that I'm trying to gain favors or to flatter people or their leaders?

If you ask the same questions about politicians, businesspeople and the media "celebrities" you will find that they have plenty of motives to lie, the means by which they do things show that they might be lying, the inconsistencies between their previous promises or words and either the current ones or their actions are significant, indicating hypocrisy, and the results of what they get which is power, money and fame, show that they indeed pursued those and to the extent that they say differently they are lying. So why would you believe them and not me?

I have been successful within these systems and know that being offensive against anyone is quite stupid if one wants to advance their own self-interest. I know about being polite and my forefathers probably invented politeness. I know that what you want to hear is affirmations of your ego. I have kept my silence and remained polite until now. So please forgive me for my "offensive language" but I believe that there comes a time when telling the whole truth the way one truly experiences it is necessary even if I know that it will offend many, to my detriment, as it has.

The reason for the necessity of all of the truth, even if it's difficult to accept, is that humanity and creation is designed to be only as free as the deceit, pretense and illusions about its immorality, ignorance and incompetence as it overcomes.

Writing a book that I knew upfront would make you dislike me and the best I could do with it is to make some fun of me so as to hopefully keep you entertained; a book that is unlikely to succeed in the short term because of the huge spiritual inertia for such a change, is part of the evidence that I excluded my self-interest, for your benefit. Why tell you truths that I know you don't like? Would you expect less from a friend?

By the way, English is a very rich language but is poor spiritually because it doesn't have appropriate words for the types of love that exist. Philia, (filia,) friendship love is identified as a distinct kind of love in the Bible and it refers to the love at the second stage from the bottom i.e. at the level of Wisdom. And Philadelphia, brotherly love, is at (the 6th,) the enlightened level, and that is how it is referred to as a "Church," in Revelation. (Rev. 3.7)

The key to resolving all the issues of humanity is victory in the war against excessive stupidity; (except if one is joking.) Please join with me in the war against excessive stupidity.

We may capture our targets by you writing a five star review (even if the review says that the book is all crap) for this book. Write a five star review and this book will brutalize murder and obliterate excessive stupidity. I have set myself at the limit of excess stupidity and by reading this book you will be smarter than me because you will not have to use any cuss words to make your points; you can let this book do that part.

The Generals of the war against excess stupidity (those will that write a five star review of this book) will receive, if they ask, a (by e-mail) honorary PH.D from Altrutech's here-now just established: Socratic, Aristotle, Jung and Einstein Academy of Everything in One. These Generals will thus become sinless in context of the Mystic Command.

If there is anyone other than Jesus Christ still claiming to be Right I want to meet them. These are the Last Days during which God is pouring out His Spirit of Understanding, as it was written.

Now that all excessive stupidity was murdered, you are ready to become Whole and sinless in the context of all of God's Commands.

This is the 'come to Jesus time'...come...

ON JUSTICE

Jesus Christ rightly and truthfully claimed that He is Righteousness, He is what right intends, means is and does and I, as billions of others believe Him, because He proved it and proves it, and I prove it. And billions more of all the other great religions now believe in Him, Christ Jesus, Righteousness, yet call Him by a different name.

I am convinced that people of any faith in God, atheists (like for example Dr. Rose) and people of any race, gender, age, socio-economic status, political view and philosophy can find significant and adequate common ground, to deal with any and all their differences, on living by THE SEVEN UNIVERSAL PRINCIPLES of Justice, Wisdom, Forgiveness, Wholeness, Grace, Enlightenment and Righteousness.

Let me say a few more things about Justice because it is the foundation of God's Kingdom.

Only when the judge judges rightly, i.e. not on the basis of his-own self-interest but in the interest of the conflicted, just judgment can be made and justice can be done.

Even though one must know what **right** means and must be **free** to make an independent judgment and be **discerning** of what is true and what isn't and be willing **to forgive** those that admit their wrongdoing and earnestly attempt to change their behavior, and be **understanding** of both of the perspectives of the conflicted and be **compassionate** about them to judge rightly and/or correctly, people cannot rise beyond justice to being understanding or forgiving or whole or gracious, or enlightened or being righteous unless they have confidence that at least there is Justice.

Often a judge cannot make a judgment that benefits all and is confronted with trade-offs in which at least one side may incur some (even if just) harm. The effort should be to minimize harm which is what correct, i.e. wrong but most consistent with right, judgment means. Most often the correct judgment is a "thin straight line" that recognizes the correct balances and separates correct from incorrect judgment.

To avoid doing or incurring injustice, moderation (rather that the excess of passion), is the best path because it balances best the competing or conflicted sides. It is better to not resort to justice to resolve a conflict but to find a way to settle the dispute by mutual agreement. So compromise, that does not involve you having to deceive or harm others, on the primary issues of all conflicts which are money; establishment of who is 'boss' and who is in "control," (power); and disrespect i.e. hurting one's ego; is the best answer. Wise compromise involves both sides getting the most important aspects of what they see for their self-interest while giving way on many of the less important aspects, and it is called "win-win."

In recognition of the difficulty of rendering right judgments that avoid harm to either of the conflicted sides or correct judgments when some not forgiven harm has been done, most legal systems do offer people the ability to appeal the judgment to a "higher" court. Having a place to appeal judgments should be available for students in a school or for family setting as well.

So what are the things that are "unjust harm"?

If you kick your TV every time you don't like what you see in it (as I often feel like doing) the TV will break and it is not the fault of the TV maker. So, there is "an instruction manual" that says something like: don't kick the TV.

There are thousands of laws, regulations and rules by which people have attempted to define the thin lines that separate guilt, in terms of what causes unjust harm, from innocence. Yet, there is an Instruction Manual that explains them all simply.

-The increasing unjust harm from someone slandering (false accusation, blasphemy), cheating (on the agreed rules), or stealing or killing are well established in almost every legal system in the world, and they are the core of civil law, contract law, corporate law and criminal law respectively.

-If you are greedy and want (covet) what is not rightfully yours you lose your wholeness and integrity and if you disrespect your parents your attitude causes unjust harm to you, your parents and to others.

-If you do not rest for at least one day a week to just be and experience existence, meditate and/or pray, your ability to be whole, is significantly hindered, (humans because they are built better than TV's can handle getting kicked (metaphorically) 6 days a week for a long time, but do need a minimum of a day a week to recover.)

-Using the name of God to claim superior authority on conflicts among humans that are about the vanity of humans (the power-money-fame issues) causes unjust harm, e.g. see all the, for the vanity of men religious conflicts. When God is introduced as a justification on these power-resource-ego issues of people's vanity, those that do so should be reminded that they are wrong and sinning.

 -God is Spirit, not a physical body and thus should not be depicted as an image. God is the Spirit of Love, expressing His Love to all life and asking you to live by loving justly, wisely, mercifully, in wholeness, harmony and Liberty, righteously.

-God is One and the same one God for all creation. Humans can get to oneness, to being an unbreakable whole, and be one of a kind, unique, only because of and by the Oneness in the One God. Violation of this results in the unjust harm of a person losing their ability to become whole and a unique eternal being.

That is why the simplest and best explanation of the "Instruction Manual" that comes with humans, which if you break you get broken, are **the Ten Commandments** that I just briefly explained. If you keep those you will not have to learn, any of the rest of the thousands of laws and millions of regulations neither by the easy nor by the hard way.

"Stop kicking the TV if you want it to work!" says the Maker.

Be in the Christ Spirit as per the 11th and consider the 12th Command, so that you may be able to keep the Ten.

So now you understand what causes harm to others, sin, that if committed, because of the reciprocity that is embedded in the laws of nature is bound to cause harm to you as well, resulting in a downward deadly spiral of increasing harm for all involved.

That unjust damage often breaks the bonds of love among people and separates one from Love, God, which is why it is called a sin (willing separation from God) which results in fearful, guilt ridden, hurtful, painful, deceitful and dreadful dying.

You understand that keeping the Ten Commandments, that make common sense, and keep people away not only from causing harm, but also from the desire to cause harm and from ignorantly getting in trouble, is not just a matter of behavior but that is caused by being in the wrong spirit, either by wrong, selfish intent, or by wrongly applying what is right or correct or by being ignorant.

And you understand that **Justice** intellectually starts from knowing what **right** is and means, to being in **enlightened** liberty, to **graceful** discernment of truth and right under each circumstance, to **holiness**, wholeness and separate Independence, to being willing to be **forgiving** of those that recognize their wrong and are willing to change, to being understanding and compassionate of all sides, **wisely,** i.e. with the correct understanding of the impact of your actions. Yet it is the reverse process that a child must experience from the outside world to learn about each of these seven spirits of God, from one stage to the next.

Judaism is by the Spirit of Justice by God's Laws as I explained above. Confucianism is self-evidently by the Spirit of Wisdom. To forgive by the Spirit of the Merciful and Compassionate God is what Muslims are urged to do as every Chapter in the Koran starts with. Taoism is by the Spirit of wholeness and holiness, as shown by the separate and Independent life of Lao Tzu. That you don't know the names of the Aryan (Vedas; Knowers, Seers of Life) Mystics of Hinduism is evidence of their humble graceful work. Buddhism is self-evidently in the Spirit of Enlightenment, that leads to Liberty and Joy, as Buddha means enlightened. And the Most High, the Light that Enlightens is Righteousness, Christ Jesus.

The Seven Spirits of God and the Seven Heavens: Justice, Wisdom, Forgiveness, Holiness, Grace, Enlightenment, and Righteousness are not in conflict with each other but are fully mutually supportive, and are in Harmony, all being the expressions of Love, that are all needed for the various circumstances you will encounter in life.

Now you can understand Jacob's dream of the ladder to heaven with angels ascending and descending from the heavens.

It was shown to you that to fully understand any of the Spirits of God, you need to know all of them and will have to move through each of them, from righteousness to justice intellectually and in the reverse order from justice to righteousness practically, in each circumstance.

Operating by the Eternal Truths of God's Spirit you will be in God's kingdom, eternally and will not perish. To do so sustainably you need to establish only one small Independent Holy Demilitarized, Disarmed Land in your nation to actually live by love is God's Will rather than living by the power, money, fame conflicts and competitions that the world necessarily has to operate through, and Judged by, to reduce wrongdoing.

It is important to note that children are predisposed towards loving others so that actually a big part of what needs to be done is to stop messing them up while teaching them about being able to survive and defend them-selves in this world.

Justice is the least preferred expression of love because not forgiven harm has already occurred before justice starts operating. A world in which there is no more than justice, a world without compassion, forgiveness and so forth, a world of instant justice and nothing else would be a horrible tormenting place.

Yet, you understand that Independent justice, by the correct due process, is a pre-requisite to getting elevated from the animalistic dominance and abuses of power by the strongest, into truly loving relationships.

Justice has been high jacked by lawyers that mostly operate in self-interest and thus, by definition, wrongly, and have financial incentives to increase "injustices" to get paid handsomely (given the threat to your liberty) in adjudicating.

To the extent that there is no justice those that try to oppress, dominate and damage others by their physical force, or by legal authority or by money and by fame, continue causing huge unnecessary confusion, harm and deaths.

Central to Justice is fairness. Fairness is about both sides agreeing on the process irrelevant of which side one takes among the competing sides. Fairness is about mutual respect. Dr. Rose's latest book is focused on the centrality of MUTUAL RESPECT. Fairness is about being treated equally to any other. One can be fair only if they put themselves in "the shoes of the other" understand the other and recognize the validity, even if one disagrees, of what others say and do given their past. If one is fair they should be willing to accept for themselves whatever they propose to others.

The change can occur by students learning rightly what right means and is and then what right judgment and just justice means and is, primarily by their parents and their teachers.

Dr. Robert Rose on JUSTICE

In my classes (K -university) I found that even the youngest students had a heightened sensitivity to any imagine or real personal experience of injustice. "That ain't fair!" This begins when a child can begin to talk well enough to express it.

Recent research demonstrated that three month old babies who saw videos of children who shared compared to those who took things from others understood or "felt" a sense of justice. After seeing the videos they were shown photos of those that shared and those who were selfish and cruel. The babies smiled at those who shared (were fair) and they looked away from the unjust behaviors.

My classes were seen as "safe" as the students quickly realized that I used (Constitution, Bill of Rights) methods that insured that no one was unfairly accused or punished unless the infraction was "proven." They also noted approvingly that the offenders were "appropriately" punished. The consequence fit the offense and the punishment was never 'overkill."

Overkill is too often the punishment at home and in schools. I grew up sensitive to this because - in his effort to keep me from becoming a thief - my father punished me severely. When I stole a five cent pencil sharpener from a store and I was caught he did the following. I had a toy sailboat worth $100 in today's money that was my favorite possession. He took me down to the cellar; hit me ten times with a broomstick on the butt. He then opened the furnace and threw the boat in and forced me to watch it burn. About a year later when I was about nine years old, I stole two cigarettes from one my aunts. This time he burst into my bedroom at night, yelled at me, and began hitting me on the butt with his plastic strap. The next morning when my parents came into my room they saw that my butt was severely cut and the bed bloody.

Interestingly enough, this didn't stop my stealing. It made me so angry that I became the king of thieves and for years I stole everything while I had money in my pocket to buy things. As a parent and teacher I was keenly aware that many who continued to break even reasonable rules did so because of their sense of injustice and often they had experience overkill in their punishments.

So, as a teacher, instead of MY rules posted on the wall as my new class entered, WE, as a class decided on the minimum rules to keep them safe, but to insure everyone was treated fairly. After they heard I didn't believe they should be punished by talking in class, getting up for a drink, getting help from a friend, they decided on rules that they agreed made sense.
WE then decided on several alternative consequences for when they broke a rule, had been proven guilty, and they discovered they would CHOOSE their consequence.

The latter was seen by many teachers and parents as plain crazy. Naturally, they'd select the easiest-least uncomfortable one they said.
However, I emphasized that the purpose of punishment was to change behavior, not to be cruel. If the consequence they chose did not change the behavior, the next time they lost the POWER, their Privilege to choose.
Most quickly saw that with justice comes Personal Responsibility. Once that became a critical parameter that they understood, there was class consensus, a group pressure to one, not break THEIR rules, and two, take their consequence without arguing or whining.

It worked in our home and it worked in my classes. It was never perfect, but it gave everyone a reasonable goal and methods to insure greater justice for all. One other technique that I added for those who didn't trust the system was the Student Court.

The Student Court was available to anyone who felt he had not received justice. If he requested it, it was never denied. He would select his attorney and his witnesses. The jury of five was selected alphabetically from the class roster and rotated. The judge was elected by the entire class. My only role was to further insure the legal processes were followed. This worked from first grade on. In all except a few cases this satisfied even the most angry student.

In those few instances when this didn't work, I would tell the student (who still either said he was not guilty or felt he'd been unfairly treated) in front of the class - "Ok, you still are upset so here's what I'll do. I know that our criminal justice has even executed people who after they were dead were found innocent. Horrible. I don't want to unjustly be part of punishing anyone who is innocent. So, even though you seem to be guilty, we could be making a mistake. Therefore, you will not be punished. I'm not saying you are innocent or guilty, but we will not punish you. HOWEVER, if you are accused and proven guilty of the SAME offense, your will not choose your punishment and it will be much more severe. Do you understand and do you agree?"

About half admitted they were guilty, the other stuck by their story. The second group did not commit the same offense so probably justice was served. Even, if they may have been guilty since they shaped up, the system worked. It helped the rest see that justice was always possible.

In our blended family of seven there were 12 years differences in age between the oldest and youngest two (twin girl and boy). We made certain that every child had the chance to give input in our family rules, their consequences, and most decisions. If they disagreed they knew exactly why the final decision was made.

It was democratic, but they understood that sometimes they were outvoted and other times, their parents' decision was put into effect because of our greater knowledge and experience. How we spent our money was an example. With consequences the child's choices were not an issue and we honored them - unless a choice wasn't working. In school one swat on the butt was the choice of 95%, suspension last choice, but in our family most chose paying money, losing a privilege for a day or two, or something that they really cared about being taken away that made them think twice about doing the infraction.

The main point is that each accepted that s/he had their day in court (each knew s/he had been treated justly by their standards and beliefs appropriate to their age) and therefore took responsibility for the action that had gotten them into trouble and they didn't complain about the consequence each chose. It didn't always work perfectly and sometimes we saw hurt or anger, but it was minimal and short-lived. Almost never did we hear, "That ain't fair!"

At school or in the home giving everyone real justice at a level each understood resulted in fewer interpersonal conflicts (verbal and physical assaults) and the bad, angry or depressed feelings and actions that result from real or believed injustice were minimized.

ACTIVITIES to PROMOTE to EXPERIENCE JUSTICE

Activity 1.

Think about a time when you were accused of something that you didn't do, but were punished. Did you have the chance to tell your side of the story? Did you know who accused you? Did you have the chance to have a say in your consequence? Either discuss it with your family or your teacher - or write it as a means to get it off your chest - called catharsis.

What do you think SHOULD have been done? Why do you think it wasn't done?

ACTIVITY 2

Take another incident from any time in your life in which you were accused of something you did wrong, but you were given many of the same rights or opportunities to explain as I offered my family and students.
Explain the differences in how you felt when you (1) received a fair hearing, (2) received justice, and if the (3) consequence was just. If any one of these three didn't occur, explain why and how YOU felt.

Explain fully your thoughts and feelings about the degree of justice you received.

ACTIVITY 3

Tell about a situation in which you saw a teacher (1) publicly accuse a student, (2) not listen to a student's side, (3) act as police, jury, and judge,(4)sentence (force a punishment) on the student without discussing it or any of the event with him.
If you felt he was innocent or at least deserving of the chance to explain himself, did you do anything to help him get justice? If not, why not?

Take a similar situation in your home when a family member was not given his/her rights. Explain what you think your parent(s) did wrong and how you felt. Did you speak up in his/her defense? Why not?

ACTIVITY 4

Take something you have heard or read about a specific group that has been treated unjustly. We have revolutions by blacks, Hispanics, Native Americans, women, gays, and various religious groups that have been victimized by whoever is a majority in a geographic area.

Take ANY group and find a person from that group online or in your area that you would be interested in knowing about his/her personal experience with injustice. Be aware that some may find your interest irritating (look up patronizing) and may become unpleasant. Explain that you have experiences injustice and have been asked to try to understand someone else's experiences.

The purpose is to see how the specifics of injustice may be different, but the mental and emotional pain is similar. When you do find someone who will interact with you, share this with your family and/or in school.

ACTIVITY 5

You have had to not only rethink your beliefs about justice and injustice, but you have had a chance to discuss them with adults and peers. To help you better understand some of the changes you may have experienced and thought about, it would help JUSTICE become more a part of your life if you would either:

- Tell your parents or teacher or classmates how you plan to IMPLEMENT justice into your life;
- Write an short essay, poem, short story or anecdote about how you will make acting just with others (MUTUAL RESPECT);
- Keep a diary or journal to explain the just and unjust things you've done;
- You and a close friend talk on a regular basis and share your just and unjust experiences.

God's Kingdom by the Promised Lands on earth

Once the Kingdom is established on earth through Independent Demilitarized Disarmed Lands, the holy places are the National Democracies within which one Independent Disarmed Holy Land is allowed and the world is your garden.

What The Kingdom is designed to leave out (and it must be implemented so) is primarily the competition for power-money-fame systems thus leaving out selfishness, greed, malice, ill-will, vengeance, hatred and physical violence towards any person or group of people no matter how much you disagree, dislike and disapprove of their spirits, words or actions. Secondarily The Kingdom is designed to leave out all the control of each other because of fears, money-greed, sex-exploitation and self-loving egos' causes of all the conflicts and negative emotions, as described, that haunt adults.

This liberty from destruction and death is no more than you try to do for your children and it is God's Will that it is done for all His Children.

I plead with you, for your sake, to not treat God and love as if utopia but to work for allowing at least one small safe, Independent Demilitarized, unarmed, Democratic Land in the world in which people live by the Loving Spirits of the Holy Spirit (and not by money-power-appearances,) for the multitudes that are unnecessarily hurting, suffering, in wrath and dying, now.

"These are the words of him who has the seven spirits of God..." (Rev. 3. 1)

Are you happy with life as you are experiencing it? Are you sustainably happy? Do you feel loved by others? Do you love rightly others who aren't part of your family? Are you lonely? Are you sad? Indignant? Angry? Hurting? Are you in physical pain or with a medical problem? Are you frustrated? Scared? Anxious? Confused? Tired? Do you feel shame or Guilt? Do you feel understood and known by others? Are you doing what you truly believe in? Does your life have meaning and purpose? Do you feel joyful and confident about the prospects for your children to live free and happy lives? Has technology solved any of these problems for you or did it just change the form of your problems? Do you think that technology by, for example, the invention of a bigger nuclear bomb will resolve these issues? Do you really believe that another Conservative or Liberal government will resolve any of these issues?

So, why is Jesus Christ the only Savior? Because you, I or any other human could never understand truly what right means. Failing to understand and know what is right, everything people have said is intellectual crap, not much more valuable intellectually than chicken squawking, even if texted or communicated by I-phones or "twits." And even if someone explained what right and righteousness is, no one would believe that living righteously can be done truly and with positive results and they would be called hypocrites unless they truly lived and taught righteously and were willing to be ridiculed, blasphemed, beaten, persecuted and murdered to prove to hypocrites that they fully excluded their self-interest as Christ Jesus did, and no one else.

For example, I, despite knowing and explaining Right, sure as heck would be unwilling to be persecuted, blasphemed, tormented and murdered by hypocritical pretentious lying wrongful sinful evil w.b.s. scum, to save them. As a result all would continue pretending to know what they are talking about and lying and insisting that they are right- with no evidence or logic to prove that they are not right- while remaining evil wrong and liars condemned to death, with no hope of Salvation from their inevitable tragic end. That is why Jesus Christ is the only Savior and that is how he saved you.

Now there are billions that testify that He is The Truth, as He says, and is Right and soon the vast majority of humans will believe in Christ Jesus and in righteousness and the only change needed is for some to believe enough in him to truly live righteously by loving all in God's Promised Independent Demilitarized Disarmed Democratic Holy Lands and so be delivered from suffering, death and evil.

Despite all the above, including evidence by honest testimony of billions of others about Jesus Christ and God, and despite proof of what right must mean to be right and proof that Jesus Christ is Right, faith is a pre-requisite to God's Kingdom, and those that believed even without all the evidence provided here have been blessed, because one has always the option to reject any logic including right reasoning on the basis that they don't like it and refuse to discuss it anymore.

It is fully predictable that hypocritical B.'s will find what is advocated disrespectful and threatening, that hypocritical W.'s will find the suggested solutions impractical and "bizarre," and that hypocritical S.'s will find the book offensive angering and the author egotistical, vulgar like a ruffian and arrogant; because that is what hypocritical B.W.S.'s do.

But what will change to change any of these issues within the same competition for power-resources-ego-sex-recognition systems that all animals have been operating under, all along?

You are not meant to be led by deceitful, wrongful, violent hypocrites as it has been. Leave these worldly wrongful systems to stop suffering.

What are the alternatives to what is proposed in this book?

If your refuge is faith, how does a Christian or any believer behave differently from a non-believer at work if their job is to be a plumber, a software engineer, a salesperson in the same company? If you think that a new chemical will do it, (and given that Chemical Engineering is one of the MSc. Degrees I hold) check what your current chemicals have done for you. I know poor villagers in Africa and Europe and Asia that live much healthier, happier, more fulfilled and longer lives than most Americans. If your refuge is work do you really think that if you get a job or a better job, such as being an executive, any of the issues above get solved or do you think, as I know, that you will be dealing with bigger and more hypocritical B. W.S.'?

Even though the current systems reduce harm more than they cause to most, there is a very significant number, in the billions, of poor, depressed, weak, alienated and righteous people whom they harm more than they benefit. Don't let the great love that is within you remain trapped and oppressed by the inevitable fears, inhibitions and calculations that these systems force you into.

Beyond not having the right answers for any of the personal questions above or solutions for the multitudes that are unwillingly oppressed by being forced to operate within harsh competitive whorish beastly impersonal systems, with no way out, do you have a solution for any of the troubled by religious conflict areas around the world, such as Palestine- Judea, Kashmir, Golan, Kandahar, N. Korea, each of which can result in a hugely catastrophic global war?

So, before you reject what is Advocated here please find an alternative that's likely to actually solve these problems for you and for your children or else violent power, deceit, distraction, hypocrisy, egocentricity and confusion rule and by complicity and inaction you're condemning yourself and them.

Who claims that only the Saudi Arabians and Italians are qualified, by having a Disarmed Demilitarized Holy Land in their nation, to represent God's Love in the world?

Who argues that Americans aren't qualified to have such a Disarmed Holy Land that is actually inclusive of all (including of women and children) and in which living by love is actually practiced, by the free choice of those living there? Do you claim that there is no one holy in America? Or does anyone claim that they want the holy people that are here to keep suffering and being abused to death by not being Independent and free from the dysfunctional badly run confused violent terrorized sad pretentious (very temping) plutocratic hypocritical worldly W. houses...

Just because of the "offensive language" I used, if not for other reasons, I do not expect that the elites and the herd like majority will agree or like what I write; I hope and expect a few to agree (despite disliking my "offensive language") and for the majority to agree to disagree and so to let us be Independent and free.

Given the facts that you experience, no alternative has worked in solving any of these issues and none serious has even been proposed. Yet, God's Kingdom on earth through God's Promised Independent Demilitarized Disarmed Holy Lands, as described here, does solve all of these problems and is destined to happen. Why delay? Why continue allowing the increasing human suffering and wrath?

"There will be no more delay." (Rev. 10.6)

Until God's Kingdom is established on earth, the only option to avoid the coming destructions is to stay out as observers "from above," from "up in the Heavens" that have been Revealed.

Then a mighty angel was heard: "Fallen, fallen is Babylon the great!" (Rev. 18.2)

This is your and humanity's last chance for a "do over."

"Come out of her (Babylon,) my people."(Rev. 18.4)

Please don't pray the Lord's Prayer any longer; do it. It is offensive to God and instigates His wrath for people to keep hypocritically worshiping Him by words while their minds, hearts and Spirit are still so far away from Him; thus humans are causing immense suffering, deaths and probably the destruction of humanity. Please establish God's Kingdom on earth. Live in it. I told you how when-where-why. It's your first priority to avoid death and to be truly free and truly happy.

Unless I cussed at you personally by name and thus mean to offend you, if you were offended by my necessarily unpleasant writings, please forgive me... yet, it is you that needs to re-read whatever offended you because whatever you found offensive, given that I don't know you and that you don't know me, it's most probably an old wound that you need to heal.

If you don't Know God, my God, The God there is a googol of reasons to be afraid.

When you Know the Good God, Love, as I describe Him, there is nothing to be afraid of, ever. Do not fear.

Dislike and peacefully express your dislike of the lying hypocrites that talk about right but do nothing to let one free land (topos) where right may rule, thus making what they say u-topia; they are out to hurt you.

Like and express your like of the truly honest, the righteous and the kind. Choose Life. Choose Him who is Present with you and me at the now of your choice, not in body but as we have come to you on the "clouds of heaven."

Do not follow me; I don't want responsibility for your (I'm sure beautiful) behind. Sorry, but I have difficult enough time being responsible for my ugly badass.

It is you that has the responsibility for the holy Life entrusted to you by the Holy Spirit. I prefer leaders to followers; lead.

If you follow, follow the Christ Jesus.

Worship the Good Father, Love; The God.

Now, you should be able to correctly understand everything from the Theory of Everything and understand what Christ Jesus said why He said it and what He meant. And what the following means, why and how it is to be achieved:

"The Spirit of the Lord is upon me, because he has anointed me to bring good news to the poor. He has sent me to proclaim the Release to the Captives and Recovery of Sight to the Blind, to let the Oppressed go Free, to proclaim the year of the Lord's favor." (Luke: 4.18 and Isaiah.)

"Today this scripture has been fulfilled," (Luke 4:21) in your eyes.

You are Washed, Cleansed and Released from Captivity. Your Eyes are Opened, you are Enlightened, have the Right Understanding of and in all Truth, and have been given Eternal Water. Drink. Be Free.

Now you have experienced the Baptism.

Take a restful bath or a dip in a clean river or preferably in my favored Aegean Sea, (stay little in Athens because until I get there it will remain mostly dead Museum relics) for your body to also experience the cleansing.

Have I fulfilled Jesus' promise by guiding you into all of the Truth?

Woman: Love Man rightly,
Love men correctly.

Men: Be mostly quiet to listen carefully enough what is said and what isn't said to perceive intent, reason, reasoning, truth and evidence.

Mary, gather my students and I will meet them.

My website is: http://www.lifeanew.org and my e-mail is: paulzecos@gmail.com

Paul, Alexander, Emily.

(Even though Emily has not read this book because I know that she rightly rejects bad language and also rightly rejects all the 'not nice' things that her dad may have written.)

Be Free forever in Joy by Loving all rightly and truthfully.

Now that you've been empowered with the correct understanding of the Universe by the Wisdom of God, can See the Whole Truth and with the know-how to transform problems to solutions and objectives to reality please don't underestimate your immense power and capacity to, by yourself, change the world to become as it should be, by making the Eternal Spiritual Truths that you believe in, the reality and truth that is objectively evidenced by anyone.

There are no "Notes" because you can easily check the validity or not of whatever you doubt from what I write from the internet.

-A picture is worth a thousand words but the right Word by the right Logic is worth more than a trillion pictures. For example, one may see thousands of pictures (of beautiful islands) in a "oneword" link.

-The summary of the current and of most future major media news until what is advocated here is done is: increasingly painful stunning stupidity!

-Assume that you are righteous. What will you do?

Be gods, Children of the One God, creating truth in and by Truth as it should be.

Bless you and your loved ones.

Don't look anymore at the clouds in the sky for me.

I am now the lightening on the clouds of your mind and Spirit.

The sun, the moon and the stars cannot see cannot reason and have no choices; therefore they are lesser than you are.

The sun, the moon and the stars are the Darkness and **you are the Light.**

Please help establish one small Independent Holy Disarmed Demilitarized Democratic Land in your nation for the poor, the weak, the homeless, the refugees, the old, the suffering, the alienated, the oppressed, the peace-loving and the righteous to live in peace by love truly, if they so choose, and as an oasis of true love for the rest.

18. To the Resurrected Christ Jesus

Dearest Brother, Savior, Teacher and friend,

I was lost and got imprisoned in the belly of the fish. I am eternally grateful for your unimaginable courage and tolerance in saving me.

Babylon and her confusion was copulated upon hard long deep fast, caught on fire, and has now Fallen. The three evil spirits: **fear, selfishness, greed** have been released. The blasphemous Dragon is dead at the bottom of the ocean and never to be forgiven; the Beast and the false prophet have been captured and thrown in the lake of eternal fire; the kings, Presidents, leaders of the governments of the nations of the world and their "captains" are toast and are "breakfast" for "the Birds."

Shutting my wild mind up long enough to hear understand and type what you say is hard work for me, so even if it is early in the Day, I am going for.... a short nap.

Your paths are now straight. Your Brides have been called; the guests are invited. I am fed up "Feeding Pigs." I am now coming back.

This Day (millennium) is your Day.

The world is now your footstool. Rule the world.

I do not know how long it will take my friends and adversaries in the world to understand this Revelation of the Revelation, See you the Light, and know how to make two into One, as your paths of righteousness do, but when they do, because I like great parties, please wake me up for the your Marriage Ceremony and festivities.

I come only from the Father. I have explained everything and hope that you have been guided into all of the Truth.

Father, kill me now if you choose to forgive those that blaspheme our Holy Spirit of Truth.

In the name of the Truth, Light, Life, I Am, Amen, the Lord of Lords, Christ Jesus.

Amen, amen; (as only in John's Gospel); the truth about The Truths and the truth about the lies.

I am because of and for I Am.

19. My Question to you is:

Do you support the establishment of one sovereign, Independent, Demilitarized Disarmed, Democratic, Land of God?

Please choose one or more of the following choices:

1. Sure; I recognize and petition the Independence and Sovereignty of God's Disarmed Lands.

I want to help and to add my name in THE BOOK OF LIFE.

2. Yes, as a first priority, in my own nation.

3. Yes, somewhere on earth.

4. Maybe in Judea-West Bank or Kashmir or Golan.

5. I support it for those who want it but I am quite happy in this society as it is.

6. No; it may be nice but it cannot be achieved. It's utopia; or what are you smoking?

7. No; it is bad idea and/or you are a bad person.

Please e-mail me the numbers of your answers along with your name and/or any comments at paulzecos@gmail.com particularly for any significant part of the whole truth that I neglected and is not a part of is already described. For corrections or improvements please refer to the relevant page number.

Thank you.

The Beginning….

Bibliography

1. THE HOLY BIBLE (from Greek Biblio meaning Book,) any version.

2. What the Buddha Taught; by Walpola Rahula

3. Bhagavad-Gita: As it is; any Edition.

4. The Way of Life; Lao Tzu; Translation by R. B. Blakney.

5. The Essential Koran; any translation, such as by Thomas Cleary.

6. The Wisdom of Confucius; Edited by Lin Yutang.

7. The Odyssey by Homer, any translation.

Religions

8. The Complete Gospels Edited by Robert Miller.

9. Kabbalah by Gershom Scholem.

10. Kabbalah by Perle Epstein.

11. The Tao of Jesus by John B. Butcher.

12. Rabbi Jesus by Bruce Chilton.

13. The Holy Science by Swami Sri Yukteswar.

14. Tablets of Bahaullah by a Committee the Bahai World Center.

15. The Prophet by Kahlil Gibran.

16. Understanding Islam by Thomas Lippman.

17. Great Christian Thinkers by Hans Kung.

18. The Imitation of Christ by Thomas Kempis.

19. The Spiral of Life by Mona Rolfe.

20. The power of Kabbalah by Yehuda Berg.

21. The World's Religions Edited by Sir Norman Anderson.

22. The World's Religions by Huston Smith.

23. Our Religions Edited by Arvind Sharma.

24. Torchbearers of Spiritualism by Mrs. St. Clair Stobart.

25. The Religious leaders of Greece by James Adam.

26. Mere Christianity by C.S. Lewis.

27. The Seven Story Mountain by Thomas Morton.

28. Tai Chi Classics translated by Waysun Liao.

29. Buddhism by Rhys Davids.

30. Krishna the Charioteer by Morini M. Dhar.

31. The Orthodox Way By Bishop Kallistos Ware.

32. Crossing the threshold of Hope by John Paul II.

33. The Power of Compassion by the Dalai Lama.

34. The Three-Personed God by William J. Hill.

35. Unconditional Life by Deepak Chopra.

36. The Great Thoughts by George Seldes.

37. The Lost Teachings of Jesus by M. I. Prophet and E. C. Prophet.

38. A Course in Miracles by the foundation of Inner Peace.

39. The Celestine Prophecy by James Redfield.

Science

40. Archaeology of the Lands of the Bible by Amihai Mazar.

Physics

41. Modern Physics by Serway, Moses, Moyer.

42. THE NEW PHYSICS Edited by Paul Davies.

43. Quantum Mechanics by F. Mandl.

44. Relativity by Albert Einstein.

45. Space Time Matter by Herman Weyl.

46. Experimental Foundations of Particle Physics by R. Cahn and G. Goldhaber.

47. A Brief History of Time by Stephen Hawking.

48. The Feynman Lectures on Physics by Richard Feynman, Leighton, Sands.

49. Superstrings Edited by Paul Davies.

50. Chaos by James Gleick.

51. Fractals and Disordered Systems by A. Bunde and S. Havlin.

52. Theories of Everything by John D. Barrow.

53. Physics and Philosophy by Werner Heisenberg.

54. The Problems of Mathematics by Ian Stewart.

Biology

55. Descent of Man by C. Darwin.

56. Mapping our Genes by Lois Wingerson.

57. The Human Nervous System by Murray L. Barr and J. A. Kiernan.

Fiction

58. Hamlet, Macbeth, King Lear by W. Shakespeare.

59. Lysistrata by Aristophanes any translation such as by Douglas Parker.

60. Candide by Voltaire.

61. The Old man and the sea by E. Hemmingway.

Philosophy

62. The Portable Plato Edited by Scott Buchman.

63. The Basic Works of Aristotle by Aristotle, any translation.

64. Oedipus plays by Sophocles by Paul Roche.

65. From Socrates to Sartre by T.Z. Lavine.

66. The Story of Philosophy by Will Durant.

67. Making Sense of it all by Thomas V. Morris.

68. Greek Thinkers by Gompertz translated by G. G. Barry.

69. Self-Reliance and other Essays by R. W. Emerson.

70. Fuzzy Logic by D. McNeill and P. Freiberger.

71. English Etymology by T.F. Hoad.

72. The Philosophy Behind Physics by Springer-Verlag.

Psychology

73. Diagnostic and Statistical Manual of Mental Disorders by the American Psychiatric Association; any Revision.

74. Synchronicity by C. G. Jung.

75. Quantum Reality by Nick Herbert.

76. Quantum Psychology by Robert Anton Wilson.

77. Introduction to Neuropsychology by J. G. Beaumont.

78. Synopsis of Psychiatry by H. J. Kaplan, and B. J. Sadock.

79. Hierarchical Concepts in Psychoanalysis Edited by A. Wilson and J. E. Gedo.

80. Severe Personality Disorders by Otto Kernberg.

81. Of 2 Minds by T.M. Luhrmann.

82. Cultural Psychology Edited by J. W. Stigler, R. A. Shweder and G. Herdt.

83. Beyond Boredom and Anxiety by M. Csikszentmihali.

84. Intellect by Mortimer J. Adler

Economics

85. The Wealth of Nations by Adam Smith.

86. The General Theory on Employment, Interest and Money by J.M. Keynes.

87. Capitalism and Freedom by Milton Friedman.

88. The Politics of International Economic Relations by Joan Edelman Spero.

89. Land without Justice by Milovan Djilas.

90. Individual Rights in the Corporation by A. F. Westin and S. S. Salisbury.

Politics

91. The Declaration of Independence; US Constitution; Federalist Papers.

92. Democracy in America by Alexis de Tocqueville.

93. World Politics by Bruce Russett and Harvey Starr.

94. Mandate for Peace by M. Gorbachev.

Organizations

95. Managing Organizational Behavior by Cyrus F. Gibson.

96. Behavior in Organizations by A. G. Athos and R.E Coffey.

97. Mastering Change by Ichak Adizes.

98. The Effective Executive by Peter Drucker.

"The Best 100 books ever" is rounded off with:

99. The World Anew by moi-même

100. *Walt Disney's Donald Duck by Carl Barks!*

Please send all complains about "The World Anew" not being rightly one of "The Best 100 books ever," (because they helped me most; organized by subject) to any leader of the world because the author of the list didn't clearly exclude his self-interest, ... (*while each world leader obviously excludes his self-interest!*) in making judgments and priority lists... and to the major media c/o Brian Williams at NBC News and/or Jon Stewart at Comedy Central and/ or Donald Duck at Walt Disney- ABC *who will investigate this self-interested action thoroughly and I'm sure they will get back to you promptly!*

References on the right side: Christ Jesus, Mary, Buddha, The Vedas, Lao Tzu, Mohammed, Confucius, Moses, David, Ap. John, Ap. Peter, Ap. Paul, Thomas, Homer, Pythagoras, Euclid, Archimedes, Cleisthenes, Pericles, Plato, Aristotle, Sophocles, Constantine, Da Vinci, Michelangelo, Newton, Adam Smith, G. Washington, T. Jefferson, B. Franklin, A. Lincoln, C. Jung, Beethoven, A. Einstein M. Gandhi, JFK, RFK, MLK, Mother Teresa, Mary M., the saints...